SOFTWARE DESIGN DECODED

The MIT Press
Cambridge, Massachusetts
London, England

SOFTWARE
DESIGN
DECODED

66 Ways Experts Think

Marian Petre and André van der Hoek
Illustrations by Yen Quach

First MIT Press paperback edition, 2025

© 2016 Massachusetts Institute of Technology

Illustrations © Yen Quach

This book was set in Milo by the MIT Press. Printed and bound in the United States of America.

Library of Congress Cataloging-in-Publication Data

Names: Petre, Marian, 1959– author. | Hoek, André van der, 1971– author. | Quach, Yen, 1992– author.
Title: Software design decoded : 66 ways experts think / Marian Petre, André van der Hoek, and Yen Quach.
Description: Cambridge, MA : The MIT Press, [2016]
Identifiers: LCCN 2016008329 | ISBN 9780262035187 (hardcover : alk. paper), 9780262553049 (pb.)
Subjects: LCSH: Computer software--Human factors--Popular works. | Computer software--Development--Popular works.
Classification: LCC QA76.76.H85 P48 2016 | DDC 005.1--dc23 LC record available at https://lccn.loc.gov/2016008329

10   9   8   7

For more information and background about the book,
as well as additional insights contributed by the community,
see https://mitpress.mit.edu/software-design-decoded

PREFACE

What makes an expert software designer? The typical answer—experience and innate ability—is less than satisfying. While it carries elements of truth, it offers little from which we can learn and generalize. Experts clearly do not just approach their work randomly. Quite the contrary, they have specific habits, learned practices, and observed principles that they employ deliberately during their design work.

This book offers a look at those habits, practices, and principles, one rooted in many years of studying professional software designers and their ways of working. It offers 66 "things that expert software designers do," each of which can be traced back to academic literature that documents expert behavior and each of which has been confirmed to us time and again by those working in the field.

Some may be familiar, others not. Some are easily put in practice, others not. Some have immediate impact, others not. A constant, however, is that expert software designers are keenly aware of *all* of these practices and draw on them when the situation calls for it.

Today, software is no longer limited by technology, but rather by imagination. Yet the software that turns the imagined into reality can be complex, and the context in which this transformation must happen can be even more complex. This places extraordinary demands on software designers, demands that can be met only if we collectively "step up" to achieve sustained excellence in design.

We hope this book plays its part.

ACKNOWLEDGMENTS

This book would not have been possible without the many software designers we have been able to study, observe, interview, and simply talk to over the years. We appreciate your generosity, and hope that you might still be able to find a practice or two to adopt. Our sincere gratitude.

In addition, we thank the following individuals for their contributions to the book: Alex Baker, Clive Baldwin, Gerald Bortis, Randi Cohen, Grace Petre Eastty, Max Petre Eastty, Peter Eastty, Thomas Green, Jasper Grimm, Uwe Grimm, Michael Jackson, Christopher Keller, Kimberly Keller, Crista Lopes, Consuelo Lopez, Tamara Lopez, Marie Lufkin Lee, Clara Mancini, Nick Mangano, Lee Martie, Martin Nally, Peter Petre, Edgar Weidema, Greg Wilson.

SOURCE NOTES
FOR ILLUSTRATIONS

3—Experts divide and conquer

Trygve Reenskaug (1979). Models - Views - Controllers, Xerox PARC Technical Note, December 10, 1979. Based on Tryvge Reenskaug, THING-MODEL-VIEW-EDITOR—an Example from a Planning System, Xerox PARC Technical Note, May 12, 1979. Available at http://heim.ifi.uio.no/~trygver/2007/MVC_Originals.pdf [Accessed June 15 2016].

6—Experts use metaphor

J. M. Carroll and C. Carrithers (1984). Training Wheels in a User Interface. *Communications of the ACM* 27 (8):800–806.

7—Experts prefer working with others
Used by permission, drawing based on photograph
from: A. van der Hoek and M. Petre, eds. (2013). *Software
Designers in Action: A Human-Centric Look at Design
Work*. CRC Press / Taylor & Francis Group, 452 pages.
ISBN 978-1-4665-0109-6.

10—Experts involve the user
Based on dog-appropriate switches designed by Clara
Mancini. http://www.open.ac.uk?blogs/ACI/.

13—Experts prefer solutions that they know work
R.T. Fielding and R.N. Taylor (2002). Principled Design
of the Modern Web Architecture. *ACM Transactions on
Internet Technology* 2 (2):407–416.

28—Experts invent notations
Example provided by Jasper Grimm, based on a notation
developed by Jeff Walker: J. Walker (1982). Variations for
Numbers Jugglers, *Juggler's World* 34 (1):11–14.

38—Experts address knowledge deficiencies
Based on *The Wizard of Oz*, 1939, Metro-Goldwyn-Mayer.

54—Experts test across representations
Used by permission, drawing based on photograph
from A. van der Hoek and M. Petre, eds. (2013). *Software
Designers in Action: A Human-Centric Look at Design
Work*. CRC Press / Taylor & Francis Group, 452 pp.
ISBN 978-1-4665-0109-6.

EXPERTS
KEEP IT
SIMPLE

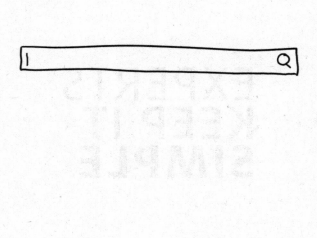

EXPERTS PREFER
SIMPLE SOLUTIONS

Every design problem has multiple, if not infinite, ways of solving it. Experts strongly prefer simpler solutions over more complex ones, for they know that such solutions are easier to understand and change in the future. Simplicity is so important to them that they often continue to search for simpler solutions even after they have a solution in hand.

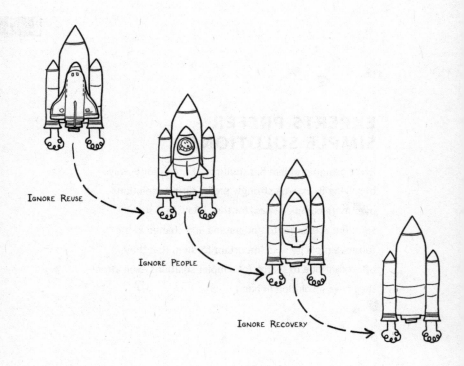

Ignore Reuse

Ignore People

Ignore Recovery

EXPERTS SOLVE SIMPLER PROBLEMS FIRST

Experts do not try to think about everything at once. When faced with a complex problem, experts often solve a simpler problem first, one that addresses the same core issue in a more straightforward form. In doing so, they can generate candidate solutions that are incomplete, but provide insight for solving the more complex problem that they actually have to solve.

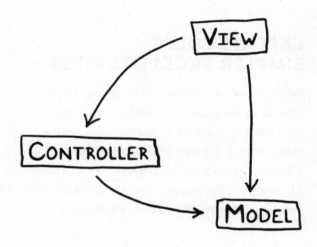

EXPERTS DIVIDE
AND CONQUER

Experts know when and how to break down a complex
problem into smaller problems that can be solved
independently. In addressing the parts, however, they
do not forget about the whole: they reflect on the
relationships between parts. When what emerges
in solving one part affects other parts, they make
adjustments. Indeed, they sometimes repartition the
whole problem and solution as a result.

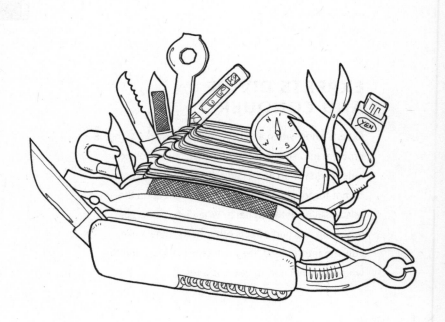

EXPERTS DO NOT OVERGENERALIZE

General solutions are preferred over less general solutions, both for the design as a whole and for its constituent parts. Experts, however, avoid *over*generalizing, which constitutes wasted effort and leads to solutions that are more complex than necessary. The balance is important. Experts use what they know about the practical constraints of the design context to decide whether to generalize for reuse or to optimize for the immediate situation.

```
$ls -l | grep "Jan" | sort +2n | more
```

EXPERTS DESIGN ELEGANT ABSTRACTIONS

While all developers create abstractions, experts *design* them. A good abstraction makes evident what is important, both in what it does and how it does it. Through a single lens, it communicates the problem it solves and the machinery of its solution.

Experts are not satisfied with just any abstraction, they deliberately seek elegant abstractions through which complex structures can be introduced, understood, and referred to efficiently.

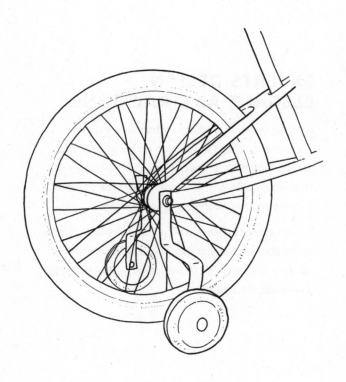

EXPERTS USE METAPHOR

Experts frequently use metaphor to discuss parts of a design and how it works. By invoking metaphor, a more vivid and immediately available picture is evoked of some aspects of the software, which particularly benefits collaborative design work in quickly and succinctly communicating ideas and assumptions.

EXPERTS
COLLABORATE

EXPERTS PREFER
WORKING WITH OTHERS

To experts, the image of the designer as a lone genius who has flashes of brilliance is a fallacy. Experts know that stimulation through working with others is key to their own design performance. Moments of surprising or deep insight do happen, but experts know that those moments are more likely in a rich, collaborative environment.

QUICK QUESTION ABOUT YOUR SECURITY MODULE

 YEAH I CAN HELP

 HOW DO I ADAPT FOR...

EXPERTS REACH OUT

Experts deliberately involve others outside of their team when they have a purpose for doing so, often to obtain specialized technical or domain knowledge. Experts do not wait to contact others when they need them; they know that "sooner is better."

EXPERTS CHECK
WITH OTHERS CONTINUALLY

Experts know to check with collaborators regularly to coordinate mutual efforts, goals, ideas, and assumptions. They know that individual work may diverge within a collaboration, and that spotting divergence is crucial, both to identifying errors and seizing opportunities. Frequent ad hoc communication (rather than formal meetings) is a feature of high-performing teams.

EXPERTS INVOLVE
THE USER

Experts are acutely aware of users. They deliberately
involve users in the design process, studying them,
talking to them, engaging them in testing intermediate
designs, and even asking them to take an active role in
the design team.

Yet experts do not take everything users say at face
value. They realize the potential limitations, as users'
thinking is often colored by current experiences.
Experts look beyond what users ask for, to what users
actually need.

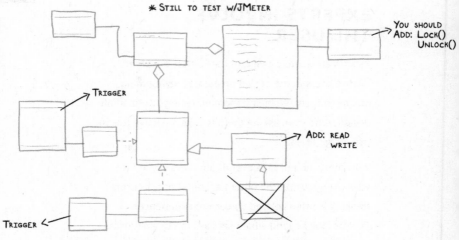

* COOL DESIGN, SOME FLEXIBILITY NEEDED THOUGH
* STILL TO TEST w/JMETER

YOU SHOULD
ADD: LOCK()
     UNLOCK()

TRIGGER

ADD: READ
     WRITE

TRIGGER

* TRIGGERS SHOULD USE OBSERVER PATTERN

EXPERTS SOCIALLY EMBED AND REINFORCE GOOD PRACTICE

Experts know that the interplay between designers plays a crucial part both in nurturing creativity and in promoting quality and rigor. They consciously embed and reinforce good practice in their team. They use knowledge of the group, of both individual and combined strengths and limitations, to structure activities, provide systematic checks, and share knowledge. This collective safety net liberates individuals to extend themselves.

Experts especially take care over the induction of new members into local culture and practice, while eliciting fresh perspectives from them.

EXPERTS AGREE TO DISAGREE

For the benefit of the design project, experts often agree to disagree. They know that divergence of opinions can drive innovation and excellence in design. They also know that many decisions made early are adjusted, retracted, or refined later on, and so prolonged haggling tends to be counterproductive if there is more design to do. Instead, experts accept temporary disagreement and proceed in designing other aspects of the project. More information resulting from further design activity will help them resolve their disagreement.

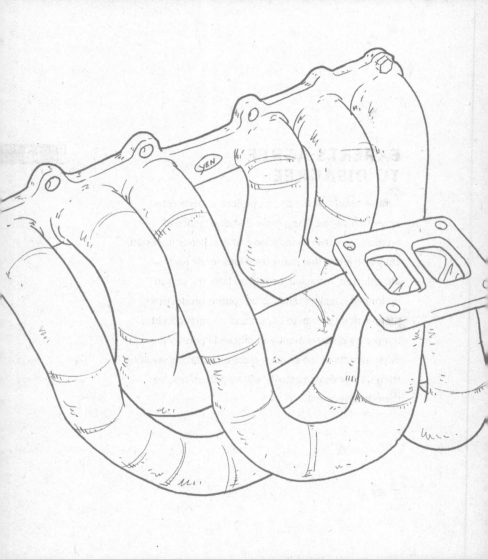

EXPERTS
BORROW

REST

EXPERTS PREFER SOLUTIONS THAT THEY KNOW WORK

Experts have no desire to "re-invent the wheel." If they have a solution that works, or know of one elsewhere, they will adopt that solution and move on to other parts of the design task. Of course, they know to re-assess the existing solution within the context of the current project, to make sure that it actually fits. As long as it does, and as long as it is legally and ethically allowed, they choose to borrow rather than build, reuse rather than re-implement, and copy rather than draft.

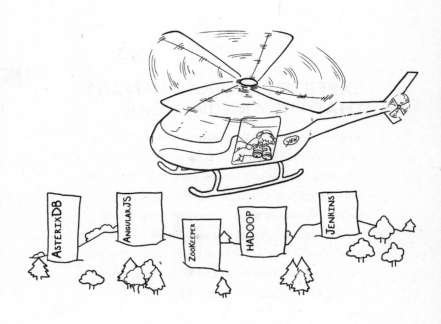

EXPERTS
LOOK AROUND

In the same way that architects walk cities to examine and take inspiration from existing buildings, software experts examine the designs of other software to "see how they did it." They frequently do so in response to a particular challenge they face, but they often also spend time looking around just to add to their repertoire of possible design solutions to draw upon in the future.

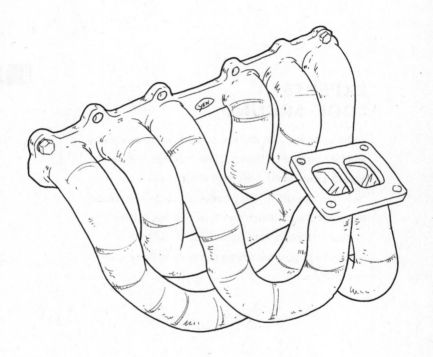

EXPERTS TAKE INSPIRATION FROM WHEREVER THEY CAN

Experts live with their heads up and their eyes open. They are aware of their surroundings and "try on" any ideas they spot. They take inspiration from other people, from other areas (photography, astronomy, literature, model railways), and from their wider environment (a whiteboard drawing, a blog post, a toy, a game). They continually collect ideas that might be useful.

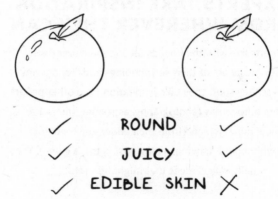

EXPERTS USE ANALOGY

In dealing with intractable problems, experts sometimes turn to analogy, levering likeness and unlikeness to other situations to shift their thinking. They carefully examine where the analogy holds and where it does not, and especially use where it breaks down to drive their understanding of the design problem at hand.

ARCHITECT

Focus on security

Perfectionist

Programs essential,
most difficult parts

Knows code inside-out

NEWBIE

Focus on basic functionality

Fearful

Programs small bug fixes

Knows code barely

SENIOR PROGRAMMER

Focus on extensibility

Somewhat sloppy

Programs major new
features

Knows major parts well

RELEASE ENGINEER

Focus on stability

Detail-oriented

Programs patches

Acquainted with
most of the code

EXPERTS USE DESIGN METHODS (SELECTIVELY)

Experts do not re-invent how to go about design. While they know that design is a creative process that involves impromptu activities, they also use structured design methods to advance their project when appropriate.

They know of and apply a host of methods (world modeling, tradeoff analysis, refactoring, storyboarding, test-driven development, cognitive walkthrough). However, they also know the limitations of such methods and apply them only if they believe their project will benefit. Experts balance systematic practice with freedom of invention.

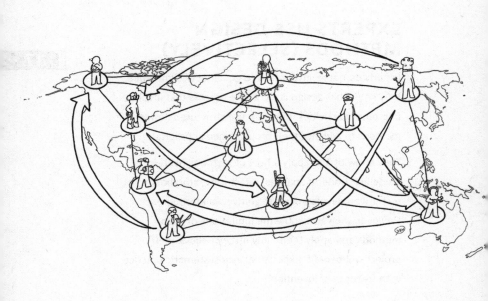

EXPERTS NETWORK

Experts are very aware that they do not know everything—far from it. They compensate by building a network of people who know things, have special expertise and domain knowledge, or know how to think and question. They know to whom to turn when they need something.

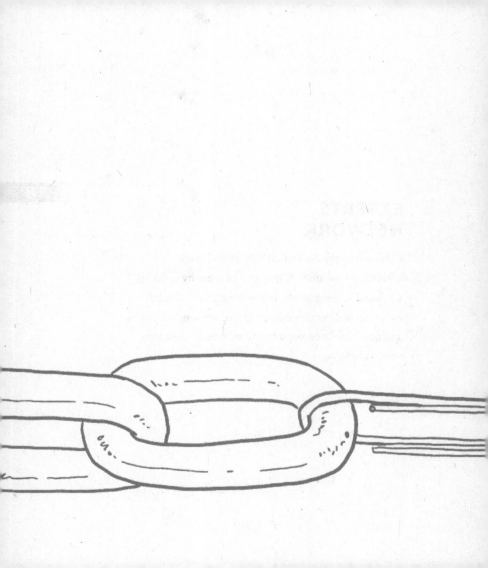

EXPERTS
BREAK
THE RULES

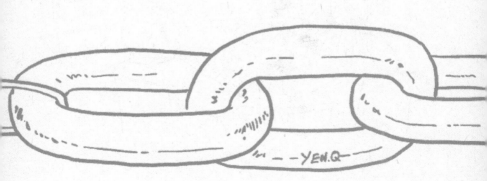

EXPERTS RELAX CONSTRAINTS

Experts do not take much for granted, and for tough problems they will reconsider just about anything, including hard constraints. They relax these constraints in order to explore a broader range of possibilities, sometimes relaxing different constraints successively so as to challenge their understanding and promote insight.

Experts particularly break constraints early, when creativity and exploration are needed. Of course, as they progress and begin to form a more comprehensive solution, they want clarity and completeness, and re-introduce the genuine constraints they previously ignored.

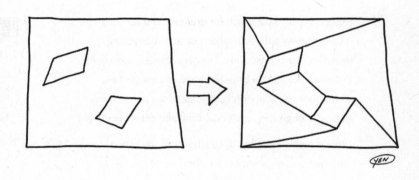

EXPERTS RESHAPE
THE PROBLEM SPACE

Experts often step back from the stated problem and consider the problem space more broadly, looking for alternative ways of understanding "what the problem is." They may change direction by reconceiving the problem space, or by addressing a different problem in the same space. They intentionally choose somewhat different goals from the original design problem, as this leads to insights either into where the real problem lies, or into how to overcome key obstacles.

EXPERTS USE NOTATIONS AS LENSES, RATHER THAN STRAIGHTJACKETS

Experts understand the true value of notations: they serve as lenses to examine a design problem or advance a design solution from a particular perspective. Experts are not married to any one notation and will use whichever notation best suits the task at hand.

As any notation emphasizes some information at the expense of other information, experts remember to complement the leverage a notation gives them with engaging with what is outside of it.

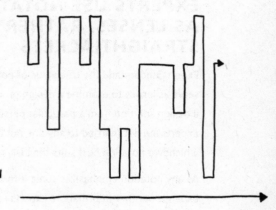

REQUIREMENTS DESIGN

INTERACTION DESIGN

ARCHITECTURE DESIGN

IMPLEMENTATION DESIGN

TIME

EXPERTS DESIGN THROUGHOUT THE CREATION OF SOFTWARE

Experts do not subscribe to the vision that design is merely a phase during which requirements are transformed into an architecture or implementation design. Rather, experts know that requirements are designed, that interactions are designed, that architectures are designed, that code is designed, and—most important—that all these forms of software design inter-relate and are often worked on in parallel. They know it is therefore frequently important to break out of a prescribed software development process and engage in design activities where and when necessary.

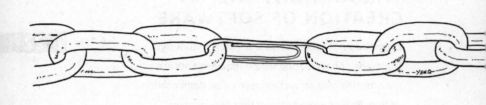

EXPERTS DO NOT FEEL OBLIGED TO USE THINGS AS INTENDED

Experts use what is useful to them and no more. Because they understand what they need and why, they adopt things on their own terms. They may apply a methodology selectively, recombine process steps, cross paradigms, alter model solutions, or use methods in unexpected ways.

EXPERTS
SKETCH

EXPERTS EXTERNALIZE THEIR THOUGHTS

Experts sketch when they think. They sketch when alone. They sketch in meetings with colleagues or clients. They sketch when they have no apparent need to sketch. They sketch on paper, on whiteboards, on napkins, in the air. Experts know that sketching is a way to interact with their own thoughts, an opportunity to externalize, examine, and advance what they have in their minds.

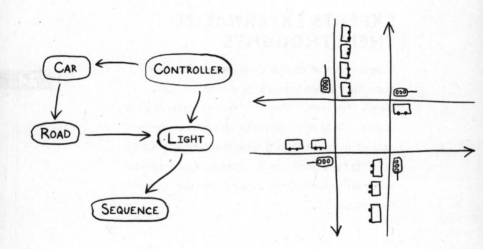

EXPERTS DRAW THE PROBLEM AS MUCH AS THEY DRAW THE SOLUTION

Experts know that their understanding of the design problem and their understanding of its solution inevitably deepen and co-evolve as they design. Experts therefore draw the problem as much as they draw the solution: by moving back-and-forth, they not only ensure that both stay in sync, but also explicitly use advances in the understanding of one to drive advances in the understanding of the other.

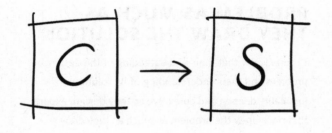

EXPERTS DRAW WHAT THEY NEED AND NO MORE

Experts are frugal in creating their sketches. Experts draw what they need to support their thinking, discussion, argument, communication, or other design activity—but no more. A sketch consisting of a few boxes, a few arrows, and a few annotations is not uncommon, as is a diagram that is later uninterpretable because of its sparseness. Providing detail when it is not needed is a waste of effort and distracts from the task at hand.

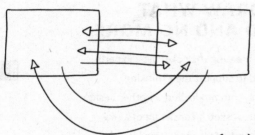

$(s,t) \text{ Send } (s',t') \Longleftrightarrow$

$(s \cap t = \emptyset) \wedge (s' = \emptyset) \wedge$

$(t' = t \cup S)$

EXPERTS SHIFT BETWEEN FORMAL AND INFORMAL

Experts are not lazy. When the situation calls for it, they employ much more formal diagrams than the sketches they typically create. To model certain phenomena more clearly—with more precision and completeness—they may well work out a state machine in all of its detail, edit pseudocode on a whiteboard, or meticulously specify all of the entities, fields, keys, and relationships in a database schema. Once done, however, they will quickly return to sketching, employing a more informal style that abandons much notational detail.

4 BALL

NOTE: ASYNCHRONOUS

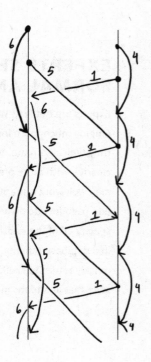

EXPERTS INVENT NOTATIONS

Experts choose a notation that suits the problem, even if the notation does not exist. New notations arise when, in the heat of design, shorthand symbols are used that take on a meaning of their own. This meaning typically persists for the duration of the design meeting, but in some cases use of the symbols becomes more pervasive in the design project.

EXPERTS
KEEP SKETCHES

Experts prefer to keep their sketches rather than discard
them. Their desks are cluttered with paper sketches.
Their whiteboards are full of drawings. They may have
an archive full of old sketches. All for a reason: they
know they may need to revisit a sketch, whether
to consult it to re-invigorate their understanding or to
evolve it because some goal or constraint has changed.

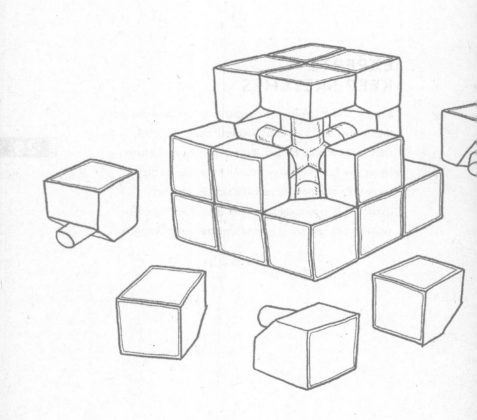

EXPERTS
WORK WITH
UNCERTAINTY

EXPERTS KEEP OPTIONS OPEN

Although a natural inclination might be to solidify any
design decision that can be made as early as possible,
experts do the opposite: they prefer to keep their
options open. They know that any decision they make
now may need to be revised later if they wish to explore
an alternative direction. Therefore, if they do not
have to make a particular decision yet, they simply
will not make it.

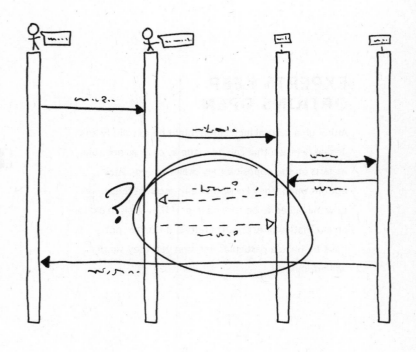

EXPERTS MAKE PROVISIONAL DECISIONS

To further a design solution, experts often make decisions provisionally. They keep track of which decisions are firm and which are provisional, as well as the conditions under which the decisions are made. This way, they acknowledge explicitly where their design is still tentative and where it is more definite.

EXPERTS SEE ERROR AS OPPORTUNITY

Design regularly involves error: things that "go amiss," misunderstandings, obstacles, wrong turns, emergent issues. Rather than fearing error, experts embrace error as opportunity. They accept it as an inherent part of design and take time to explore both the failure and the context around it. Understanding what happened often reveals insights about the problem—or about the solution—such as assumptions, misconceptions, misalignments, and emergent properties.

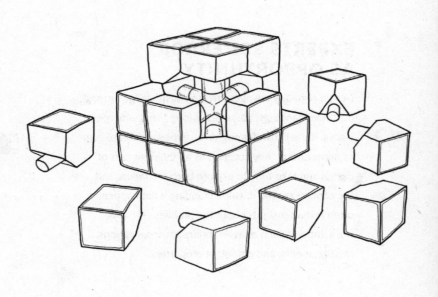

EXPERTS KNOW
HOW THINGS WORK

Experts have a huge, accessible store of knowledge.
They know how things work in general. They know
how specific things work. They know how the current
design works. When something is uncertain, experts
bring that knowledge to bear, extending from the
known to the unknown.

 33

	Design Alternative 1	Design Alternative 2	Design Alternative 3
Development time	****	**	******
Cost of acquiring COTS components	******	***	****
Reuse of our existing Codebase	******	*******	****
Compatibility	******	****	*******
Performance	******	******	*******
Security	****	*******	****

EXPERTS MAKE TRADEOFFS

No design problem can be solved perfectly. Experts realize that designing is making tradeoffs, with each decision they make favoring some aspects of the design solution over others. Experts inform their decisions by collecting as much information as possible and considering how each potential decision trades off among their design goals.

EXPERTS PRIORITIZE AMONG STAKEHOLDERS

The history of software is littered with examples in which the wrong stakeholders were prioritized (usually managers over end users). Experts cut through issues of positions of power and human preference, opinion, and bias to identify the real stakeholders—the people who in the end determine whether or not the system will be adopted successfully. By focusing on them, experts can set the right design priorities for the project.

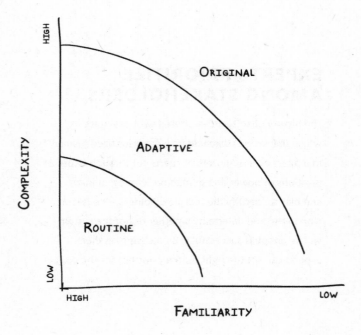

EXPERTS ADJUST TO THE DEGREE OF UNCERTAINTY PRESENT

Different design problems incur different amounts of uncertainty. Experts know which type of problem they are dealing with and adjust their practices accordingly. Routine problems have less uncertainty and are handled in a standard, informed manner, with many decisions made early. Adaptive and original problems involve more uncertainty and require exploration and invention. This entails maintaining more alternatives, deferring more decisions and making provisional decisions, and backtracking as necessary.

EXPERTS
ARE NOT
AFRAID

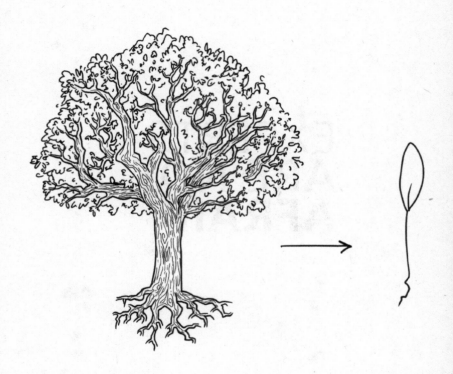

EXPERTS FOCUS ON THE ESSENCE

Every design problem has an essence, a core set of considerations that must be understood and "nailed" in the design solution for it to solve the problem successfully. This essence can be disruptive: changes in the core drastically alter the peripheral decisions that need to be made. Experts focus their efforts on the essence first, and delay expending effort designing on the periphery.

EXPERTS ADDRESS KNOWLEDGE DEFICIENCIES

Experts make every effort to find out and fill in what they do not know. In fact, experts explicitly look for gaps in their understanding of a design problem and its possible solutions, and they try to address those deficiencies as early as they can. They know that "not knowing" is worse than knowing that something is problematic.

A particular form of knowledge deficiency is assumptions. Experts know that making assumptions is an integral part of design practice, but make every effort to verify whether or not their assumptions hold.

EXPERTS GO AS DEEP AS NEEDED

Experts are not afraid to get their hands dirty in nitty-gritty details. If code must be written to understand whether a particular algorithm is sufficiently performant, they write code. If model checking is needed to guarantee a certain property in their design, they build and check the model.

Experts know that any abstraction they make is eventually put to the test by its transition to code, which is why they often engage with implementation—even during conceptual design. Aligning abstraction and implementation enforces discipline and accuracy.

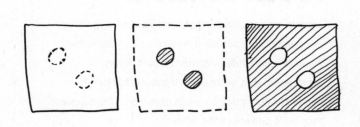

EXPERTS TRY
THE OPPOSITE

Experts take drastic measures when needed. When they
are stuck, they might try the opposite. This may not lead
to a satisfactory solution, but it almost certainly leads
to new insights that help them free their minds, identify
new possibilities, and decide on how to press forward.

EXPERTS DO SOMETHING (ELSE)

Most design projects bog down at some point, when every suggestion seems to lead to further problems. Rather than continuing to "bang their heads" against the same problem, experts switch their focus to another part of the design. It often does not matter what they choose to work on, as long as they change focus for a while. Doing so is likely to reveal considerations that help them overcome the obstacle.

41

EXPERTS KNOW WHEN TO STOP

Experts are sensitive to when the incremental benefits
of revisiting the same issue diminish. They have
a strong internal gauge as to when it is time to stop
and move on.

42

DesignSketch = Box* + Relationship*

Box = Name Port*

Relationship = "("Box Box Arrow")"

Arrow = "$\longrightarrow$" | "$\longleftarrow$" | "$\longleftrightarrow$" | "$\rule{1cm}{0.4pt}$"

Name = [a-zA-Z0-9]+

Port = ...

EXPERTS BUILD
THEIR OWN TOOLS

Experts go to great lengths to surround themselves with
the right tools for the job. This includes not only finding,
evaluating, and appropriating external tools, but also
creating special-purpose tools (intermediate languages,
testing tools, visualizations) that fit the design situation.

43

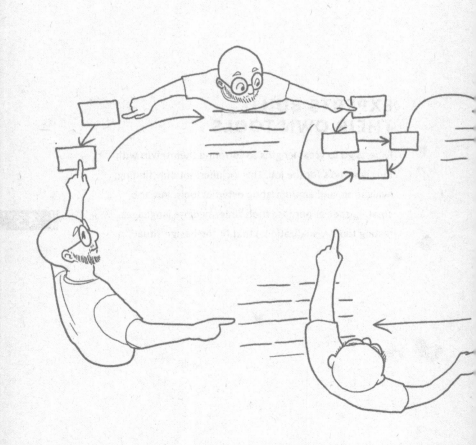

EXPERTS
ITERATE

EXPERTS REPEAT ACTIVITIES

Experts ask the same questions multiple times, of different people, but also of the same people. Experts test their designs, not once, but multiple times. Experts draw a diagram, then draw it again, and perhaps again and again. Experts repeat these activities because they know that, each time they do so, they must re-engage with a fresh mindset and re-explain to themselves or others. Variations in how they engage, think, draw, and communicate, as well as variations in what they choose to focus on, uncover new issues and opportunities.

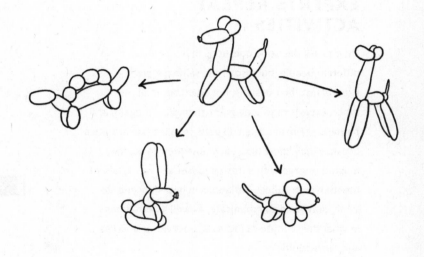

EXPERTS GENERATE ALTERNATIVES

Experts explicitly seek, develop, and evaluate alternatives throughout design. They do this at all levels. By probing these alternatives, even just in their minds, they maintain as much flexibility in the design solution as possible. Alternatives make explicit where and how the design might be able to "give" in the face of future decisions.

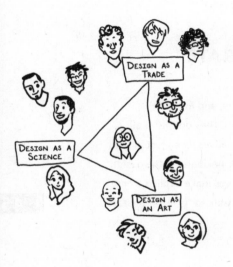

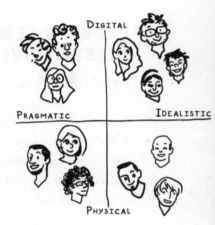

EXPERTS EXPLORE DIFFERENT PERSPECTIVES

Experts examine a design problem, and its possible solutions, from different perspectives. They examine the problem from both a human and a technical perspective. They assess architectures for their structural quality, implementability, and deployability. They look at both the usability and the accessibility of different interface mock-ups. Because they know that focusing narrowly on a single perspective is guaranteed to miss important considerations, they explicitly iterate over multiple perspectives.

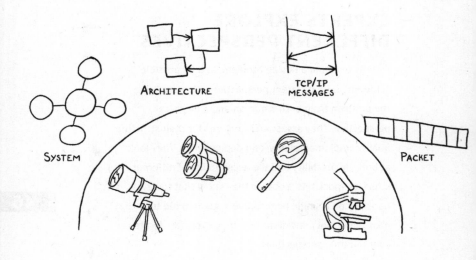

SYSTEM

ARCHITECTURE

TCP/IP MESSAGES

PACKET

EXPERTS MOVE AMONG LEVELS OF ABSTRACTION

Experts design their solutions at multiple levels of abstraction, concurrently. They know that focusing only on high-level models is likely to omit important detail and that working only on low-level code is likely to lead to inelegant solutions. In exploring a design solution, they deliberately move up and down among levels of abstraction, and use resonances among them to spark insights and identify problems.

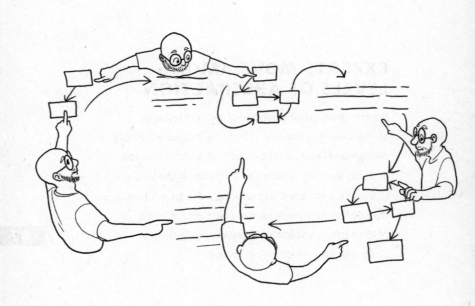

EXPERTS ROTATE AMONG SUBJECT PAIRS

Even in the throes of working on detailed issues concerning a design, experts iterate through issues in combination. They know that it is futile to consider a single issue in isolation for a long period of time. Rather, they juxtapose them: experts choose to focus on two (occasionally three) separate issues, consider them together, make some progress, and move on to the next pair of issues fairly quickly. In cycling through and iterating over pairs of issues, they ensure that different aspects of the design stay in sync with one another as they formulate the overall solution.

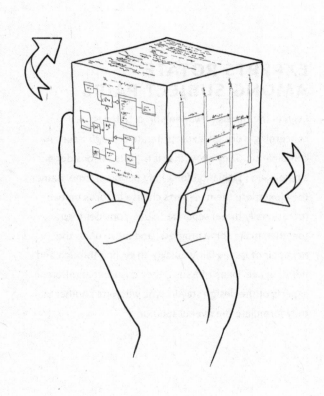

EXPERTS CHANGE NOTATION DELIBERATELY

Experts ask themselves what would happen if they remodeled what they have in a different notation, using somewhat different modeling concepts or somewhat different semantics. Differences in expression can prompt them to consider additional issues.

EXPERTS PAUSE

Experts prefer to build discontinuity into the design process: by taking a break, they are more likely to uncover fresh issues the next time.

50

EXPERTS
TEST

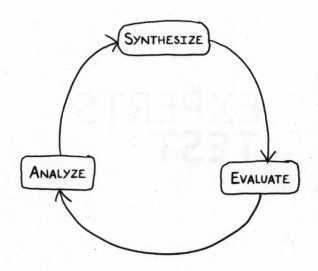

EXPERTS ARE SKEPTICAL

Where others are content, experts remain skeptical. They are skeptical that they explored the necessary breadth and depth of possible solutions. They are skeptical that the current leading solution is good, or even just good enough. They are skeptical of others', and their own, ideas. That is why they test their designs. Testing can provide instructive evidence: whether the design meets its objectives, whether there are emergent issues, or whether assumptions are justified.

EXPERTS SIMULATE CONTINUALLY

Experts imagine how a design will work—simulating aspects of the envisioned software and how the different parts of the design support a variety of scenarios. When working with others, experts regularly walk through a design by verbalizing its operation step-by-step. When alone, they simulate mentally, exercising the design repeatedly over time.

```
IF (CAR APPROACHES INTERSECTION)
  IF (INTERSECTION.LIGHT IS RED)
      CAR.SPEED = 0
  ELSE IF (INTERSECTION.LIGHT IS YELLOW)
      CAR.SPEED += 10
```

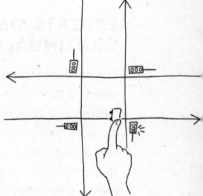

EXPERTS DRAW EXAMPLES ALONGSIDE THEIR DIAGRAMS

On their own, design diagrams remain passive abstractions. This is why experts draw examples alongside the diagrams when they simulate a design. Externalizing their thoughts, juxtaposing the simulation with their design, and envisioning the execution in context, forces them to interpret what they drew and to test their design more thoroughly in the process.

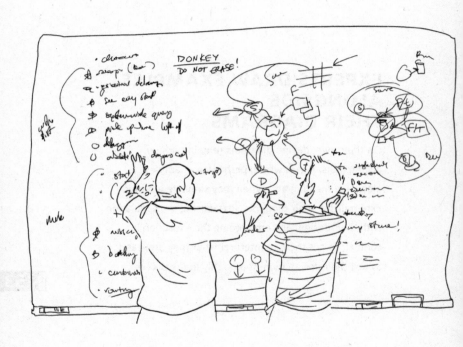

EXPERTS TEST
ACROSS REPRESENTATIONS

Different aspects of a design solution are often
represented in different diagrams—commonly in
different notations altogether. Rather than testing each
of these in isolation, experts know to juxtapose them
in order to examine their dependencies, constraints,
interactions, and other alignments.

54

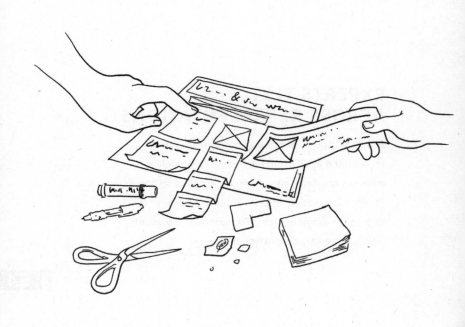

EXPERTS PROTOTYPE CONCEPTS

Experts know that people struggle to engage with abstractions and therefore frequently turn to prototypes to elicit feedback. Prototypes, whether on paper or as more realistic mock-ups, show concretely how the proposed design will behave. They allow stakeholders to engage with and respond to the design concepts, potentially providing important contextual information.

EXPERTS
PLAY THE FOOL

Experts pretend to be ignorant, purposely setting aside
what they know about the design in order to expose
assumptions and flaws. Similarly, they place themselves
in the shoes of a novice user, or a co-worker
unfamiliar with the design, and imagine the questions
they would ask.

56

EXPERTS ARE ALERT TO EVIDENCE THAT CHALLENGES THEIR THEORY

Experts remain alert to anything that might challenge what they believe about their design. They are open to information that is unexpected, and are particularly sensitive to any indication that their design might be wrong. An offhand comment from a future user that does not align with the current design might well prompt a significant shift in design scope.

To experts, no issue is too small to investigate, for they know that small issues can be indicative of much larger problems lurking beneath the surface.

EXPERTS
REFLECT

EXPERTS CURTAIL DIGRESSIONS

It is not uncommon for designers to realize suddenly that they have been discussing an at-best marginal issue for half a meeting. Experts know that, in the midst of design, it is easy to lose sight of what is happening, and they make it a practice to check regularly where they are and where they are going. They use this information to abandon unproductive work, and focus effort where it needs to be focused.

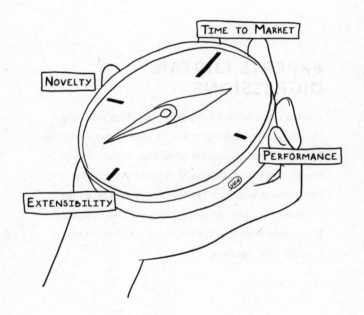

EXPERTS RETAIN
THEIR ORIENTATION

After many meetings, changes, and enhancements, losing track of how the design at hand actually works is not unusual. Experts know the importance of understanding fully the essential underlying concepts of a design, and they make every effort to ensure that they remember the decisions that have already been made, the ones that still need to be made, and why this is so.

EXPERTS THINK ABOUT WHAT THEY ARE NOT DESIGNING

While it is natural to focus on what a design must accomplish, experts also spend time thinking about what a design is *not* intended to do. In articulating and considering boundaries, they discover where they are over- and under-designing.

60

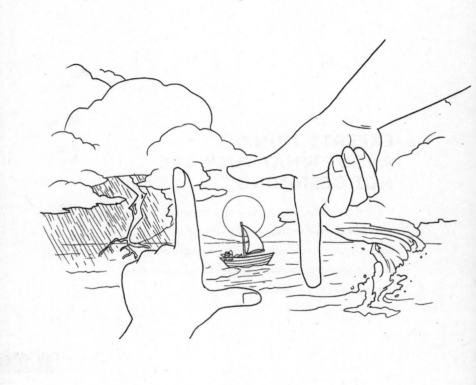

EXPERTS RE-ASSESS THE LANDSCAPE

Experts periodically step back, not just to examine progress, but also to reflect on the project as a whole. They question whether they are still solving the right problem. Have client goals changed? User perceptions? Technology? Deployment context? Market? Experts ask these questions with regularity, to ensure the software they design is fit for purpose.

EXPERTS INVEST NOW
TO SAVE EFFORT LATER

In reflecting on an ongoing design project, experts also anticipate what issues might emerge later. They foreshadow alternative futures, and perform cost-benefit analyses to determine whether investments now—in methods, tools, resources, design alternatives—could save effort later.

EXPERTS
KEEP GOING

EXPERTS DESIGN ALL THE TIME

Experts design at their desk, when taking a walk, on their way to work or back home, in the shower, in the gym, and anywhere else—including in design meetings and conversations. They mull over a design whenever and wherever they can—through habit or preoccupation—as they know that inspiration can strike at any moment.

EXPERTS KNOW DESIGN IS NOT DONE UNTIL THE CODE IS DELIVERED AND RUNNING

The success of a design is determined largely by the experiences of the users. Experts know that any design decision can drastically influence perceptions. They do not consider their designs done until the code is delivered and running. That is when the users finally experience the software.

EXPERTS
KEEP LEARNING

Experts do not take their expertise for granted. They
are continuously on the lookout for new knowledge
to add to their repertoire, and they explicitly seek out
and make time for opportunities to learn.

EXPERTS
PLAY

Experts play with new hardware and new programming languages. They play with toys and technology of all kinds. They play with mathematical and logical problems. They play with random new design challenges they make up for themselves. Play is invigorating; it helps keep their minds fresh, exposes them to novel designs, prompts them to reflect on classic designs, and opens their minds to invention and imagination.

AUTHOR BIOS

Marian Petre "picks the brains of experts" to find out what makes expert software designers expert, how people reason and communicate about design and problem solving, and how they use representations in their reasoning. She is a Professor of Computing at The Open University in the UK; she holds degrees in Psycholinguistics and Computer Science.

André van der Hoek is a programmer at heart, who loves talking to and working with software designers and developers to create new tools that help them be more effective and efficient. He is a Professor of Informatics at the University of California, Irvine; he holds degrees in Business-Oriented Computer Science and Computer Science.

Yen Quach loves to draw. She is an award-winning freelance artist and illustrator who works in both digital and traditional media. Reflecting the world with curiosity and creativity, she began the #draweveryday challenge in 2013, and she has not missed a day yet. Yen holds a degree in Illustration and Animation.

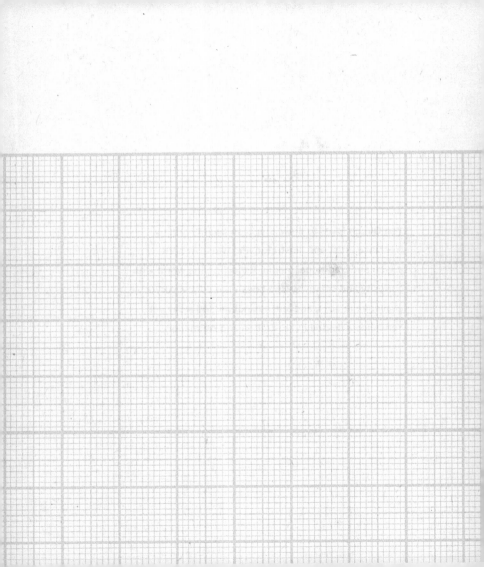

Publisher contact:
The MIT Press
Massachusetts Institute of Technology
77 Massachusetts Avenue, Cambridge, MA 02139
mitpress.mit.edu

EU Authorised Representative:
Easy Access System Europe, Mustamäe tee 50, 10621 Tallinn, Estonia
gpsr.requests@easproject.com

Printed by Integrated Books International, United States of America

"Did your ex not want children?"

Practically the moment he spoke, he tilted his head back with a groan. "Sorry. That's none of my business."

"I don't mind answering. The reason is nothing too personal. First we wanted to wait. Then it was obvious that we weren't going to last." Thinking about that decision, her chest felt tight. Catching her breath, she added, "It was for the best."

Sean's blue eyes settled on her. Then he smiled. "Thanks for the offer about Jackson. I appreciate it."

"You're welcome."

"Hey, I almost forgot to ask how you liked volunteering over at Loaves of Love."

And just like that, all the progress they'd made in their relationship evaporated in an instant.

At least for her.

Doubts set in. What was she doing, talking bad about her job and offering to babysit his son when she couldn't even afford a trip to the grocery st

Dear Reader,

Many years ago, I used to volunteer at my church's food pantry. Several times a day I would either walk people down a long hallway to drop off donations or guide them into the neatly organized pantry so they could get whatever items they needed. Helping both groups made my heart full. Everyone who walked down that hall had a story to tell, and if there was one lasting thing I learned, it was that both the donors and the recipients were a lot alike.

All that—and a newspaper article about a special food pantry in New Brunswick, Canada—is the inspiration behind the A Matchmaker Knows Best Romance series. I loved the idea of creating a trio of romances around a town's food pantry.

I hope you enjoy *Their Surprise Reunion.* Thank you for giving it a try! And, if you ever have the time or the opportunity, I hope you'll consider donating something to your local food pantry. I feel certain that someone will be very glad you did.

With blessings and my thanks,

Shelley Shepard Gray

THEIR SURPRISE
REUNION

SHELLEY SHEPARD GRAY

HEARTWARMING

**Harlequin®
HEARTWARMING™**

Recycling programs
for this product may
not exist in your area.

ISBN-13: 978-1-335-05149-3

Their Surprise Reunion

Copyright © 2025 by Shelley Sabga

For questions and comments about the quality of this book, please contact us at CustomerService@Harlequin.com.

TM and ® are trademarks of Harlequin Enterprises ULC.

 Harlequin Enterprises ULC
22 Adelaide St. West, 41st Floor
Toronto, Ontario M5H 4E3, Canada
www.Harlequin.com

Printed in Lithuania

MIX
Paper | Supporting
responsible forestry
FSC® C021394

New York Times and *USA TODAY* bestselling author **Shelley Shepard Gray** has published over a hundred novels for a variety of publishers. She currently writes Amish and inspirational romances for Revell, Kensington and Harlequin. With over two million books in print, and translated into more than a dozen languages, her novels have been HOLT Medallion winners and Inspirational Readers' Choice and Carol Award finalists.

Shelley has been featured in the *Philadelphia Inquirer*, *Washington Post*, *Time*, *Woman's World*, *First for Women* and *USA TODAY*.

She currently lives in northern Ohio, walks her dogs, bakes too much and writes full time.

Acknowledgments

I'm so grateful for the Harlequin Heartwarming team for their help and guidance. The entire team, especially my editor, Johanna Raisanen, is a joy to work with. I continually feel grateful and blessed for the opportunity to be a Harlequin author.

No acknowledgment letter would ever be complete without thanking my agent, Nicole Resciniti, and the team at the Seymour Literary Agency. It's because of their belief in me that I'm able to spend my days doing what I love.

Finally, I'd like to thank my husband, Tom, for cooking, cleaning and going to the grocery store when I say yes to too many things.

CHAPTER ONE

THE BUILDING, located just off Medina's historic downtown square, didn't look all that scary. Built at the turn of the last century and sporting three floors, nine windows and a gorgeous door painted shiny black, it was actually rather inviting. So were the neatly trimmed boxwoods lining either side of the walkway, the whitewashed bricks that surrounded every window, and the matching brick walkway leading up the front stairs.

Kayla Harding had walked by the building at least a hundred times. She'd even dropped off items in the back on occasion.

Back in another life.

Somehow, none of that mattered. All that did matter was that she was holding an empty canvas bag instead of a full one, and she was trying to gather the courage to get out of her car and enter the front door instead of the back one.

That was the problem, she decided. The back door was for people who had too much and were donating. The front? Well, that was for the person she'd recently become. Someone who was hungry enough to need a helping hand.

"Sitting in the car bemoaning your situation isn't going to help you any," she told herself.

The ache in her stomach only reinforced that fact.

Making the decision at last, Kayla got out, carefully locked her vehicle and, with her purse in one hand and the canvas bag in the other, headed toward the food bank.

"Hi!" a blonde lady called out. "You going in, too?"

This woman was also going inside? Taking in the small gold hoops in her ears, the well-fitted jeans, designer tennis shoes, T-shirt and tailored coat, Kayla nodded.

"Good. That's great." Leading the way, the lady strode up the steps and opened the door. When Kayla continued to hesitate, she said, "Come on now, don't be shy. Everyone's so nice here. You're going to love it."

She was going to love it? It was hard not to frown as she followed the woman up the stairs and through the door. When it shut behind her, Kayla was immediately overwhelmed with the scent of fresh bread and the sound of laughter.

Obviously, she'd come to the wrong place.

You're an idiot, she silently scolded herself, giving herself another mental slap. Only yesterday she'd told her therapist that she was going to stop putting herself down. Just because Jared had done that for the three years they'd been married, didn't mean she was going to continue it. *Jared didn't give you any money*, she reminded herself. *His lawyer made you feel horrible for expecting anything at all. Why are you still lugging around the low self-esteem he hoisted onto your shoulders?*

"Carol, who do we have here?"

Brought back to the present, Kayla realized that there was a long table in front of them. In the middle sat a spry-looking lady with short gray hair, good cheek bones and a warm expression.

"I'm Kayla," she said. Lowering her voice, she added, "Harding. I'm Kayla Harding."

"It's nice to meet you. I'm Edna." With one look, Edna seemed to take in everything that Kayla was. Corduroys that were now a size too big. A teal wool sweater that was well-made but old. Her light brown eyes, dark blond hair and the tote bag clutched in her hand. "Carol, why don't you go on ahead?"

"Are you sure? I'd be happy to show Kayla the ropes."

"I've got it." Edna's voice was firm.

And with that, a new tension filled the room. Mixing with the scent of fresh bread and the sound of faint laughter. An awareness previously missed. "Oh. Sure. See ya, Kayla."

Unable to speak, Kayla tried to smile, but her lips felt too tight.

Ten steps later, Carol was through another door, this one with stained glass in the center.

Edna stood up. "Are you here for some food, dear?"

The embarrassment was excruciating. But the truth couldn't be denied. "Yes." She lifted her hand. "I brought a bag."

"I'll make sure that's filled before you leave." As another burst of laughter floated through the crack of the door behind them, Edna cocked her head to one side. "Any chance you have a couple of free hours? We're baking bread today. We could use the help...and you might enjoy it."

"Baking bread?"

"Teams of volunteers come in two to three times a week and make loaves of bread together. It's a lot of fun."

"Well, now..."

"The bread is for the food bank, of course," Edna continued in a smooth—but firm—tone of voice. "Everyone who comes in for food will receive a loaf or two, depending on the size of their family. But everyone who comes in to help gets to leave with a loaf, too."

"I've never baked bread."

"No worries. Someone will teach you."

Kayla felt like she wasn't exactly getting her point across. "I was serious. I came for food."

"I know, dear. But you might find making bread for an hour or two will feed your soul, too." She paused. Seemed to study Kayla's expression. Then, she smiled. "If you prefer, we can go down this hall to our right and pick out whatever items you'd like. There's even a door out the side. No one has to know you were here."

That was tempting. If she took that option, then she could take some food, slink out the side door, hurry to her car and drive to her apartment. In the privacy of her kitchen, she could open a box or a can or whatever she got, heat it up and eat.

Her stomach might be filled but the same gnawing ache inside her would still be there. If she baked bread, she might have something else to think about besides making the food last four more days until she got paid.

"I'll give it a try."

"I'm so glad to hear that. I think you'll enjoy it." She stood up. "While the loaves are baking, we can take care of your shopping."

"All right."

"Let's go now. I seem to remember there was an open spot near a couple of very nice people. I think you'll get along great with them."

After they crossed through the doors, Edna showed Kayla where to stow her coat, purse and tote bag. Then she directed her to the sink and pointed to the directions, which were to slip on an apron, tie hair back, carefully wash hands and forearms, and put on gloves.

Then she walked Kayla to an open spot at a long

wooden table that could probably seat twelve people. There were three of these tables in the large area. She thought it looked a bit like the tables in the dining hall at Hogwarts. Except there were no benches to sit on. Or magical creatures.

Just a lady wearing sweatpants and a T-shirt and a man wearing jeans and a long-sleeve T-shirt in a vibrant shade of green. Across the chest, in bold, white lettering, was Medina Football. She smiled at them both...just as she realized that she knew the guy. He was Sean Copeland, their high school's former football star.

Sean glanced at her, then stilled.

Her heart sank. It was obvious that he remembered her. And why wouldn't he? It wasn't like their high school in Avon Lake had been that big.

Oblivious to the tension flowing between them, Edna performed the introductions. "Sean and Wyn, this is Kayla. Kayla, Sean and Wyn have both been baking bread here for quite some time. They'll be able to show you what to do better than I can."

Kayla smiled. "Hi."

"Good to meet you, Kayla." Wyn winked. "We're glad you're here. Be careful around Edna, though. She's a whiz of understatement." She paused to chuckle at her own words. "The truth is that our director can bake like nobody's business. However, we let her feel good about herself by running the place."

Smiling at Kayla, Sean added, "We're not will-ing to do anything to give up our free loaves."

"That is pretty special," she said softly.

"Don't forget to find me when you're done, Kay," Edna said. "I'll be looking for you."

"I won't forget. Thank you."

Edna's expression softened. "Anytime, dear. You two take care of her now," she tossed out over her shoulder as she headed back to the front.

"Kayla Harding. It is you, isn't it?" Sean asked.

"Yeah. How are you, Sean?"

"I'm good. I moved south for a while but now I'm back. I'm working at Medina High."

"Coaching football?"

"Yeah. I'm the assistant. I coach football, wres-tling and teach American history."

"Wow. That's wonderful." And now she was even more embarrassed by her situation. She'd never gone to college. Instead, she had married a jerk and now couldn't even afford to buy her own groceries. Her stomach tightened. Any sec-ond now, Sean was going to ask what she'd been up to and she would have to try to decide just how much to divulge.

"Have you ever made bread before, Kayla?" Wyn asked.

"No. I mean, I've made banana bread, but noth-ing with yeast or anything." Looking at the rect-angular wooden cutting board in front of her, she continued her fumbling explanation. "What I'm trying to say is that I've never kneaded bread."

Whether Sean was starting to sense that she was nervous or that it wasn't the right time to catch up, he lifted his chin. "Don't worry. It's easy. If I can do it, anyone can."

"We've got directions written out, too," Wyn said. "After your first loaf, you're going to wonder why you haven't been baking bread at home all your life."

"I'm anxious to get started."

The two of them spent the next fifteen minutes showing her where to get all the ingredients, reminding her how to correctly measure flour and helping her sprinkle flour on her cutting board. Before long, Sean was demonstrating how to knead the bread.

Kayla found it all easy enough, but the kneading did take a bit of getting used to. Especially since they used enough dough for two loaves at a time. It took a bit more muscle than she'd realized.

Sean noticed. "Let me know if you need a hand."

"Thanks. I've got it, though." With some dismay, she realized she sounded a bit out of breath. "You make it look so easy."

Wyn chuckled. "That's because Sean here has been lifting weights his whole life," she quipped as she walked toward the ovens.

"Who would've ever thought being a dumb jock would have its benefits?" he joked.

As she kneaded the dough, Kayla allowed her mind to drift back twelve years. She and Sean hadn't been great friends. They'd had a couple of classes together and had even been partners in a biology lab one semester. While he'd played sports and hung out with the popular kids, she'd been in the choir, helped take care of her younger sister and worked at her uncle's pizza place. She vaguely remembered everyone making a big deal about Sean earning a scholarship to a university, but that was it. "You played football in college, right?"

"Yeah. For OU."

Ohio University. "I couldn't remember."

"We went to high school together," Sean said. "How long have you been in Medina?"

"Not long. Just a couple of weeks." It had actually been closer to three months. After her divorce was finalized, she'd lived with her parents for a couple of weeks until they'd helped her get the small apartment she was living in now.

"This is just my second year here. I was down near Cincinnati teaching and coaching at a small prep school until the head coach at Medina called."

For the first time since they'd started talking, she thought that Sean sounded subdued. She wondered if something had happened.

"Talk about a small world!" Wyn exclaimed. "What a nice coincidence that you came in today and there happened to be a space next to us."

"It sure is," Kayla said as she covered her bread

so it could rise. "So, now we wait for thirty minutes?"

"Well, you wash your area, and then go help bag bread," Wyn said.

Following their directions, she washed dishes, wiped counters, divided her dough into loaves and helped bag cooled loaves while hers was rising again.

Finally, just as the two loaves she'd made went into the oven, Wyn announced it was time to go. Another group would come in to take care of the last loaves of bread and clean the space so it could be used for other purposes during the week.

After waving goodbye, Wyn walked out the door, leaving Kayla alone with Sean. "Hey, I feel like we barely caught up. Can I walk you out?"

"Thanks, but I have to see Edna."

"Oh, yeah. I forgot. Sorry, but I don't have time to wait for you. I've...well, I've got a kid I need to go pick up from my parents' house."

"You have a child?"

"Yeah, a boy," he said with a look of pride. "His name's Jackson. He's six."

"That's wonderful." If she wasn't so happy for him, it would have been difficult to keep a smile on her face. How had his life gone so right and hers gone so wrong?

He rolled his shoulders, obviously uncomfortable. "Listen, I don't like to talk about it, but um, my wife...Dannette. Well, she passed away three years ago. She got sick." He swallowed. "Anyway, that's really the reason I moved here. I needed a change."

Hating that she'd just been feeling so jealous, Kayla softened her voice. "I know all about needing a change."

"Yeah?"

"Yeah. I...well, I'm recently divorced."

"I'm sorry."

"Me, too." She swallowed. "All I'm trying to say is that I think Medina is a good place to start over. I mean, at least it has been for me."

"Me, too."

There was a new tightness around his lips, like he was trying to hold it together. "I'm so sorry for your loss, Sean."

"Me, too. But, like I said, it was a few years ago." Squaring his shoulders, he added, "Jackson and I are doing all right now."

"I'm glad."

"Kayla, are you ready?"

Looking at the doorway, where Edna had just appeared, Kayla said, "I'm sorry. I've got to go. It was good to see you."

"You, too." Taking out his phone, he swiped a few screens. "Here, let me have your number. I'll let you know when I'm coming here again."

She was about to say she didn't have time to exchange numbers but figured knowing when he was going to be at Loaves of Love would be a good thing. That way she wouldn't have to worry about running into him. Quickly she pulled out her phone and they exchanged numbers.

"I'm glad I saw you, Kayla. I mean it," he said before heading out the door.

"Looks like you already made a friend," Edna said when Kayla reached her side.

"It's more like we were getting reacquainted. Sean and I went to high school together."

"I don't know him well, but he volunteers here once or twice a month." She winked. "Depending on his football schedule."

"That's good to know." Maybe it would be easier than she thought to avoid him.

"Let's go down to the pantry and get you taken care of. Ready?"

"Yes, ma'am." As she followed the older lady down the hall, Kayla realized that coming here hadn't been the worst thing she'd done in days. It had been one of the best. The simple act of baking bread and doing something for someone else in her situation made her feel like she wasn't quite so alone. "Thank you for encouraging me to stay," she whispered before they entered a large room filled with shelves.

Edna lightly squeezed her shoulder. "I hope you come back. Both to help with the bread…and if you need a hand, Kayla."

"Thanks."

"No, I mean it. Please don't hesitate to return. A

lot of businesses and people in the neighborhood donate food and necessities regularly. We always have full shelves."

"That's amazing."

"It is. But helping others is what we're here for. If you don't take advantage of the food bank, everyone's efforts go to waste, right?"

Feeling like she was in a daze, Kayla nodded.

"Good. Don't be a stranger."

"I won't. Thank you again," she whispered. Until things got better, she had a feeling she was going to have to return.

But she promised herself that things were finally going to get better for her. If she and Sean crossed paths again, she was going to want to hold her head up and feel good about herself.

Somehow, she was going to do it. That was a promise she intended to keep.

CHAPTER TWO

SEAN COPELAND MISSED Dannette all the time. But he especially missed her at eight o'clock in the evening. Eight o'clock was after school, after football practice, after he'd gotten home, cooked dinner, washed dishes, supervised Jackson's shower and tucked him into bed.

Eight o'clock was when he sat next to his six-year-old, read him a couple of pages out of whatever book they were reading and realized that no matter how hard he tried, he was never going to tell the story as well as Jackson's mother had.

His boy never complained, but Sean knew Jackson thought the same thing. He could see it in the pinch of his lips. The way his eyes would glance around the room. The way he never put up a fight when Sean said it was time to call it a night.

It was the exact opposite of how Jackson had been with his mother. No matter how long Dannette read, he'd want her nearby a little longer. "Just one more page," he used to say. Even back when he was three years old.

Now, as he finished the last page of the fifth chapter of their current book, Sean knew this evening wasn't going to be any different.

"That's all for tonight, sport," he said as he closed the book and put it on the nightstand. "It's time for you to get some rest."

"All right, Dad."

Bending down, he pressed his lips to his boy's forehead. "Sleep tight. Love you."

Jackson, wearing a soft white undershirt and a pair of flannel pajama bottoms with Labradors printed all over them, nodded as he scooted farther into the depths of his twin bed. "Love you, too."

Then, his little boy turned onto his side, so his back was facing the door.

A lump in his throat, Sean stared. Tried to remember if Jackson did that when Dannette would leave the room. He couldn't remember. With an inward sigh, he turned off the light and closed the door.

Moving back to the kitchen, he contemplated getting a beer but decided a glass of water would do just fine. He carried it into the living room and sat in his dark gray electric recliner. It was covered in supple leather, had a cup holder and was big enough to fit his large frame. For years he'd coveted it. More than once he'd dragged Dannette over to the model in whatever furniture store they were in and encouraged her to try it out.

She'd laughed and said the thing was bigger than

her car. Of course, then she'd also given him a soft look. It was the kind of look that told him everything she was thinking. It said how sorry she was that they couldn't afford such a thing, not with her choosing to stay home with Jackson for a couple of years and him on a probationary teacher's salary. How sorry she was that his wants somehow always seemed to come in last.

He used to shrug and say it didn't matter. It was just a chair. But that hadn't stopped him from walking over to admire the beast every time they were in the store. Why had he thought such a thing would make him happy?

When his brother, Jack, his sister, Meg, and their spouses had delivered the thing on Christmas Day a year after Dannette's death, it had felt like a kick in the gut.

They'd been so excited to give it to him that it had taken everything he had not to start crying like a baby. Instead, he ran his hand over the leather once again and tried to look impressed. And thrilled. Especially when Jackson had been jumping up and down and cheering and announcing that it was what his dad had always wanted.

Sean hadn't had the heart to tell any of them that it was just a chair. That, yeah, he'd once thought that chair was everything, but now he knew better.

What he really wanted was his wife back.

That moment had been a turning point for him, though. Even though he was a widowed dad, an assistant football coach, a history teacher and had next to no extra time, he knew he had to do something to get out of his head.

That was why he'd ended up volunteering at Loaves of Love. He'd wanted to force himself to count his blessings.

It did do that. But what it also had done for him was give him a few hours a month to do nothing but chat with some nice folks. They were friendly and didn't ask him about Dannette, and they didn't pester him about their kids' grades in his history class or their sons' chances to start on Friday night.

Instead, the folks there shared simple stories and discussed the weather. Gave each other pointers about making really great loaves of bread. They laughed when he'd admitted to trying to make his own pair of loaves at home—and that they'd ended up feeling as heavy as bricks.

The hours he spent at Loaves of Love were nothing and they were everything.

And now, he couldn't believe it, but the place had given him yet another gift. Because of the food bank, he'd been able to reconnect with none other than Kayla Harding. He'd known it was her from the moment their eyes met. Of course, Sean also would have known that hair of hers anywhere. Kayla Harding had been pretty in high school and she was pretty now. But she also happened to have the most gorgeous head of dark blond hair he'd ever seen. It hung about halfway down her back in a thick mass of curls. He was glad she hadn't cut it all off. That would've been a shame.

He felt bad that she'd gotten divorced but there was a part of him that was glad she was available. Oh, his heart was still Dannette's, but if Kayla had been married, that guy would likely never want her connecting with Sean again.

If Kayla had been his, Sean knew he wouldn't want some guy texting her. Not even as "just friends." Kayla had an aura about her that was all sweetness. He wouldn't want anyone taking advantage of that.

Of course, he wouldn't be thinking any of that if he still had Dannette.

Lost in thought, Sean sipped his glass of water, and instead of watching television like he'd planned to do, he stared out the window and allowed himself to think about Kayla. And then, before he lost his nerve, he pulled out his phone and texted her.

Hey. Want to grab lunch together on Sunday afternoon? It will be great to catch up.

He watched his screen, secretly hoping that she would respond right away. But she didn't.

Staring back out the window, he tried not to care about that.

"HEY, COACH?"

Looking up from his computer screen where he

was inputting grades, Sean stilled. It was Jamison, his talented kicker who had yet to meet a set of goalposts he couldn't kick a ball over. Jamison was also shy and quiet.

"What's up, J?"

"Have you graded those midterms yet?"

"I have."

Jamison swallowed. "Do you remember what I made?"

"I can look." He studied the junior. The kid looked nervous. "What's going on?"

"Well, um, homecoming's coming up. But my dad's been on me about my grades. He said if I didn't get at least a B on my midterm he wasn't going to push back my curfew."

Sean kept his expression even, but inside, he was shaking his head. Jamison's dad was so intent on his son getting a scholarship he micromanaged the kid. Sometimes, Sean was afraid Jamison was going to snap, he put so much pressure on himself. "Got a date for homecoming?"

"I think so." He looked down at his feet. "I mean, I'm planning on asking Alicia, but not if I have to go home at eleven like a loser."

"I've seen Alicia look at you in the halls, J. She's never going to think you're a loser. Not even if you have to take her home at eleven."

"Yeah, well." He stuffed his hands in his pockets.

"Let's see how you did, then." A couple of clicks

of the mouse brought him to third period. Scanning down, he located Jamison's name, his grades... and yesterday's midterm. Feeling the muscles in his neck ease, he looked up at the boy. "How does a ninety-five sound?"

It seemed to take a second for the number to register. "I made an A."

"You did. I'm proud of you." He grinned. "Looks like you better figure out how you're going to ask Alicia." He never could get over how all the kids now went to extremes when it came to asking girls out these days.

"I know how." Looking even happier, he added, "And because I got an A, my parents are going to give me money to take her out to dinner, too."

"That's great. I'm happy for you."

"Thanks." Just as he started to turn away, he added, "And thanks for doing this. You're pretty cool, Coach."

"Thanks, but all I did was tell you your grade. You're the one who earned it. See you at practice."

Jamison gave him a salute as he walked off.

Glancing at the clock, Sean figured he'd better get himself together, too. He had the last block free so he could head over to the field house to confer with Coach Crowder and the rest of the staff.

Just as he started shutting down his laptop, his phone buzzed. Wondering if he was finally going to hear from Kayla, he pulled it out of his back pocket. And grinned when he saw her name.

Clicking on the message, he eagerly read her note.

That's so nice of you to ask. But I'm sorry. I can't.

He read it twice. Just to make sure that he hadn't mistakenly skipped a couple of words or phrases. But of course, he hadn't. She'd given him twelve words. Kept things polite. Simple.

No rain check.

No explanation.

Frowning at his screen, he started overthinking. Was Kayla not interested in seeing him again? Like, ever?

Or was she not a chatty texter?

No worries. Maybe another time.

He stared at the screen, willing her to reply. When she did, he read it immediately.

Yes. Maybe another time.

So, maybe she really was busy and she didn't like texting much. She hadn't said *never*.

But a sixth sense was telling him that she was shutting him down. She wasn't interested in seeing him again. Not unless they both happened to be volunteering at Loaves of Love at the same time.

And man, if that wasn't a bummer.

CHAPTER THREE

IT HAD BEEN hard to say no to Sean, but Kayla had
no choice. She wasn't in a good place. Not emotionally, and pretty much not in any other way. She
felt like she was barely existing and she didn't see
those circumstances changing anytime soon.

Sitting in the storage room during her lunch
break at Tami's Cards, Kayla forced herself to not
give Sean a reason for declining his invitation. She
didn't want to make something up and she'd never
been good at lying. It was better just to keep things
simple.

But boy, it was hard. There was a part of her
that wanted to spend some time with the guy her
younger self had had a bit of a crush on. More importantly, she would love to give herself an hour
or two of simple conversation. It had been a long
time since she'd done that with anyone. Even when
she'd thought she and Jared were happy, they'd
never had an easy or relaxed relationship. Jared
had been far too driven for that.

So simply enjoying a cup of coffee while reminiscing about old times would've been nice.

Pushing the dream away, she took another bite of her peanut butter sandwich and smiled happily. Both the peanut butter and bread had come from Loaves of Love. Peanut butter had recently become her go-to food. It was filling and wasn't completely bad for her. It sure tasted better on the homemade bread. Her meal felt almost fancy.

She was swallowing her last mouthful when the door opened and Tamera, her manager, stepped in.

"Oh, good. You're done."

Kayla hastily swallowed that last bite and washed it down with a sip of water. "Good?"

"I need you to come on out and man the counter. We have several customers out there and I have to go to an appointment."

Kayla glanced at the clock. She still had ten more minutes of her lunch break. If Tamera was leaving, then she wouldn't be able to run to the bathroom, make a phone call or simply sit down until the end of her shift.

When Kayla had first started working at the gift shop, she'd pretend that things like getting the breaks she deserved didn't matter. Instead of reminding Tamera about her time owed, she'd jump to her feet any time her boss asked her to.

Unfortunately, it wasn't long before she realized that Tamera didn't appreciate anything she did to go above and beyond. She would never let Kayla leave early if she worked half of her lunch and usually acted annoyed if she tried to get her missed break in the afternoon.

Worse, she was pretty sure that her boss had known that she was going to leave and had kept Kayla on the floor instead of allowing her to have her lunch break early.

All that was why she remained in her chair. "I'm sorry, but I still have ten more minutes of my lunch break."

"You're going to have to take that ten minutes later today."

Seeing that Tamera was already walking toward her office, Kayla said, "When?"

She stopped and turned to face her. "When?"

"Yes. I mean, it's one o'clock now. I'm only working until three. When do you think I'll be able to have those ten minutes that I'm owed? Will you be returning at two?"

Tamera's expression pinched. "Kayla, we don't have time for this game. Customers are waiting."

"I'm sorry. I don't know what else to do. You've taken advantage of me more than a handful of times and have refused to give me more hours or even the raise you promised."

The bell that Tamera had placed at the cash register rang. She sucked in a breath, obviously ready to yell at her. When the bell rang again, she walked back out.

When she was alone again, Kayla realized her

hands were shaking. What had she done? She'd be lucky if Tamera didn't fire her this afternoon.

Just imagining how that would impact her life made Kayla's stomach clench. Standing up, she threw away her trash and replaced the lid on her thermos of cold water.

But still, there was something inside of her that made her stand her ground. She was pretty sure it was the memory of making bread with everyone and being treated so kindly by Edna. If Edna could make her feel so good when she came into Loaves of Love to get food, shouldn't her boss allow her a lunch break without making her feel guilty?

After running into the washroom, she hurried out to the counter. Two customers were there, and neither looked like they needed help. Tamera was standing behind the counter and texting on her phone. She looked up when Kayla approached. "Are you finished now?"

"Yes."

"I called Amy. She's coming in at two. She'll be with you until you leave at three."

"All right." She held her breath, half expecting Tamera to tell her not to return.

Instead, her manager just picked up her handbag and headed out the front door of the shop.

Watching her leave, Kayla made a mental note to think again about working someplace else. There had to be another job where she could, at the very least, have a better work environment.

"Excuse me, miss?"

She turned to a lady with a gray perm. "Yes?"

"Can you help me choose a condolence card for my neighbor? I forgot my reading glasses."

"Of course," she replied as she walked to the lady's side. "That's why I'm here."

"You are my favorite employee, dear. Always so kind and genuine. You make shopping here so pleasant."

"Thank you for saying that."

Glancing at the door that Tamera had just strode out of, the lady continued, "I know that woman is your boss, but she's not very nice, is she?"

It was so tempting to agree! But knowing the right thing to do was to take the high road, she said, "I think Tamera's having a tough day today."

"Humph. Aren't we all? My neighbor of thirty years just lost her husband. Personal problems don't give folks the right to take out their bad moods on everyone else, though."

The comment surprised a chuckle out of her. The customer was right. "Let me show you some of my favorite cards. I think when you hear the sentiments, one might feel like the right fit."

Later, after the two customers had left and the store was empty, she decided to take another risk. That sweet lady had been right. A lot of people go through tough times but they continue on.

It would be nice to have something good to think about, something new and different to look for-

ward to. That would be an excellent change of pace.
Quickly, she pulled out her phone and typed a text.

Sean, I could meet for a cup of coffee sometime
if you are still interested.

   She pressed Send before she could change her
mind.
   And then she felt a warm glow flow through her.
She seemed to be getting braver by the second.

CHAPTER FOUR

His sister, Meg, might be thirty-three years old, but she still entered a room like she had when she'd been thirteen. She blew in like she was in the middle of a hurricane. On some days, their mother had claimed, she was just as disruptive.

Sean had always loved her zest for life, though. He might be outgoing, but he also tended to be thoughtful about what he said. It wasn't uncommon for him to wait a second or two before replying to a question.

Dannette had often teased him about it, saying just once she would like to experience his unfiltered self. Now, he wished he had given that to her a lot more often.

"Who are you going to see, again?" Meg asked as she tossed her purse on the top of his dining room table.

"Way to make yourself at home, Meg."

"Oh, please. You could care less." Looking fondly over in Jackson's direction, his sister added, "Half the time I come over here, I'm in danger of cutting my feet on scattered Legos."

He'd done that more than once. "We've been working on that."

She waved off his words. "You know I'm joking."

"Okay…"

She groaned. "Sean, I want to know about this coffee date you have this afternoon. Who is she?"

After quickly looking Jackson's way, he said, "Keep your voice down, Meg. I haven't said anything to Jackson about it."

Confusion, tinged with a heavy dose of worry, entered her expression as she gripped his hand and pulled him to the table. He let himself be dragged.

"How come?" she asked. "And does Jackson need to know about you going out for a cup of coffee on a Sunday afternoon?"

Sitting down across from her, Sean did his best not to look as flustered as he felt. "Of course not. It's just coffee with an old friend."

Meg was staring at him intently. "You've got my attention now. So…you said her name was Kayla Harding?"

"Yeah. She went to Avon Lake High, too."

"I don't remember her."

"She and I were in the same grade. So she was three years younger than you."

Meg wrinkled her nose. "Nope. Her name still isn't ringing a bell… I know! We should look her up in a yearbook." Jumping to her feet, she scanned the set of bookshelves on the wall across the room. "Where are yours?"

"In a box in the basement."

"Sean. You need to dig yours out."

"There's no need. It was a long time ago." Plus, he still had boxes of Dannette's things down in the basement. Boxes that he'd promised his sister he'd sort through and get rid of but never had. "I should probably give them away one day."

"You can't do that. Jackson is going to love looking at them when he gets older."

"I doubt it."

"He will. I promise. Just like you will one day get a kick out of looking back at your high school years."

"Why is that?"

"You were practically on every other page of the yearbook."

"I wasn't." Though, he kind of had been. He'd been going out with the yearbook editor and she'd put his pictures throughout. It had been embarrassing, especially since their relationship had fizzled out long before the yearbooks were available.

And all his friends and family teased him about it mercilessly.

"I'm not getting out a yearbook just so you can see what Kayla looked like when she was fifteen. It really was a long time ago, Meg." They'd been different people then. At least, he had been.

"Come on. I bet she looks the same."

"Maybe." He shrugged. "Like I said, the year-books are in a box. And no, you are not allowed to go down there and dig through my stuff."

"That's too bad. I wouldn't mind seeing all those old pictures of you." She winked. "You were quite the guy around campus, you know."

"Please." Back in high school, he'd been all about football, scholarships and making his parents proud. He'd also been just full enough of himself to take for granted all the attention he'd gotten just because he'd been one of the stars of their football team.

Now he was a teacher, a coach, a single dad and a widower. He was also constantly tired. There weren't a whole lot of similarities between his current self and the cocky kid he'd been all those years ago.

"Okay, since I can't see a picture, you need to tell me all about her. What's her story? Where does she work?"

No way did he want to start sharing what little he knew about Kayla. Or give his nosy sister any ideas about spying on her at work. "Meg, listen. The clock is ticking and I've got to go. Don't make a big deal about this, okay?"

She must have seen something in his expression because everything about her softened. "Okay."

"I won't be long."

"Take your time. I promised Jackson that we'd make cookies and watch *Scooby-Doo*."

"I don't think kids watch that cartoon anymore."

"Jackson and I do. He loves it." She pointed to the door. "If there's a problem, I'll call. Go and relax. And have fun."

TWENTY MINUTES LATER, standing outside the coffee shop where they'd agreed to meet, Sean was wondering how he'd ever thought he'd be able to relax. When he'd arrived and didn't immediately see Kayla, he'd realized he was nervous. He knew he wasn't ready to actually start dating, but it was pretty evident that he wasn't even sure how to hang out with women as friends.

He'd met Dannette his freshman year in college. Back then, he was still riding the high of obtaining a scholarship and being on Ohio University's football team. She'd been in his English composition class. She'd been adorable, with her dark hair in a pixie cut, dancer's build and studious eyes peeking out from a pair of silver-framed eyeglasses.

When he'd asked her if he could borrow a pen, she'd given him one. And then had barely given him the time of day. For weeks.

And that had been all it took for him to become smitten.

His roommates had been sure that as soon as Dannette finally consented to go out with him, his interest in her would lag. It didn't. Every time she let him in a little bit deeper, he fell harder into her world. They'd gotten engaged the day they both graduated.

Looking back, Sean realized that their relationship had been based on his infatuation and a bunch of dumb luck. Of course, Dannette had been smart enough for both of them, which was why they'd gotten along so well.

Or, maybe it was because there had been a hundred reasons why they'd fallen in love.

All he knew now was that he had no idea if he was supposed to wait inside for Kayla, keep standing in the cold or check his phone constantly to see if she had texted to change her mind.

"Hey, Coach!"

Seeing one of his players approach, his arm tossed around his girlfriend's shoulders, Sean felt his cheeks burn with embarrassment. And, yes, envy. The kids looked relaxed and content. Pretty much the exact opposite of the way he was currently feeling. "Hey, Brandon. And…Eve, yes?"

Eve nodded. "How are you, Mr. Copeland?"

"I'm fine. Just, ah, waiting for someone. Are you two having a good Sunday?"

Brandon flashed his trademark grin. "Yeah. I went to church with Eve's family and then we went out to brunch at Kennedy's."

"I've been meaning to try out that place. How was it?"

"Great."

"I hope you didn't eat them out of house and

home," he teased. His lineman was a big boy and never shied away from second helpings at team dinners.

"Nah, I took it easy on Mr. and Mrs. Park." Glancing just beyond Sean, the senior's smile turned slick. "I think the person you're meeting just arrived, Coach."

"Oh?" When Eve pointed to his left, Sean felt like throwing his head back. Kayla was standing there with her hands stuffed in her pockets. Probably for a full minute. "Kayla. Hey. I'm sorry. I was talking to one of my players and, um, Eve here."

She smiled at the young couple. "I didn't mind. It's nice to meet you both."

"You too. Hope you have a great time on your date," Brandon said with a sly grin.

Kayla's eyes widened as she glanced his way.

Pure embarrassment engulfed him. That was all he needed—for word to get around that he was dating. Hoping to laugh off the awkward moment, he chuckled, "Sorry, buddy, but Kayla and I are not on a date."

"That's right," she added. "We're just friends."

"Oh. Sure. See ya, Coach," Brandon said before reaching for Eve's hand and guiding her away.

"Yeah. See you tomorrow, Brandon," he muttered as he opened the door to the coffee shop. "Here. Come get out of the cold."

Following her inside, he gestured to the line. "Let's order our coffees before we find a seat."

"All right." She stared at the menu and the bakery case with wide eyes. "Boy. There's a lot of choices here."

"Everything's great. Especially those peanut-butter-and-oatmeal cookies."

"Hmm."

As they moved up, he said, "Look. Um, I know it's just coffee and cookies but this is my treat."

"I can't let you do that. There's no need, anyway. We're just old friends, right?"

"Absolutely, but I want to take care of it. I'm not going to badger you to meet me for coffee and then not pay."

"Are you sure?"

"I'm sure." He was almost tempted to tease her about making a big deal out of something so small, but he held his tongue. They didn't really know each other, so he had no idea if she'd had a difficult experience with her ex.

"All right, then. Thank you."

"What will you have?" the guy behind the counter asked.

"Kayla?"

"I'll have a vanilla latte. Thanks."

"Anything to eat?"

After darting another look at the case, she said, "One of those peanut butter oatmeal cookies, please."

"Make that two cookies, a brownie and a large Americano."

"Size of the latte?"

"Large also," he added before Kayla could reply.

After paying, the cashier said that someone would bring their order to their table. Which brought forth yet another question. "How about that table for two in the corner? It's quiet and near the fireplace."

"That would be perfect."

Following her across the room, he finally took in the way her blond curls fell against her shoulder blades. How she was still as slim as she was in high school. He liked how she was wearing running shoes with her jeans and how her ivory sweater looked soft and well-worn. She looked comfortable and unpretentious.

But most of all, he liked that she looked as nervous and awkward as he felt.

If they were on the same page, then chances were good that they were going to get along fine.

CHAPTER FIVE

KAYLA SUPPOSED THE Blue Door Coffee Shop lived up to its name. It had an indigo-blue door. Inside, the baseboards surrounding the worn wood floors were painted the same shade of blue. It was pretty.

Actually, the entire space was pretty. The owners had adopted a retro vibe. Framed posters of past Medina High School musicals kept company with black-and-white photographs, an assortment of modern-looking clocks and antique furniture. Jazz music drifted from the speakers and the three college-aged people behind the counter looked happy and were joking with each other and the customers.

But what seemed to be the focal point was the gorgeous glass-and-chrome bakery case with no less than a dozen different scrumptious-looking choices inside.

All in all, the place, located kitty-corner to Loaves of Love, was adorable.

Kayla was almost sad that, after only looking in the windows for months, she'd finally stepped inside. Everything about it appealed to her. It was going to be hard to not come back anytime soon.

No, it was going to be hard because she knew she wouldn't be able to afford to return anytime soon. She shouldn't even be there now.

But at least she'd have this coffee date to look back on.

"Well, what do you think of the cookie?"

She realized then that she'd been slowly chewing that cookie while staring off into nothing. Like a dolt.

Recovering herself, she said, "Would you think I was exaggerating if I told you that it's probably one of the best things I've eaten in the last year?"

He laughed. "I thought the same thing. Whenever I take Jackson down here, he always wants to stop in for a frosted sugar cookie. I get one of those, though." He shrugged, indicating her cookie. "Even though it's getting harder and harder to not put on the pounds, I can't help it. They're just that good."

Kayla liked the way his expression softened when he talked about his son. "Tell me about Jackson."

"He's great and he's all boy." Looking sheepish, he added, "I guess I sound like a proud parent, huh?"

"There's nothing wrong with that. So, he's six?"

"He is. He just turned six. He loves to play with Legos and ride his bike and color and chat about everything under the sun."

"He sounds adorable."

"He is. Well, I think he is. He's a good kid, too. Sometimes I take him with me to practice. He knows that he has to stay out of the way and listen to me so he doesn't get hurt."

"I bet he enjoys just being there with you."

He nodded. "And being around the guys. He watches the big kids like they're superstars and passes out water when I let him."

"Do your players treat him okay?"

Sean looked surprised that she would ask. "Of course." When she raised her eyebrows, he added, "They're not only good boys, they know better than to mess with a coach's kid."

"Oh. I guess you're right." Remembering that it was Sunday afternoon, she asked, "Who's he with now?"

"My sister, Meg. Do you remember her? She was three years ahead of us."

"I don't think so. But if she wasn't in the choir or one of my classes, we probably didn't have a reason to know each other. Freshmen and seniors don't hang out together all that much."

Sean took another sip of his drink. "You've got a point," he murmured as he sat back. "Back then, we were all in our cliques, weren't we?"

"I suppose. But sometimes I think it had more to do with all the activities we did. We didn't have time to know a bunch of kids who we never saw."

"You're right. I see that now in the high school.

They're all so busy. It's rare to see kids with a lot of free time on their hands."

"You like being there, don't you?" She couldn't help but notice the rapport he'd had with Brandon and his girlfriend.

"Teaching and coaching high school?" When she nodded, a fierce look entered his eyes. "Oh, yeah. I love it. I love the way all their emotions are practically written on their faces. Everything is amplified. It's 'great' or 'horrible' or 'boring.' It keeps me young."

"You're lucky." When she realized how envious she sounded, she added, "I mean, everyone remembers the teacher who went the extra mile for them. You're going to be that person for some of your students."

"I don't know. I hope so." Obviously uncomfortable, he added, "Better than the teacher who everyone knew didn't give a damn."

"True." Giving into temptation, she took another bite of the cookie.

"What about you?"

"Hmm?" She swallowed fast.

"So far I've told you about Jackson and my job. I've told you about Dannette, too, at Loaves of Love. I want to know about you."

Like an old friend, her insecurities engulfed her. "I'm afraid there's not much to tell," she said. "I'm divorced, don't have any kids and I moved here fairly recently."

"Where do you work?"

"At the card and gift shop a couple of blocks from here." Not wanting him to ever visit her there, she decided not to share the name.

"Do you like it?"

Even though it would have been easiest to smile and say she did, Kayla couldn't do it. "I don't want to sound negative, but I don't."

Sean leaned back a bit as his voice softened. "You don't sound negative when it's the truth. So... why don't you like it? Is it boring?"

"It can be. But I don't mind the actual work. I like cards and I really like helping all the customers. They're sweet. It's...well, it's my manager that's the problem. She's kind of a jerk." Which, of course, was a huge understatement.

"Really? What does she do?"

Wishing that they'd never started talking about her job, she blurted, "Nothing too crazy." When Sean frowned, she added, "I mean, it's nothing for you to worry about—or that I can't handle."

"Oh. All right."

But it wasn't. She'd somehow made a big deal out of a basic question about her job. Forcing herself to add a little bit more info, she said, "I'm sorry, it's, ah...a sore subject with me because my boss does a weird thing with my lunch breaks. She always finds a way to shorten them but never allows me to make up the time missed."

"Man."

Realizing she sounded petty, Kayla waved a hand. "We don't have to talk about this."

"I want to. How does she manipulate you into giving up your lunch?"

She took a sip of coffee as she weighed her words. "Well, um, say she asked me to come back to the counter ten minutes early and I do. If I tell her an hour later that I need to go make the phone call I didn't have a chance to take during my lunch, she lectures me about being conscientious or something."

"Wow. She is a jerk."

"She really is." She smiled at him.

"What are you going to do?"

"Last week, I would have told you nothing, but I think I'm going to have to find a new job. I finally stood up to her on Friday."

Sean grinned. "Good for you!"

"It would've been good if she'd been impressed with my gumption. She was not."

"Man, I'm sorry."

"That's okay. If it wasn't for that, I probably wouldn't have changed my mind about meeting you here. She made me so mad that I decided that I needed to have something fun to look forward to." She moaned. "And now I sound pretty boring. And like a bad employee, too." And, maybe, like she was making something more of this meeting than there was.

He laughed. "Not at all. You sound sweet."

Kayla doubted that, but now she felt embarrassed. Here, he'd asked her something about herself and all she'd done was complain about her job. Since she didn't want to apologize again, she tried to move the conversation along. "When I'm not complaining about my job, I like to go walking. There are a lot of nice parks and walking trails in the area."

"I've discovered that, too. Maybe one day we can meet to go for a walk."

"I'd like that, as long as walking doesn't actually mean running," she teased.

"I promise, it's just walking. My knees have told me loud and clear that they have no need to run five miles ever again."

Pretty sure he wasn't in as bad shape as he was letting on, she chuckled. "It's a date, then. I mean, as friends."

"Yeah. Of course." He paused. "I might not be free for a couple more weeks, though. We've got homecoming coming up, and then a chance to make it to playoffs."

"I understand." Thinking of how busy he was— and how she had nothing but time on her hands— she added, "Listen, if you're ever in a bind and need a hand with Jackson, feel free to reach out. I'd be happy to hang out with him."

Sean stared at her intently. "You mean that, don't you?"

"I do. I like kids."

"Why don't you have any? Did your ex not want children?" Practically the moment he spoke, he tilted his head back with a groan. "Sorry. That's none of my business."

"I don't mind answering. The reason is nothing too personal. First, we wanted to wait. Then, it was obvious that we weren't going to last." Thinking about that decision, her chest felt tight. Accepting that they were never going to live happily ever after had been so hard. Catching her breath, she added, "It was for the best."

Sean's blue eyes settled on her. Then he smiled. "Thanks for the offer about Jackson. I appreciate it."

"You're welcome."

"Hey, I almost forgot to ask how you liked volunteering over at Loaves of Love."

And just like that, all the progress they'd made in their relationship evaporated in an instant.

At least for her.

Doubts set in. What was she doing, talking bad about her job and offering to babysit his son when she couldn't even afford a trip to the grocery store?

"Kayla, you okay?"

"Sorry, I, um, just thought of something I was going to do today." She shook her head, as if she was trying to clear it. "I liked Loaves of Love a lot. It's a great organization."

"Edna is a powerhouse, isn't she? I don't know

how she accomplishes so much at once. She must not sleep."

"She is impressive. I mean, what I know about her so far. I didn't get a chance to talk to her much, but she seems very nice."

"I think it's such a worthy organization. I like how people in need can help others while they help themselves."

With each second, she was feeling more and more like an imposter. "Yes. I like that, too."

"I mean, there's nothing wrong with needing a helping hand from time to time, but it's probably a good idea if people don't get into a habit of getting something for nothing."

And now she felt even worse. Though she was pretty sure that Sean had no idea how callous he sounded, she felt as if he'd emotionally slapped her. "I doubt anyone there for food shows up because they want to take advantage of others."

"Well, no. Of course not."

"I mean, asking a stranger to help so they can eat...well, that's got to be hard."

"You're right." Looking more miserable, he added, "I'm sorry. You're exactly right. I spoke without thinking."

"You have every right to have an opinion. And, um, it's not my place to tell you how to think. I'm sorry for jumping all over you."

And...it was time to call it a day. Looking at one of the numerous clocks on the wall, she reached for her purse. "Gosh, look at the time," she said as she stood up. "I hadn't realized it was so late."

"Hey. Wait—"

"I'm sorry. I really do have to go." She picked up her empty plate and half-drunk latte. "Thanks again for the coffee and the cookie. It was great. I'll go take this to the counter."

Sean was on his feet, too. "Kayla. Listen, I'm sorry for sounding so full of myself. Maybe it's because I hang out with teenage boys all the time—or maybe it's me—I don't know. I do know that I've started speaking more and more without thinking. I'll do better. Please, don't rush off."

"I'm not rushing off anywhere. I've just got to go." She smiled, though she was pretty sure it looked more like a grimace. She turned, hurried to the counter and handed the guy her dishes. "Thanks."

Turning back to Sean, she noticed he was still on his feet, but hadn't moved. His expression was blank.

He probably had no idea what to think. No doubt about it, she'd made a real mess of this meeting.

Face burning, she hurried to the door. "Bye, Sean."

"Yeah, bye," he said.

And then she was out of there. Practically race-walking down the sidewalk.

Glad that she'd walked there instead of driving,

she turned right, needing some space away from the town square.

Needing the time to reflect on just what a mess her life had become. She hated her job. She didn't have a lot of hobbies. She was still hurting and dealing with emotional scars from her divorce. And yet she had no problem giving Sean a piece of her mind for having the nerve to utter a careless comment. Instead of being honest and telling him why she'd been at Loaves of Love in the first place.

"You, Kayla Harding, need an attitude adjustment," she proclaimed under her breath.

Her conscience merely informed her that what she really needed was a new life.

And here she'd thought she'd already accomplished that.

Boy, she had a ways to go.

CHAPTER SIX

AFTER SPENDING A few hours every afternoon looking for other jobs but finding nothing that sounded better than her current situation, Kayla woke up on Friday morning determined to adopt a more positive attitude. At least she knew what to expect at Tami's Cards. The few other jobs that she was qualified for were either thirty-to-forty minutes away or sounded far more stressful. She decided it would be much better to grin and bear her current situation while she explored more options.

Unfortunately, all her good intentions deflated when she arrived at work and discovered that Tamera had cut her hours for the following week and for that very day. She was only scheduled to work four hours. To make matters worse, Tamera ignored every attempt Kayla made to talk to her while she was in the shop. Her manager either focused on customers, chatted on the phone or disappeared into her office.

Knowing her next paycheck wasn't going to be

enough to make ends meet, she knocked on her manager's door at the end of her shift that afternoon.

"Yes, Kayla?" Tamera asked after giving Kayla permission to enter.

"I don't understand why you cut my hours."

"It's fairly obvious, don't you think? We're not all that busy so everyone's hours got cut."

"But when I spoke to you about my need to have at least thirty hours a week, you said you understood."

"I did." Folding her hands on top of her desk, she continued. "I understood that you were disappointed."

"But my pay—"

Tamera sighed. "Kayla, there's nothing I can do. The store needs to make a profit. I can't do that if I'm paying folks to stand around and do nothing. Surely, even you can understand that." She smiled, just like that should have made plenty of sense.

Boy, that "even you" comment burned, but Kayla did her best to focus on her bills. "Now I have even less hours than I did before. I have bills to pay."

She exhaled. "Kayla, I'm sorry, but that's not my problem. There is nothing else I can tell you."

"I see." And, finally, she did see. She was in a bad situation. Every day, it was getting harder and harder to find anything in her job that she enjoyed. It was going to get worse, too, if she didn't do something about it.

Kayla turned around, walked straight to the storage room and picked up her lunch bag, coat and purse and then headed out.

Amy, who was opening a large box of cards to sort, looked up as Kayla approached. "Uh-oh. I'm guessing Tamera didn't understand your concerns?"

"Not even a little bit. I'm barely going to make enough to pay my gas and water bills," she confided.

"I'm so sorry. I'm only doing this job to get a little bit of extra spending money, but her cutting everyone's hours is tough."

"Yeah." It was a struggle to keep her expression neutral when the jealousy she was suddenly feeling felt like it was eating a hole in her stomach. Amy was a nice lady but had no idea what she was going through.

"What are you going to do?"

Or…maybe she did understand. "I don't know. I'll think of something, though."

Amy's expression brightened once again. "Good luck. I'll see you in a couple of days. Have a good weekend."

"Thanks, you too."

The chilly air kissed her cheeks when she stepped outside. The weather was getting colder. Halloween was in a couple of weeks. Soon, they'd have their first snow. Usually, she got excited about the change of seasons, but all she could seem to think about was how much the gas bill was going to be if she had to turn on the heat.

For about the hundredth time, Kayla wished things were getting easier. She felt so alone, too. She was so embarrassed by her circumstances, she was reluctant to burden anyone with her worries.

Her friends would be uncomfortable and would feel like she was sharing her news because she wanted money. Her parents would offer to help her out again but there was no way she was going to accept help from them. Not with her father recovering from radiation treatments for prostate cancer. And there was no way she was going to ask her sister, Meredith, for anything. Meredith was a buyer for a big store in Seattle and led a glamorous life. Even though Meredith would Venmo her some money before they got off the phone, that would be something neither of them would ever forget. It would be a really low point in Kayla's life if she had to ask Meredith for help.

Taking a deep breath, she was just about to head for her car when she spied the Loaves of Love building and remembered that Edna had said that they baked loaves several days a week. Maybe she could stop by and see if they needed an extra pair of hands.

And, sure, she might be able to take home a loaf of bread if she helped. But that wasn't what was on her mind. No, she needed to do something that made her feel good. Her heart needed that more than anything.

Next thing she knew, she was walking inside.

And there was Edna, sitting at the desk just like she had two weeks previously. She had a pencil in her right hand and was obviously checking off a list, but when she lifted her head and spied Kayla, she smiled.

"You came back! I'm so glad."

"I remembered today was bread-baking day. I just got off work and decided to see if you could use an extra pair of hands."

"You came at the perfect time," Edna said as she got to her feet. "All the loaves are in the ovens, but we could sure use some help bagging loaves of bread and wiping down countertops. What do you think? Are you up for that?"

"Absolutely."

"I'll walk you inside and introduce you to Mike. He's supervising everyone today."

"Okay."

She paused in the doorway. "How are you doing, otherwise?"

"Okay." Her bottom lip trembled but she didn't want to make this visit about her.

But still Edna noticed. Lowering her voice—even though there wasn't anyone around to over-hear—she said, "How's your food situation?"

"It's not bad." It wasn't good, but she could survive a little longer.

"You sure about that?" Edna asked in a kind way.

Unable to lie anymore, she shrugged. "I still

have some food left. Plus, I didn't bring a canvas bag."

"You know what? I seem to remember a couple of things that were brought in this week that you might be able to use. While you work in the kitchen, I'll put them in a sack and place them next to your coat and purse."

"That isn't necessary. I didn't come in for a handout. I came to help."

"And your help is appreciated." As those words sank in, Edna gave her a long look. "Do you hear what I'm saying, dear?"

"I think so."

"Loaves of Love is here for a reason. It is possible to want to help out and accept a helping hand at the same time."

"I hadn't thought about it that way."

"I hope you will now. So…may I fill a bag for you and set it next to your things?"

There was only one answer to give. "Yes." Releasing a ragged breath, she added, "Thank you, Edna. Your help is appreciated, too. Very much."

Edna beamed. "There you go, Kayla. That's much better. Being able to accept a gift is a wonderful thing." Turning to an elderly man with a mustache, she said, "Mike, this is Kayla. She's here to help bag bread and wipe counters."

Mike waved. "Come over here, young lady, and wash your hands. You walked in at the perfect time. I was just wondering how I was going to get all these loaves bagged up. I'm going to put you right to work."

Kayla decided those words were the best things she'd heard all day.

CHAPTER SEVEN

FEELING PLEASED, Edna sat back, stretched her legs, and looked out the front window. It had been an especially calm day at Loaves of Love. The volunteers had arrived on time, they'd been pleasant and had done a good job making bread. The phones had been quiet, and her flour supplier had even called to say that they were sending over an additional fifty pounds of flour with this month's order. They wanted to do their part for the organization.

To top it off, Edna had only had a handful of folks come in for food. That should be a good thing, she supposed. It might even mean that some of her clients' situations had improved and they no longer needed a helping hand.

She should be writing notes about this in her journal. At the very least, describing the day in glowing terms—proof that this organization she used to dream about actually could be a successful venture.

She'd begun to record one or two sentences

about each day when she'd opened the building. She could write all that down.

Instead, she continued to look out the front window.

Several people walked by. One little boy looked in, caught sight of her and waved. She waved back. Other than that, nothing.

Restless, she stood up and turned around. She knew she could go into the kitchen and help the volunteers bag the last of the bread and clean. A lot of times she did that.

But they had things handled. Edna had learned that if she got too involved in other people's work, they'd step aside, feeling like she should be the one handling things. That didn't empower them. All it did was make them feel like they weren't doing a good job.

Plus, Kayla was smiling. She was talking to a pair of old-timers who'd just walked in and they were making her giggle. The poor girl had looked like she had the world on her shoulders when she'd walked through the door. For some reason, she'd needed to volunteer today.

And, Edna suspected, she was going to need some groceries to get her through the week as well. She'd almost forgotten to get those for her.

Pleased to have a task to do, she put up a sign that said she'd be right back, and walked down a back hallway to the "store." When she'd taken over the food bank, the first thing she'd noticed was that the area where all the food was stored looked like someone's abandoned basement. The space was dark, uninviting and cramped. She'd hated that.

So, she'd rearranged the whole space and even added two windows. They had frosted glass so no one could see inside, but they did make things a whole lot cheerier.

She'd also painted the walls a buttery yellow and replaced the worn linoleum floor with some luxury vinyl tile that looked like big planks of wood. Every time she walked inside the space, she smiled.

Picking up a paper bag, she began pulling items from up and down the aisles, then grabbed a plastic bag for some bars of soap, foil and other items that folks on a budget had a hard time buying.

Two hard raps to the back door made her jump.

Opening it up, she saw Wayne Bradshaw.

"Wayne?"

He looked just as dumbstruck as she probably looked. "Edna? Wow." Taking two steps in, he wrapped her in a hug.

She hugged him back, pleasantly surprised. Stepping back, she gripped his arms. "How long has it been? What are you doing here?"

"It has to be at least eight or ten years since I've seen hide or hair of you," he teased. "And, to answer your other question, I'm here to deliver some ground beef."

"What?"

He looked around. "This is the food bank, right?"

"Well, yes."

"Long story, but I was with my son. He and one of his friends bought a cow. They decided to donate some of the ground chuck instead of storing it in their freezer for four months. I was headed this way so I offered to drop it off."

"I can't believe it. But I'm so happy you did. My clients are going to be so excited. Fresh ground beef is a treat these days." Remembering that Kayla was probably just about done and that there might be someone else waiting in the lobby, she glanced toward the hallway behind them. "Speaking of which, I probably need to go to the front. People are in the kitchen and I also have someone waiting on some items."

Wayne's expression warmed. "I understand. Do you trust me to bring in the meat myself?"

"Of course." She pointed to the freezers. "If you could stack the meat in there, I'd appreciate it. And, if you don't mind, maybe even bring a pound to the lobby? There's someone there who could use your gift."

"I can do that. I have twelve pounds of meat in one-pound bags. After I get eleven in the freezer, I'll come see you with the last bag."

"That sounds good. Thanks." She hurried back to the front, Kayla's bags in each of her hands.

No one was waiting there. A glance inside the

kitchen showed that Kayla was helping to stack chairs. She'd be done soon.

Sure enough, ten minutes later, all five of the volunteers wandered out.

"Everything's cleaned up, Edna," Phyllis called out. "The space is ready for the next group."

"Thank you. Have a good afternoon."

After exchanging pleasantries with the other three volunteers, she was alone with Kayla. She, like the others, was holding a loaf of bread.

"Is it okay that I kept a loaf like I did last time?"

"Of course. That's what it's there for."

"Thank you."

"Are you doing all right? You seemed a little frazzled when you arrived."

"I'm okay. Better. I just needed to get out of my head for a little bit."

"I know the feeling. Listen, I have some items for you, but an old friend of mine just stopped by with some fresh ground beef. He said he'd be here shortly." Hearing footsteps, she smiled. "And here he is."

Kayla's eyes widened.

Looking at Wayne, she figured he was a bit intimidating at first glance. He was tall and rather imposing. His resting face looked like he was about to bite somebody's head off. But when he smiled, his appearance completely changed. He looked a little like a big teddy bear.

Luckily, he was smiling at Kayla. "Kayla, please meet Wayne. Wayne, this is Kayla."

"Nice to meet you." Handing Edna the bag of ground beef, he added, "Here you go."

"Kayla, do you eat meat?"

"I do."

"Then this is for you," she said as she placed the meat in one of the bags.

"Wow. Thanks."

Kayla was looking pretty confused that Wayne had brought out a pound of ground beef. Chuckling, Edna said, "There's a story about how the hamburger got here, but I'll wait to share until the next time you come in to volunteer." She added smoothly, "Here you go, dear." She handed both bags to Kayla, who placed the loaf of bread into the top of one. "Have a good night."

Kayla was looking at the two bags like Edna had handed her the moon. "I don't know what to say. Like I said, I only came in to help out."

Not wanting to rehash her earlier words, Edna said, "Dear, all you have to do is tell me that you'll be back again."

"I will."

"I'm glad. Now you take care, honey."

After Kayla walked out and the door closed behind her, Wayne spoke. "I think you just made that girl's day."

"I hope so. Kayla looked pretty stressed out when she walked in a little while ago. She is a sweetheart, but I fear she's got a lot on her plate. I hope she has someone that she can talk to. I hate the idea of her carrying all her burdens by herself."

Wayne crossed his arms over his chest. "Edna, this facility, this place you have?"

"Yes?"

"Well, it's amazing. I remember when you used to talk about doing something like this."

"Do you?" A melancholy wave of emotion settled in her chest, but it wasn't unpleasant. Wayne had been one of her husband Phil's best work friends.

Edna had liked him, too. She'd gotten along with his wife, Georgia, all right, but it had been obvious that they were never going to be best friends. Georgia had been a sporty woman and was always entered in some golf or tennis tournament. Unfortunately, Edna had always been uncoordinated.

Thinking about those old days, when there had been four of them, she murmured, "Do you remember sitting around at those business dinners and dreaming?"

"I do. I remember like it was yesterday." His mouth tightened. "We had big dreams back then, didn't we?"

She knew what he was referring to. They'd talked about trips the four of them would take for fun. The guys used to say that they were going to go on long fishing trips when they were old and retired. She and Georgia used to say they'd go on vacations and sleep late and play with grandchildren. None of them had imagined that two of their lives would be cut short.

"I've long since stopped asking the Lord why He made me a widow at fifty-two. He just did."

Some of the tension in his expression eased. "I asked some of those same questions." After sharing a commiserating smile, he looked down at his boots before meeting her gaze. "Did you ever remarry?"

"No. You?"

"Nah. I figure I'm probably too set in my ways for anyone else to want to put up with me."

She chuckled. "Same."

He pursed his lips, seemed to consider his words for a spell, then added, "That said, I still like to eat dinner. When do you get off? Want to grab a bite to eat?"

Working in a food bank, she'd thought she'd seen it all. She didn't think many things could surprise her anymore. But getting asked out to dinner by an old friend who was looking at her like she was still attractive?

Well, she sure hadn't seen that coming.

Trying it on for size, she realized that she didn't hate the feeling. "Where were you thinking?" Gesturing to her usual uniform of jeans, tennis shoes and sweater, she added, "I'm not dressed for anywhere fancy."

"I'm not, either. What about that Mexican restaurant on the corner?"

"That sounds good." Telling herself that it would simply be nice to not eat alone in front of the TV, she smiled at him. "I can meet you there in about fifteen minutes. I need to walk around and close up the building. Make sure everything is locked up tight." And maybe take a moment to comb her hair or something.

"Do you need help?"

"Nope. But thanks for asking."

"I'll get a table and see you in about twenty. Sounds good?"

"Yes. Would you like me to walk you to the back door?"

"I'm good. I can walk around the building easy enough."

Watching him walk out the front door, Edna felt a shiver of anticipation settle into her stomach. Instead of pushing it away and chiding herself for acting like a silly girl, she elected to hold it close.

Sure, she was just going to dinner with her husband's old friend, but it felt like something more.

And for the first time in a long while, she decided that maybe she wouldn't be opposed to something more in her life.

No, she wouldn't be opposed to that at all.

CHAPTER EIGHT

"ZACK LOOKS GOOD," Cal Melon told Sean on Monday morning. They were watching their star running back go through a second set of exercises with the athletic trainer on the practice field. Zack Schrock looked like he was handling every movement easily. Just like he had before he'd gotten hurt.

Sean agreed with the head coach. Ever since Zack had gotten tackled and started favoring one of his knees, he'd been keeping an eye on the sophomore. Zack was a gifted athlete and a couple of scouts were already showing up at his games. If he stayed healthy, chances were very good that he would get a scholarship to a Division 1 college.

But, the guy pushed himself too hard and also lied about his pain. Sean had been debating whether to have a heart-to-heart with the kid or let Cal make that call. Someone needed to do it before Zack hurt himself again.

"He's been working hard. And supposedly resting it, too."

Cal frowned. "Supposedly?"

"I could be wrong, but I've been getting the feeling that he's not being completely truthful."

"That puts a new spin on things. So, what do you think? Can he start on Friday? We need him, but not enough to risk him being out the rest of the season."

It was a hard call, but Sean remembered being in Zack's situation. Not only was he hoping to play in college, the kid also lived to be on the field. "I think so," he said slowly. He paused, then blurted, "I want to speak with him, though. He's got big dreams. I don't want him losing his focus and damaging that knee." Feeling obligated, he added, "Unless you want to speak to him instead."

"No reason for me to get involved. You're the one with the close rapport with the boy. You do it."

"All right. Thanks."

Cal's jaw tightened. "As much as I want Zack playing hard, his family's counting on that scholarship."

"Zack is, too. Plus, I think there might be something else going on. He hasn't seemed himself." Sean paused. "It might be my imagination, though."

"We'll see. Follow your instincts, Sean. Zack trusts you. I know you'll say the right words, but don't forget to let him know that you realize what he's up against. I think some of these boys forget that we were once in their shoes."

"Will do."

"Good." Cal wrote a couple of notes on his clipboard. "Fill me in if you think there's something going on that I need to know."

"I will."

"Thanks." After glancing at his phone's screen, Cal looked back at Sean. "Before I forget, can you come to practice Wednesday night? I know you usually keep it clear for Jackson, but Nan's got a program at school. She's singing a solo. I told her I'd be there."

Nan was Cal's seventh grader. As much as Sean liked giving his Wednesday afternoons and evenings to Jackson, he knew Cal's family was important to him, too. "I'll see what I can do."

"Thanks. It's appreciated."

After speaking with a couple of the boys lifting weights, their head coach walked out. Five minutes later, the buzzer Sean had set on his phone sounded. "Good job, guys!" he called out. "You've got fifteen minutes to shower and head to class. See you at practice this afternoon."

"Yes, Coach," most of them chorused.

Seeing Zack approaching, Sean said, "You have study hall first bell, right?"

Zack pulled to a stop. "Yes, Coach."

"Come into my office as soon as you shower."

Worry entered his eyes, but he only nodded.

When Zack walked into his office seven minutes later wearing a pair of jeans, a gray T-shirt and wet hair, his worried expression was more pronounced.

Sean had been debating the best way to share

his concerns and had decided it would be best to come straight to the point. Zack was a worrier. He wasn't going to be able to talk about anything until his mind was at ease.

"Have a seat." He gestured to the two bottles of Powerade he'd put on the desk. "Help yourself."

"Thanks." He unscrewed the cap and downed half of the bottle.

After taking a fortifying sip of his own drink, Sean rested his palms on his knees. "Zack, I wanted to speak to you about two things."

"Okay."

"One of them has to do with Friday's game. The other is more personal."

"Personal? What's wrong?"

Glad that he'd put it out there, he said, "I know you've been upset about your knee, and I want to talk about it. But, I've gotten the feeling that something else is going on, too."

Zack put the half-drunk Powerade on the desk. "Going on with what?"

"You. Now, you know I check in with your teachers, so I know your grades are good."

The boy nodded. "I know they are, too."

"And, you seem to be getting along with everyone on the team just fine." He raised his eyebrows. "Am I right?"

"Yes, Coach." His worried expression was turning more perplexed.

"So, I'm guessing that whatever is on your mind has to do with home. Or, maybe a girl?"

Zack grimaced. "I don't have a problem with a girl, Coach. I've sworn off them for a while."

"So, that brings us to my last idea. What's going on at home?"

When Zack stiffened, Sean added, "You can handle my nosy questions two ways. You can tell me that it's none of my business and we'll leave it at that. Or…you can trust me to have your back and keep anything you share between us."

He scoffed. "You'd really let me tell you something was none of your business?"

"In this case, yes." He lowered his voice. "But I'd rather you try to let me help you. I'm your assistant coach, but I'm more than that. I care about you. Just like you're one of my players, but there's more to you than just being a member of the team."

And just like that, all of Zack's bluster imploded. He closed down in front of Sean. "If I thought you could help, I'd tell you. But I don't think it's possible."

Now Sean was wishing he'd said something better. Anything that had meaning, that would encourage the kid to trust him. His mouth was dry, but he forced himself to say the words. "I'm not a miracle worker. If I can't help you, I'll tell you that I can't." Remembering Cal's advice, he added slowly, "I don't mention it much, but you remind me a lot of myself, Zack."

"Why?"

"I loved playing ball, but I also wanted to go to college. I knew from the time I was in middle school that my grades were never going to be good enough to get a scholarship. The only thing that would was football. I lived in fear of messing up or getting hurt and ruining my entire future."

"But you did get the scholarship." Zack's gaze darted to a frame on the wall. It held a picture Sean's parents had taken the night his team had won a play-off game for OU.

"I did. It was never a certainty, though."

Zack's eyes darted around the room, pinging off Sean's old high school photos. A picture of him on the field after a particularly good game at OU. A photo of him holding Jackson. Zack's gaze lingered on that for a few moments, then stilled as he saw another photo, this one smaller and taped to the corner of Sean's desk. It was of Dannette and him on their first anniversary.

"That's your wife, isn't it?"

"Yes."

Zack swallowed. "And she died, right? I mean, that's what I heard," he said in a rush.

Feeling like the kid had just tackled him, Sean sucked in a breath and steadied himself. He was going to answer the boy's questions with honestly. Even if it took him off guard. "Yes. Her name was Dannette, and she did die. Three years ago."

"And now you just have your son? There's only the two of you."

"That's right, Zack." Feeling like he needed to add something, he said, "Jackson is six."

"You two ever have some hard days?"

Sean nodded. "We've had more than a couple." His muscles tightened. Where was this going? Was his mother sick? He forced himself to take another sip of his drink and be patient.

Maybe it was the silence. Maybe it was the pain that Sean had—for once—not been afraid to hide. Whatever the reason, the boy seemed to come to a decision.

"My mother is pregnant, and my dad had an accident at work." He kept his eyes averted. "We have insurance, but it's not great. And then something happened with the pipe in the laundry room. It flooded." He swallowed. "We...we don't have a lot of food in the house anymore."

"You're hungry."

Some of the vulnerability that had been shining in Zack's eyes faded. "No. I'm okay. I mean, I eat lunch here. And on game days..."

"The booster club provides dinner."

"Yeah. And sometimes the guys help me out." Zack rolled his shoulders. "But that doesn't help my mom much. Or my little sisters. And I can't help out with the bills by getting a job because I've got to get this scholarship."

It was all becoming painfully clear now. Sean

had thought Zack was feeling a lot of pressure, but it was nothing compared to what he was actually experiencing. "And then you got hit."

Zack averted his eyes. Rolled his shoulders. "I'll be all right."

"I can help you."

"I can't take a handout. No way."

"Zack, I volunteer at Loaves of Love. It's a food bank. I can help your parents get food there."

"No way will my dad be okay with that. He'd freak out."

"You don't think he'd even accept food if it was for your sisters and your mom?"

He shook his head. "He doesn't want charity."

Sean swallowed. Reminded himself that there was more than one way to win a game. "Okay, then how about this. I'm going to go over there during my lunch break and pick up some food for you. I'll put it in an extra duffle bag. After practice, you take it on home and decide what to do with it."

"You serious? You want me to sneak it home?"

He nodded. "I'm very serious."

"But—"

"Here's what you're going to do. You are going to give it to your mom. Or, keep it in your room and share it with your sisters. And if that won't go over well, then you keep it and eat breakfast and have something for when you get home."

"Coach—"

Even though the kid was looking panicked, Sean

talked right over him. "If this goes okay, we'll do it again next week." He gave him a hard look. "I can't change your circumstances or your father's mind. But I can do something about you eating, Zack. You're important to me. And, if that isn't enough for you to hear, how about this? We need you strong so you can play and help us win games and you need to be strong so you can get that scholarship."

"I...I don't know what to say."

"Yes, you do. You know exactly what to say." He hardened his voice. "You say, *Yes, Coach*."

A warmth filled Zack's eyes. "Yes, Coach."

"Good. Now get to class."

Zack tossed the empty drink in the trashcan and picked up his backpack and headed to the door. "Hey, Coach?"

"Yeah?"

"Thanks."

"You're welcome. See you at practice."

The smile the sophomore threw his way felt like he'd just received a bonus and a new car, all at the same time.

He'd done the right thing.

CHAPTER NINE

WHEN HER PHONE rang on Monday evening, mere minutes after walking in her apartment's front door, Kayla was tempted to ignore it. It had been a day. No, it had been a day and a half. Not only had Tamera been in a bad mood and seemed to find fault with everything she did, but the weather was dreary and cold. Few customers had walked through the doors, which made an already-long day even longer. Kayla couldn't believe the irony. This was one day that she would have given anything to leave early, yet Tamera had kept her until five o'clock.

Then, just when she'd thought her day couldn't get worse, it started sleeting as she left work. Even though she was so glad that she'd been able to keep her paid-off vehicle after the divorce, she wished she'd had something more suited to winter weather. The short drive home on nearly bald tires was no fun. And…she'd slipped on the unsalted sidewalk next to the grouping of mailboxes outside her building. Now, she had a sore knee and a scraped hand.

When the cell chirped a third time, she tossed her things from her purse onto the floor and answered, "Hello?"

"Kayla, is that you?"

It was Sean. She rolled her eyes. *Of course* he had to call the very moment she was about to burst into tears. "Yeah, it's me." Realizing how rude she sounded, she attempted to gather herself together. "Hey, I'm sorry. Let me try this again. Hi."

"No worries. It sounds as if I caught you at a bad time."

"Not at all," she said in a rush. "I was just getting home when my cell phone rang." After kicking off her shoes, she shrugged out of her coat and tossed it on the back of a chair.

"Are you okay?"

"Kind of." Usually she would've said she was great, but the conversation was already too far gone. She was way beyond faking a good mood. "It's been a rough day." Looking down at the spot of blood on her wood floor, she attempted to laugh. "And I just slipped and fell on the sidewalk."

"Oh, no. Are you hurt?"

"No. I mean, I scraped up my hand, but I'm fine." Hating that she'd spent the first few minutes of their conversation complaining, she reminded herself that she'd been through far worse things than a long day and a scraped hand. "How are you? Please tell me you are having a better day."

He chuckled. "You know what? I'm pretty sure I am."

Sitting down in her favorite chair next to the fireplace, she smiled. "Tell me something good, then."

"Okay...let's see. Jackson got his first A on a spelling test, made his bed today and...I think I made some headway with one of my players who's been going through a rough patch."

His examples made all her petty problems slide to the wayside. "That's great," she said. "Making a bed is a big first step. So are getting A's. And making headway with a teenager? Well, I think that sounds like a pretty big deal."

"In the grand scheme of things, it probably isn't, but I've learned not to take good things for granted."

Those were words to live by. "I feel better already. I'm glad you called."

"Well, you might not be when you realize that I didn't just call to tell you about my day."

"Oh?"

"I called to see if you were serious the other day when you mentioned that you'd be happy to help me out with Jackson if I was ever in a bind."

"I was serious. I guess that bind has happened?"

"Yeah. Cal, the head coach, has another obligation on Wednesday night. Wednesday night is usually my day off practice, but Cal asked me to work. I would usually call my brother or my sister or my parents, but my parents are out of town, one of my brother's kids has the flu and my sister just helped me out on Sunday." He sighed. "I could ask her but—"

"I'll be happy to," she said quickly.

"Wait. Are you sure?"

"Very sure." Before he could protest some more or give her more reasons that she didn't need, Kayla added, "Give me the details and I'll follow them to a T."

He chuckled. "You know, I'd probably argue further if I wasn't so desperate."

"No need."

"All right. Let's see. I usually have him take the school bus home on Wednesdays. So, he could meet you at my house. Luckily, it stops almost directly in front of our house."

"What time is that?"

"Three thirty. Can you do that?"

He sounded so worried. Glancing at her schedule, Kayla double-checked that she was scheduled to get off at three on Wednesday. So, it would be tight, but it was possible. "I can."

"You'd need to be outside, waiting on him," he warned. "The bus driver doesn't like to drop him off if there's nobody there."

"That makes sense. I'll be there. I promise."

"Thanks so much. I owe you."

"Sean, it's not a big deal. I'm glad I can help."

"All right." He took a deep breath. "Now that that's settled, I'll need to give you the key and the security code and let you know about snacks…" His voice drifted off. "Boy, I'm just now realizing how much I've taken my family for granted. They do a lot."

"I'm pretty sure you don't take them for granted at all, and that they know you appreciate their help. Why don't you text me all the details? That way they're all written down."

"I have a better idea. Do you want to come over in an hour? Say, at six? I'm going to order a pizza. Then I could show you everything and Jackson and you could meet."

Going over there sounded great. Even though the drive was going to be a little bit tough, not eating a peanut butter sandwich by herself for dinner sounded heavenly. "I'd love to."

He exhaled. "Thanks. I'll text you my address."

"And I'll be there at six," she finished with a smile.

After they hung up, she leaned back and smiled. With one ten-minute phone call, her day had gone from terrible to good.

Maybe even better than good. Despite the awkward moment when he'd said something callous about being accepting handouts, Kayla thought he was a pretty great guy.

No, he was more than that. Sean was becoming

a friend. Liking how warm he sounded whenever he discussed Jackson, Kayla couldn't wait to meet his little boy.

She also couldn't deny that it was nice to be needed. For the last six or seven months, it had felt like she was the needy one. Even though all she was being asked to do was hang out with a six-year-old for a couple of hours, she was thrilled to be given that task. She might not be a parent, but she knew no parent ever entrusted the care of their child with another person lightly.

Glancing at the clock, she realized it was going to be time to leave soon. And…she had a dirty, scraped-up hand to attend to.

She hustled to the bathroom to clean up her hand, brush her hair, and put on a pair of jeans and one of her favorite sweaters.

Thirty minutes later, she was back in the car and carefully navigating her way to Sean and Jackson's house. Noticing the telltale white lines on the road, she sighed in relief. The salt trucks had just come by. In addition, the sleet had turned into light snow. Her tires were going to be okay. When she heard the weatherman on the radio say that the snow was supposed to stop within the hour and would likely not stick, Kayla exhaled.

That was something to be grateful for, she reminded herself. Growing up in northeast Ohio meant that she was used to driving in sleet and snow.

At least the weather didn't get her down too often.

The moment she pulled into Sean's driveway, the front door opened. Both Sean and Jackson stood in the doorway until she got out, and then headed her way.

"Glad you got here in one piece," Sean said with a smile.

For a full second, she allowed herself to be wowed by that smile—and by the way his gaze seemed so warm and appreciative. "Me, too," she answered.

"Hi!" Jackson called out.

Relieved to focus on the boy, she gave him a little wave. "Hi!" Jackson was Sean's mini-me, from his blue eyes to his dark hair to his stocky, athletic build. It was as if God had decided that one Sean wasn't enough.

The little boy came to a stop right in front of her and puffed up his chest a bit. "I'm Jackson Copeland."

After sharing a smile with Sean, she held out her hand. "It's nice to meet you, Jackson. I'm Kayla Harding."

"I like your name, Kayla."

"She's *Miss Harding* to you, Jackson," Sean murmured.

"Oh. Sorry, Miss Harding."

After darting a glance at Sean, she turned her attention back to Jackson. "I like your name, too. Want to show me your room?"

His eyes lit up. "Yes. Do you like trains?"

"I sure do. I love them."

"You're gonna love my room, then," he said in an excited tone. "I have a wooden train set." Scampering ahead, Jackson ran inside the house.

Well aware that Sean was right by her side—and that he happened to smell really good—she struggled to keep her voice relaxed and friendly. "He's the cutest thing I've ever seen, Sean. Really."

"Thank you. I think he's great, but Jackson can still be a handful."

"He's a little boy. I think he's supposed to be."

"Probably so," he said with a laugh. "Here, let me take your coat."

"Thank you." Feeling the way his hands brushed against her neck as he reached for it, she tried to act as if she was used to such gentlemanly behavior. She wasn't, though. Jared had never been taught to do things like that. Or, if he had, he'd sure never decided she was worth the effort. She couldn't remember him ever holding doors for her, pulling out her chair or taking her coat.

Until this moment, she hadn't thought it was a big deal. Now, she was wondering why she'd started to believe that she didn't need her husband to treat her nicely.

"Miss Harding, I have them all out!" Jackson called.

"I'm on my way." She reached down to unlace her boots, and slipped them off before heading to the boy's side.

He took her hand and pulled her to the back of his room. There stood a wooden train table with a fancy wooden train on the wooden track. Everything was in bold primary colors, which fit in well with the bright and cheerful room.

"Oh, Jackson. We're going to have so much fun playing trains on Wednesday afternoon."

"We can play with them now if you want." He picked up a bright green one. "I'll even let you have this one."

"Sorry, sport, but Kayla worked all day and I bet she's starving," Sean said from his spot by the door. "Let me get her something to drink and relax for a spell. Our pizza should be here in a couple of minutes."

"Fine." Jackson wrinkled his nose but didn't argue.

"Wednesday will be here before we know it," she whispered.

He brightened. "Yeah," he whispered back.

"What can I get you?" Sean asked as they walked back down the hall toward a living room with a kitchen beyond. Everything in the living room was cozy looking and in shades of brown. Much of it looked well-worn. In contrast, the kitchen was bright and modern and had stainless steel appliances. "I have lemonade, water, some cans of soda and…" he paused as he stuck his head a little bit farther into the refrigerator. "We've got a couple of cans of beer."

"A soda would be great."

"Diet Coke or Sprite?"

"The diet, please."

Noticing that he took the Sprite, she smiled. She wouldn't have cared if he had a beer, but there was something easy and relaxed about them both sticking to sodas with their pizza. Maybe it made her feel a little like they were back in high school again.

"Can I have a Sprite, too?" Jackson asked.

"Nope. Milk for you."

"Dad—"

"Don't argue."

"All right," he grumbled as Sean filled a plastic cup about halfway full.

"I hope you like pepperoni or cheese pizza," Sean said. "When I placed the order, I realized I should've asked if you had a preference. So I ordered two."

It had been ages since she'd ordered a pizza. Even longer than that since she'd ordered one without regard for the expense. Realizing that she probably looked shocked, she attempted to cover it up with a wide-eyed expression. "Two pizzas for the three of us? I hope you're hungry, Jackson."

"Oh, I am," he said earnestly. "I'm starving."

"What about you?" Sean asked. "Are you hungry?"

"For pizza? Always." She smiled, hoping that it

didn't look as obvious as it felt that a delivered pizza was a special treat for her.

Feeling awkward, she picked up her soda and took a sip.

Thankfully, Sean started talking. "So, Jackson, like I told you, Miss Harding is going to be here when you get home on Wednesday. Why don't you tell her what you do first?"

He sat up importantly. "Well, first, I have to put my backpack on the table and get out my lunch box and red folder."

"The red one. Got it," Kayla said.

"My red folder is very important."

It was hard not to smile. "After we have that VIP folder…what should we do with it?"

"We have to put it in Dad's place."

She looked around the room. "Dad's place?" Maybe it was Sean's mail spot?

"I meant here, Miss Harding," Jackson said as he pointed to where Sean was sitting. "You can't sit here on Wednesday."

Sean winced. "That isn't exactly true, Jackson."

"It is. Aunt Meg and me always keep your place empty so we don't forget you."

"You worried you're going to forget your dad?" she asked with a smile. And then she noticed that Sean looked like he'd been hit with a baseball bat.

Then, right on his father's heels, Jackson's expression fell, too.

Kayla froze, not quite sure what she'd said wrong

but wishing she could go back in time about five minutes.

Struggling to make things better, she said, "Whatever I said wrong, I'm sorry."

"No. No, it's not you. You've got nothing to apologize—"

The doorbell rang.

He stood up and answered it.

Listening to him speak to the delivery person, Kayla glanced at Jackson. He was staring down at his hands, which were clenched in his lap.

"Are you all right?" she asked in a soft tone.

"Uh-huh."

"Sure?"

After glancing at his dad again, Jackson frowned. It was obvious that he was considering his emotions, like he could place them on the table in front of him and sort them like a stack of cards. "I'd forgotten that we used to keep my momma's place empty." He pursed his lips. "You know, so it would feel like she was with us."

"Ah." Of course, that was a pretty poor response to the words he had shared.

"We don't do that anymore." He was frowning. Not at her. But at her chair.

Kayla realized then that she was sitting in his mother's old spot. Though it was silly, she suddenly felt like moving. Sitting anywhere but there.

So she jumped to her feet. "How about I go get the plates?" she said brightly.

Jackson remained silent as she strode into the kitchen and began opening cabinets like they were on a time crunch.

Anything to make the awkwardness ease.

If that was even possible.

CHAPTER TEN

SEAN COULDN'T BELIEVE how quickly everything between him, Kayla and Jackson had gone south. Or how deeply he could still feel Dannette's loss.

Oh, he knew he'd always miss her, but he'd thought by now the sense of loss would only feel a bit like a healed hairline fracture. Sure, it might ache from time to time in the rain or cold, but it was essentially healed. The jolt of loss that he'd felt had been more than that. Far more.

Obviously, the hairline fracture analogy wasn't a good one. Perhaps it would never be. Maybe his grief for Dannette would catch him off guard for quite a while. He didn't know.

Recalling the bewildered, apologetic expression on Kayla's face, he knew he needed to fix the situation. Fix it well, too. Sean knew that this was one of those times when his words were going to really matter. Though he'd never thought of himself as having anything close to a way with words, he was going to have to come up with the right ones.

Unfortunately, his mind had gone blank.

After tipping the pizza-delivery guy, he turned around, hoping that he could take his cues from the way Kayla and his boy were interacting.

But Kayla was in the kitchen and Jackson was still seated in his chair, swinging his legs in an aimless way.

It was so quiet, they could all hear the delivery driver's vehicle start up and reverse down the driveway.

Looked like things were worse than he'd imagined.

Since breaking down into tears wasn't an option, all he could do was fake it. "I've got the pizza," he announced. Like it hadn't been obvious.

Kayla seemed to be working the same mindset. "That's great," she said in a chipper voice. "Are these plates okay to use?"

"Sure," he said, though he'd barely looked her way as he placed the two boxes on the countertop. "Jackson, how many pieces do you want?"

After a moment, Jackson replied, "Two."

Sean opened both boxes and put a slice from each on his son's plate. "Come get your plate, then." He looked at Kayla. "What about you?"

"One slice is fine for now. Thank you."

When she made a move to take a plate, he picked one up and handed it to her. "Here you go."

"Thank you."

Finally, he could breathe again. After placing two pieces on his own plate, he joined them at the table. And realized that the elephant in the room needed to be addressed.

"Kayla, we're glad you came over, aren't we, Jackson?" When Jackson nodded but barely lifted his head, Sean spoke to Kayla. "I went to a grief counselor a couple of months after Dannette died. I...well, I was having a hard time concentrating on much of anything. It took me by surprise, because I thought I had, you know, come to terms with it."

Feeling her gaze fastened on him, he added, "I learned a couple of things about grief. One was that there's no time limit on missing a person that you loved. The other was that grief comes in waves."

Slowly, Jackson's expression eased. "Being sad is like the ocean," he said.

"Like the ocean," Kayla repeated. "That makes a lot of sense to me. Did you go to the counselor, too, Jackson?"

"Yeah. Dad said we should learn to help each other be happy and sad at the same time. Bob and me drew pictures of the beach." Looking a little more animated, he waved a hand. "You know, how sometimes the tide comes in and everything's all covered up but then later, the tide goes back and there's old shells and seaweed stuck to the sand?"

"I do. That's the grief, isn't it?"

His little boy looked pleased to be the one delivering the lesson. Sitting up a little straighter, he said, "Uh-huh. Sometimes we're all covered up with pretty water and you feel like swimming. And sometimes, there's nothing but old shells and sea-weed in your heart." He shrugged. "It is what it is."

Jackson sounded so wise and philosophical with his little-boy voice, Sean felt the beginnings of a smile touch his lips. He tucked his chin so it wouldn't look like he was laughing at him.

"You know what, I think you boys are helping me," Kayla said as she put down her slice of pizza. "I've been sad about some things, too, but I'm going to remember what you both said about waves and the sand. I never thought about grief like that."

Looking pleased, Jackson swung his legs under the table. "Do ya think it helps?"

Kayla's answering grin was brilliant. "It does. It helps a whole lot."

Looking pleased, Jackson took a big bite and chewed. After he swallowed, he said, "Do you like dogs?"

Kayla didn't miss a beat. "Yes. Do you?"

"Uh-huh. What's your favorite kind?"

"Beagles."

"Beagles?" He wrinkled his nose. "I like wiener dogs and German shepherds. And pugs and Labs."

"That's because you like them all, buddy," Sean teased.

"Uh-huh. I mean, I like them as long as they're nice dogs. Do you have a dog?"

"I'm afraid I don't. I wish I did, though. I'd love to have a nice dog to keep me company."

Casting a sideways look at Sean, Jackson said, "I wish I did, too."

"Can you guess that we've had this discussion before?" Sean asked. "Jackson keeps forgetting that a dog doesn't want to sit at home by himself all the time."

"I think that's right," Kayla said as she wiped her mouth with a piece of paper towel, their napkins of choice in the house. "I had a beagle when I was little and she thought she was one of the kids. Wherever we went, she wanted to go, too."

"Even to school?"

"Especially school! She used to howl until my mom or dad would clip on her leash and take her to the bus stop with us."

"She howled?" Jackson grinned.

"She did." Looking a little dreamy, Kayla added, "Her name was Honey and I loved her."

Jackson snorted. "*Honey* is a goofy name for a dog."

"That's not nice to say, Jackson," Sean murmured.

"Sorry, Miss Harding, but it is."

Kayla leaned back in her chair. "If Honey was here, she'd tell you that you're wrong. She thought it was a great name."

"How do you know?"

"She was super sweet and preened every time

someone petted her and said they liked her name. That's how I knew."

"Maybe we should get a beagle dog, Dad."

"One day. Not yet."

Jackson released a ragged sigh. "That's what I thought you'd say."

"We're not home enough, buddy. Think about how sad a sweet little beagle would be if it had to sit at home alone all day."

"It would be really sad," the boy admitted.

"I'd love a dog, too," Sean said. "It's just not the right time."

AN HOUR LATER, after Jackson had gone to take a shower and Sean had written out just about anything Kayla might ever need to know in order to watch Jackson for three hours, he walked her to the door. "Thanks for coming over."

"Thank you for having me." She held up the small pizza box. "And for sending me home with lunch for tomorrow."

"It's the least I could do." He rubbed a hand over his face. "I don't know what to say about that awkward direction our conversation took right before dinner."

"There's nothing to say, because I didn't think it was awkward."

She really was the sweetest woman. "I appreciate you saying that, but come on…"

"No. I'm serious. Jackson's story about grief and

the beach? It helped me. I'm not getting over a death, but sometimes I still do feel a sense of loss about my marriage."

"I guess we all have things we're grieving, don't we?"

"From time to time, I think so. That doesn't change the fact that I wish you and your son hadn't lost Dannette. I am sorry for your loss."

"I know. We're okay, though. Jackson's speech tonight proved that."

She reached out and clasped his hand. "Tonight was a lot of fun. I enjoyed both the company and the pizza. Thanks again for asking me to come over."

Before he realized what he was doing, he squeezed her hand. And felt a little jolt. Pushing the sensation away, he looked her in the eye. "You're welcome, and I'll see you in two days."

"You will. And don't worry. I'll be fine and Jackson will be, too."

"Text me when you get home, okay?" Realizing their fingers were still linked, he loosened his grip as reality clicked in. They were friends. Nothing more. "I know you've been taking care of yourself for a long time, but do it for me, okay?"

"I'll text." Kayla's expression softened before she pulled away and headed to her car.

Sean stayed in the doorway, watching her unlock her vehicle, turn on the ignition, then slowly back out of his driveway. She waved through the window before heading down his street.

When she was out of sight, he closed and locked the door, then headed to the kitchen to clean up the last of the dishes and set up the coffee maker for the next morning. Forced himself to think about Dannette. Reminded himself that she was his wife. He'd promised to love her for the rest of his life.

Sure, she'd told him to one day move on.

But was today that day?

No. No, it was not.

Just as he finished with the dishes, Jackson came out, his hair tousled and damp. "You ready to read our book, Dad?"

"Yep." As he expected, Jackson was tired and didn't make it past two pages of their novel. After kissing his forehead, Sean left the room and checked his phone.

I'm back home. Thanks again.

Pleased to hear that—and that she hadn't forgotten to text—he texted, Thanks for letting me know. Sleep tight and have a good day tomorrow

You too

She'd added a little smiley face, which made him smile.

It was such a girly thing to do, and something

Dannette would never have done. He liked that Kayla had, though.

He liked a lot of things about her. About his new *friend*.

Setting his phone down, he thought about all the little things Kayla had done that evening that had stuck with him. Her encouraging smiles. The way her eyes softened whenever she gazed at Jackson. The look of appreciation and surprise when he'd handed her the leftover slices of cheese pizza.

The way she'd reached out and curved her hand around his when they were saying goodbye. Her hand had felt soft and smooth against his.

He shook his head. And then, *at last*, he felt the familiar wave of apprehension and guilt that was supposed to accompany any thought about another woman besides Dannette.

It seemed to settle in his throat. It felt uncomfortable and threatened to choke him.

But it was still there.

He tried to be relieved.

CHAPTER ELEVEN

AT FOUR MINUTES to three, the butterflies arrived. All day long, Kayla had been battling a bundle of emotion. Excitement, worry, happiness. And yes, a slow and steady thread of nervous anticipation, which felt both surprising and reassuring.

It was surprising because Kayla wouldn't have ever thought she'd be so concerned about helping out a friend with his son. She liked kids and had always gotten along with them. Hanging out with a six-year-old wasn't a chore. Spending time with a sweet and fun little boy like Jackson was going to be a pleasure.

So, being so nervous about babysitting him kind of caught her off guard.

But not as much as the new, almost unwanted feeling of awareness that formed inside her whenever she thought about being around Sean Copeland. Even though she was pretty sure all she was feeling were the last remnants of a high school crush, there was something about the way Sean spoke to her that eased her insides. Like she was worth his time.

After her divorce from Jared, Kayla had begun to believe that she was unworthy.

Unworthy because of her lack of education and lack of money saved. Unworthy because her life wasn't anything like the one Kayla had imagined she would have. The added insult that Jared hadn't just left her but that he'd left her for another woman had compounded those insecurities.

To her shame, Kayla had even started believing that the problem lay within herself. She should've been more lovable, attractive and successful. If she'd been any of those things, Jared would've wanted to stick around. Or, at the very least, her husband wouldn't have found it so easy to stray and eventually leave.

Even though her parents and friends had repeatedly told her that the problem with Jared's wandering eye had lain with him, there had been a part of her that hadn't completely believed it. Not even her sister's repeated phone calls and pep talks had completely erased the damage the failed marriage had caused.

Her new friendship with Sean had begun to change that. Little by little, his easy acceptance of her was helping her remember that she had a lot of things to be proud about. She'd survived a really difficult time and could still get up in the morning. Most of the time, she could smile in the morning, too. That was a blessing.

Deciding it was time to go, she turned to Susan, who had arrived two hours earlier. "I'm going to take off. I can't be late for that school bus."

Susan, who had a pair of children in middle school, nodded. "You're right. Hurry now, honey. You should've left five minutes ago."

"I didn't want to take advantage."

"Take advantage of what?" she asked with a dry laugh. "There's no one here. This store has been so quiet, I would've been bored silly if you weren't here. After you take off, I might end up pulling out my e-reader."

"Don't let Tamera see you do that."

"I won't, though I wouldn't be surprised—" Her eyes widened. "Hey, Tamera."

Tamera was frowning as she looked from one to the other of them. "What's this about reading, ladies?"

"Nothing. It was a joke." Susan giggled self-consciously. "I wouldn't do anything so unprofessional."

Sharing a knowing look with Susan, Kayla said, "Have a good rest of your day." Turning to her boss, she added, "I'll see you tomorrow."

Tamera frowned. "Wait. Where are you going, Kayla?"

"I'm leaving at three today."

"Why? You're on until three thirty."

"No, I was on the schedule until three. Plus, I told you when I clocked in that I had to leave at three on the dot." She edged to the door. "I've really got to go." No way was she going to let Jackson think for one second that she wasn't there.

Tamera sighed. "Fine, but come back to my office first. I want to show you some of the boxes you'll need to unpack tomorrow."

Feeling like Tamera was manipulating her as always, Kayla pasted a disappointed look on her face. "I'm sorry, I can't. I have to leave right this minute. I can't be late."

"Excuse me, but this is your job."

"I hear you, but I can't spare the time. I have to be someplace very important." Reaching for her purse, she said, "I'll come in a few minutes early tomorrow to see the boxes."

"That isn't what I asked."

Hating the way her muscles were bunching up in the middle of her back, Kayla forced herself to think of Jackson's sweet face. "It's the best I can do."

Just as she turned back around, Tamera called out to her. "If that is your decision, then it's the last straw."

"Excuse me?" Kayla was shaking, she was so stunned.

"You heard me. Tomorrow will be your last day."

Well aware that Susan was gaping at them, Kayla struggled to keep her composure. "You're firing me because I need to leave on time?"

"I'm firing you because you're refusing to be a team player. Yet again."

All her responsibilities swam before her eyes. The bills. Her lack of savings. Important things like gas for her car and, yes, food and her rent. She was barely hanging on.

However, she also was pretty sure that if she canceled on Sean at the last minute, she was going to lose far more of herself than she already had.

If she compromised her principles yet again, she was going to lose not only her friendship with Sean but also her peace of mind.

She was going to become the person she had never wanted to be. Someone undependable.

She wasn't going to do that.

Taking a deep breath, she said, "I guess I've made my decision, then. I have to help get a little boy off his school bus. This is important." She turned and left, not allowing herself to glance back to see Tamera's expression.

Not allowing herself to think about what she'd just done.

Her prayers must have been answered, because she arrived at the Copelands' house seven minutes before Jackson was supposed to get off the school bus. Those precious moments had been enough time for her to unlock the front door, turn off the burglar alarm and turn on a few lights.

She didn't want Jackson's first step into his house to be into something dark and quiet. She wasn't sure why she thought it mattered, but it did to her.

After looking around and deciding that everything looked ready for him, she hurried back outside to wait for the bus. She was still a couple of minutes early. She'd been tempted to run into the powder room to check her hair, but she'd been reluctant to catch sight of her expression. She knew what she'd see—all the worry and stress that was now settled in the new lines forming around her eyes.

Instead, she waited on the driveway and even waved to a couple of the moms who were standing together a couple of houses away. One of them, especially, kept glancing her way. No doubt she was wondering who Kayla was.

Remembering how close-knit all the neighbors had been in her neighborhood growing up, she didn't blame their curiosity. All the moms liked to keep tabs on the neighborhood goings-on.

But, she also was in no mood to explain herself.

Luckily, she didn't have to worry about it very long. Less than five minutes later, the yellow school bus rolled into sight and stopped just a few feet from where Jackson's driveway began.

Kayla stepped forward, scanning the little boys and girls as they clambered down the stairs, each with little backpacks on their backs and unzipped coats half hanging from their bodies.

In the middle of them all was Jackson's dark hair

and blue eyes. He was giggling with a boy and a girl. Then, when he caught sight of Kayla, the best smile appeared on his face.

"Kayla! I mean, Miss Harding!"

It was impossible not to respond in kind. She started walking toward him and waved. "Hi, Jackson!"

"You came. You didn't forget."

And just like that, everything she'd gone through in the last hour didn't matter one bit.

After waving at the bus driver, who was scanning the area, obviously double-checking that all the children had been spoken for, Kayla said, "I didn't forget for a minute."

"I was a little worried."

"I'm sorry, but I'm here," she said in a soft tone. "Jackson, I've been looking forward to seeing you all day." That was the truth, too.

"Want to play trains?" he asked as they walked through the door.

"I do. But first, we need to get you a snack and sort through your backpack, remember?"

"Yeah."

She opened the refrigerator and saw a couple of kid-friendly snacks on the top shelf. "Come look at all these choices, Jackson. What do you want to eat?"

He shrugged. "I don't know."

A moment of panic seized her before she reminded herself that Jackson was just a little boy.

He probably couldn't care less about eating. Until he was hungry.

Seeing the package of ground beef on a refrigerator shelf, she said, "What are you having for supper?"

"Dad said maybe tacos."

Noticing the taco mix and a can of beans on the counter, she made a mental note to see if Sean would like her to go ahead and make it. "I'll cut up an apple and get out some peanut butter and graham crackers, then."

After she did that and he was eating, she texted Sean. As she'd hoped, he was surprised and appreciative of her offer to make their supper.

"I'm all done, Miss Harding!"

"So I see." Noticing he had a smear of peanut butter on his cheek, she smiled. "Okay, tiger. Go wash your face and hands."

"But—"

"It only takes a few seconds."

He frowned but did as she asked.

The minute the faucet was off, she wiped dry his face and hands. "Now that we have all the hard parts done, let's go play trains before I start working on your supper."

"You know how to make tacos?"

"Yep."

"Aunt Meg never makes my meals. Sometimes she orders a pizza."

"Well...pizza is always good, right?"

"Uh-huh. But I like tacos at home, too." Reaching out a hand, he tugged hers and led her to his room.

She hid a smile as she spied his unmade bed and overflowing laundry basket. Pleased to be able to help them even more, she said, "You get the train track set up. I'm going to start a load of laundry."

"Okay."

It had been no trouble finding the laundry room. Spying a bunch of towels that needed to be washed as well, she started a load before hurrying to Jackson's room. "Which train do you want to be?" she asked.

He was sitting on the carpet playing with a couple of wooden trees. "The red. It's my favorite."

"I like the yellow one. Now, what do we do?"

He grinned at her. "You're silly, Miss Harding." Moving his trains around the track, he said, "This is what you do."

"Oh! Of course." And so it began. For the next hour, she played trains, made his bed and fussed with the laundry. They talked, he told her stories about his teacher, Mrs. White, and his favorite things to do on the playground.

Then, after setting him up with some cartoons, she worked on the tacos. She'd just grated the cheddar cheese when they heard the garage door open.

"Dad's home!" Jackson called out.

She stood to one side as he ran to the back door,

his little feet sliding every so often on the wood floor.

"Hey, Jackson," Sean said as he tossed his gym bag on the floor.

When he knelt down on one knee to give his son a hug, Kayla felt a lump form in her throat. Sean had been through a really hard time, but boy, was he blessed to have such a warm and close relationship with his son.

When Sean raised his head, he met her eyes, then got up slowly. "Sorry. I didn't mean to ignore you."

"Saying hello to your son isn't ignoring me."

"Dad, Miss Harding and I played trains. And she did laundry and made tacos."

"Laundry?" He frowned. "Jackson, did you make a mess?"

"He was perfect," Kayla said quickly. "I…well, I just happened to notice a pile of towels that needed to be washed. I guess I'm used to multitasking."

"I know you texted about cooking the hamburger, but you didn't have to do all that."

"It wasn't anything. I was glad to help." When his gaze warmed on her, she could practically feel it settle into her heart.

Which made her remember that she had problems on top of problems. Such as the fact that she'd just gotten fired today. "You know what, it's time I got out of here and let you two men enjoy the rest of your evening."

Sean frowned. "Wait. Aren't you going to eat with us?"

"I didn't make the tacos as a way to try to get a meal."

"Why would I think that?" Before she could answer, he added, "Seriously, there's more than enough for three. Right, Jackson?"

"Uh-huh. I want you to stay, Kay—I mean, Miss Harding."

"Are you two sure?"

"Positive. I mean, you're hungry, right?"

Just as she was about to say she wasn't, her stomach growled.

Jackson smiled big. "You are hungry. I heard your tummy."

"I guess I am."

"Then that settles it," Sean said. "Stay to eat and then you can go home."

"Thanks." Unbidden, tears formed in her eyes.

"Jackson, you go get out the napkins and place mats," Sean said as he walked to her side. "Hey, are you okay?"

"I'm fine." But her bottom lip had a mind of its own. It trembled.

He noticed. "No, I'm pretty sure you aren't."

"It's nothing."

He stepped closer, reached out and brushed a strand of hair away from her face. "I'm pretty sure that's not correct, either."

"How about this, then? It's nothing I'd like to talk about now."

After studying her expression for a few seconds, he nodded. "Fair enough, but I'll be ready to listen when you're ready to share."

When he turned away to wash his hands and help Jackson get out plates and silverware, Kayla pressed a hand to the center of her stomach and gave herself a good talking to. She needed to get a handle on herself. Quickly, too.

If she did, then she could make sure that Sean wouldn't be afraid to ask her to help out with Jackson again sometime.

No matter what happened in her future, she wanted to spend more afternoons with Jackson. Being with him, and being able to do things for him, made her feel like she wasn't just the shell of who she'd wanted to be. Jackson made her feel useful and valued. And that was something she hadn't felt in far too long.

CHAPTER TWELVE

SEAN NOW KNEW Kayla well enough to realize that she wasn't a big talker. She seemed perfectly content to let other people spout jokes or opinions or share stories about their day while she listened and encouraged.

Yet again, he tried to recall if she'd been that way in high school. He couldn't remember, of course. Back in those days, he'd been all about football and his big dreams. He hadn't paid a lot of attention to many people outside his close-knit group.

All he did know was that he appreciated her giving nature. Maybe it was because he'd felt a little lost after losing Dannette. Long after the condolence cards and the phone calls had ended, a new, unsettled feeling had taken root inside of him. He had been having a difficult time figuring out who he was. A widower? A former-football-star-turned-high-school coach? Jackson's dad?

All of those titles fit him, but they weren't all he was. And maybe that was how everyone in the world was—a conglomeration of titles and jobs—

but he was sure having a difficult time figuring out which one fit his life.

But ever since he'd reconnected with Kayla, he'd felt as if he was himself again. He wasn't sure what had made Kayla want to start volunteering that one day at Loaves of Love, but he was sure glad she had. She'd already made a difference in his life.

Not only was she a sweetheart, but she'd become a calming influence for both Jackson and himself. With just a gentle question and an inquiring look, she'd made both him and one six-year-old little boy feel like their thoughts and words were important.

It was pretty amazing.

He wanted to return the favor.

He was sure that she was worried about something. After they ate and did the dishes together—even though he'd tried to tell her that he could handle them—he began to grow concerned. There really was something on her mind.

Making a decision, he told Jackson to turn on a favorite show while he walked Kayla out to her car. As expected, his boy eagerly planted himself on the couch and picked up the remote.

Minutes later, when they were standing by her car, Sean said, "Why don't you warm up your car for a second before taking off?" He knew it was a made-up excuse. The night was cold, but only in the thirties. Cold enough to need a coat on, but not so bad that her car would have been frigid.

Kayla must have thought the same thing because

she looked at him curiously, seemed to debate the pros and cons of refusing, then nodded. "All right."

When she was standing by his side again, he reached for her hand.

The lights on either side of his garage cast a warm glow around them. He was able to see a faint line form between her brows. "Sean, what's going on?"

"I think we've got a problem."

Panic lit her eyes. "What? Did I do something wrong with Jackson?"

"No. Nothing like that." Realizing he was making things worse by trying to be gentle, he blurted, "Kayla, I mean this in the best possible way, but you've been lying to me tonight."

"I absolutely have not."

"Sorry, but you're doing it again." Before she could sputter another word, he squeezed her fingers gently. "Come on, now. All night, every time I've asked what was on your mind or if you've been okay, you've brushed me off."

"Has it ever occurred to you that maybe I am fine?"

He couldn't resist smiling. "Nope. Come on. I know something's bothering you. Your expression looks strained and more than once you looked like you were about to cry. I know I said I'd wait, but I'm starting to think that you need to talk about what's upsetting you before your head explodes."

"I look that bad?"

"I'm afraid so. Won't you let me help?"

"Fine." She pursed her lips, then blurted, "I need to find a new job."

"Why?" It took him a second to remember that she worked at a popular card and gift shop. "What's going on?"

"A lot of things, but my manager is unreasonable and difficult." For a second or two, it looked like she was attempting to keep the rest to herself, but then her words came out in a rush. "Plus, she cut my hours. I'm not making enough money. I mean, I already wasn't making enough. And... today was bad."

"What happened?"

"I was scheduled to leave at three. She knew that, then made up a reason for me to stay late. When I told her I couldn't, she gave me an ultimatum."

"An ultimatum?" Sean knew he sounded incredulous, but how could he not? Kayla was so sweet. He knew she was a conscientious employee. Plus, it was a gift shop, for crying out loud. They weren't saving lives in an emergency room. If he could make sure one of his players had food to eat, then the least Kayla's manager could do was let her employees leave on time.

Like a dam had burst, Kayla started talking faster. "Oh, Sean, the whole conversation was horrible. Tamera made up a choice for me when there actually wasn't a choice at all."

"She set you up to fail, Kayla."

"Yep, but knowing that doesn't make it easier." She released a ragged sigh. "When I gave her the wrong answer, she said tomorrow would be my last day."

He was shocked. Irritation, mixed with a good dose of anger that someone had treated her so unfairly, welled inside of him. "You got fired because I asked you to help me with Jackson?" Now he was feeling guilty.

"No." Looking miserable, she shrugged. "She fired me because I wouldn't jump through a bunch of stupid hoops that shouldn't have been there in the first place. There's nothing wrong with needing to leave on time."

"But leaving for me, that was the reason." When he realized she was trying hard not to burst into tears, some of that anger dissipated into concern. He squeezed her hand between both of his. "Oh, Kayla. I'm so sorry. You should have called and canceled."

"No way was I going to cancel on you. I had promised I'd be here."

Feeling increasingly guilty, he added, "I shouldn't have asked you in the first place. That was wrong of me. Did I make you feel like you didn't have a choice?"

Pulling her hand from his, she stepped away. She was withdrawing and he didn't like it.

Just when he was about to reach for her again, to

put his arms around her and give her a hug, Kayla shook her head.

"Sean, I'm fine. I'll figure everything out. Please don't worry."

She was so far from being fine it wasn't funny. "Of course I'm going to worry, Kay. This is my fault."

Her eyes softened. "It's not. That's why I didn't want to tell you. I think Tamera's been playing with me for a little while. You know. If I do this, then she won't cut my hours further. If I complain, she'll refuse to let me take a break in the afternoon. Stuff like that."

"She sounds awful and miserable to work for, but I sure hate that I made things worse."

"You didn't. Being here with Jackson was the best part of my day. I loved greeting him when he got off the bus. And, I also needed to leave that job. It didn't pay well, I wasn't getting enough hours, and my boss made me miserable. I've known I needed to look around for a while."

"What are you going to do?"

"I'm not sure." Glancing at her vehicle, she said, "But I do know that I need to go home. My car's plenty warm now."

"I don't want you to leave when you're so upset."

"You have a little boy in the house who needs to get ready for bed and school tomorrow. And I… well, I think I need some time to myself."

"All right. I understand. Can I call you later?"

"Of course, but I don't want to talk about work. Not tonight."

"Okay." He'd do whatever she needed, as long as she kept talking to him.

"Thanks." Just as she turned away, he reached for her hand again. "Hey, wait a sec."

"Sean, I really—"

"How about a hug?"

"What?"

"I know you're not a kid and I know you've got everything handled and all that. But...well, my sister's told me that sometimes only a hug makes things better."

"You grew up hugging your sister when she was sad?"

"Well, yeah. She's my sister." Dannette had been a fan of hugs, too. But for the first time, he wasn't all that anxious to bring up her name. He held out his arms. "What do you say?"

"I say..." She walked right into his arms.

When he curved his arms around her back and pulled her in even closer, he felt some of the tension in her body ease.

And he decided that she fit perfectly against him. She was slim and willowy and a little fragile feeling. The ends of her pretty hair brushed against his knuckles as he ran his fingertips down her spine.

Realizing that he was finding comfort in their

embrace, too, he dropped his hands and stepped back. "Better?"

She looked puzzled as her chin lifted and their eyes met. "Gosh. You know what? I think I actually do feel better. I'm glad you forced me to talk."

"Good."

While he stood there, she got in her sedan, buckled her seat belt and reversed down his driveway.

Seconds later, her car's taillights had blended into the night. Removing her from sight.

He was alone again.

"Dad?"

Turning on his heel, he felt his spirits lift. No, he wasn't alone at all. He had a little boy in his life who brightened every day and had given him a reason to wake up every morning.

Thank the Lord.

CHAPTER THIRTEEN

AFTER CONFIDING IN Sean last night and then speaking to him right before going to sleep, Kayla felt at peace when she arrived at Tami's Cards five minutes before ten o'clock on Thursday morning.

It was the latest she'd ever arrived for an opening shift. Usually, when she was scheduled to open with Tamera she'd try to get there about fifteen minutes before. Even though she'd never been allowed to say she'd clocked in at 9:45 a.m., she'd wanted to do a good job.

Now she didn't care.

Tamera was behind the cash register and counting cash when she walked in. Everything in her body language showed that she was angry. "You're late," she bit out.

"It's not ten yet. I'm here on time."

"I expect you to arrive early for opening," she snapped. "We can't help customers when they show up if we're still turning on the lights and counting out the register. You know that."

Even though her insides were quaking, Kayla

held her ground. "I'm sorry, but why does it matter? Today is my last day."

Twin spots of color stained Tamera's cheeks. "What are you talking about?"

"I haven't forgotten what you told me yesterday. You said if I left, then today would be my last day." When Tami was still looking confused, Kayla blurted, "Did you think I didn't take you seriously?"

Tamera slammed the cash drawer closed. "I assumed you would make up the time to me today."

"So, you're not firing me after all?"

"You are the only one scheduled until this afternoon. I need you to be here."

"What about tomorrow?" Kayla was pretty sure she'd been the only person for most of the day on Friday, too.

Tamera looked away. "I'll keep you on after, as long as you promise not to pull another stunt like you did last night. I need employees I can count on. Especially now. Halloween is next week, and then people will be ordering all their cards for Christmas. It's going to be really busy."

Kayla felt as if her bills and near-empty savings account were screaming in her ears. Warning her to promise Tamera to do whatever it took in order to stay employed.

But she couldn't. Staying and putting up with her manager's rude comments and dismissive attitude felt too much like the end of her marriage with Jared. She'd put up with a lot from him after they'd gotten separated and during the divorce proceedings—mainly because she hadn't thought she deserved anything better.

Now she knew differently. And, even though it meant she was going to have to visit Loaves of Love yet again, Kayla felt like her emotional well-being just couldn't take another moment of her manager's rude behavior. She'd gone through too much with Jared to stay.

And so, feeling like she was about to jump off a cliff, Kayla took a deep breath and said the thing she'd never thought she would. "No."

"No?"

"No. I'm not going to promise not to pull another stunt, because I didn't pull a stunt in the first place. All I did was stand up for myself and not let you manipulate me. I'm not going to let you do that again."

"So, you're quitting?"

"If you want to phrase it that way, I suppose I am. But technically, all I'm doing is responding to yesterday's threat. You did say that today would be my last day." Lifting her chin, she added, "And don't try to say that I made that up. Susan was standing right here. She heard you, too."

Tamera's cheeks flushed with anger. "Don't expect me to give you a reference when you go try to find another job. You were lucky to get this one. It's not like you have a great employment history."

Boy, those words stung. The lump that had formed in her throat started to feel like a boulder, threatening to choke her. But the small slither of pride that had begun to grow inside of her stood firm. "I understand."

Just as Tamera inhaled sharply, the front door opened and four customers walked inside.

"Kayla, I'm so glad you're working today. I need your help," Rosemarie, one of the store's best customers, said.

Kayla didn't think she'd ever been more thankful for a reprieve. "I'll be glad to, Rosemarie," she replied. "Let me just get settled. I'll put my things back here." She glanced at Tamera, waiting to see what she would say.

"I'll be in my office," she said.

As Tamera strode toward the back of the store, another one of the women murmured to her friend, "I wonder what's wrong with her today?"

The other shrugged. "No telling, but at least we don't have to deal with her."

Kayla bit back a smile as she hurriedly pulled off her coat and stowed her purse in a cabinet under the cash register. Then, already feeling like she was ten pounds lighter, she went to go help Rosemarie.

Much of the rest of the day passed the same way. Kayla helped customers without a break and Tamera stayed hidden in the back. She only emerged when there was a long line of customers waiting to pay or when one lady had a specific question about a figurine that was for sale.

When four o'clock at last arrived, Susan walked in the door. And…it was at last time for her to leave.

Taking a deep breath, she put on her coat, grabbed her purse and then knocked on Tamera's office door.

"Yes?"

"It's me," she said, using the very last of her patience.

"Come in."

When Kayla entered, she saw that Tamera was playing a game of solitaire on her computer. If she'd ever needed a sign that quitting was the right decision, this was it. "I wanted to let you know that I'm leaving."

"Fine."

Her old self might have scurried out of there, but her new, almost-assertive self knew she needed to finish things the right way. "Listen, I wanted to tell you that even though things between us haven't ended well, I do appreciate you hiring me. You took a chance on me and I will always be grateful to you for that."

Tamera closed her eyes for a moment, then said, "I don't like the way you're leaving, but I wish you well."

Surprised that she'd even said that much, Kayla nodded. "Thank you. When should I expect my final paycheck?"

"I'll mail it to you tomorrow. That would have been your payday."

"I'd prefer to pick it up."

"That won't be necessary."

"I'd prefer it."

"Fine. Whatever. I'll leave it up at the counter. You can pick it up after three tomorrow afternoon."

"Thank you." Realizing that there was nothing more to say, she walked out of the office, hugged Susan goodbye and then finally left Tami's Cards for good.

She felt an array of emotions, but mainly relief. She didn't know what was going to happen in the future, but she had a feeling that wherever she worked was going to be better.

She was going to make sure of it.

CHAPTER FOURTEEN

ON SATURDAY MORNING, Kayla slept late, took a long, hot shower then got to work looking for a new job. After three hours of scanning various sites, filling out online applications and emailing companies, she was feeling frazzled and scared to death. After thinking about calling her parents and telling them the news, she decided to do something positive with herself and walked to Loaves of Love.

As always, Edna greeted her warmly before sending her inside the workroom to make her two loaves of bread.

"Kayla, over here!" Sean called out.

Unable to believe her luck, she washed up and then joined him and Wayne at one of the tables. "Hi, guys."

"Hey, Kayla. Good to see you again," Wayne said as he headed toward the sink.

When it was just her and Sean, Kayla added, "I didn't expect to see you here today."

"I wasn't planning to come, but my brother offered to take Jackson to a fall festival up by the lake. He couldn't say yes quick enough. And, since we won last night's game, the head coach gave the kids the day off," he said with a pleased-looking grin.

Which she couldn't help but admire. "And Coach Copeland, too?"

He chuckled. "Yeah. The boys deserved it, though. One of my guys who's been struggling with an injury scored two touchdowns. It was epic."

"I wish I'd seen it!" She would've loved to have seen Sean standing on the sidelines and cheering his players on.

Amazingly, his grin got bigger. "Me, too. It was awesome."

After Wayne returned, the three of them continued to chat as they measured ingredients, greased pans and floured their work areas.

Kayla had just begun to knead her second batch of bread when Edna approached her table. At her side was a young woman wearing faded jeans and a snug T-shirt. She had the kind of auburn hair that could never come from a bottle and soft-looking brown eyes. She probably wasn't much older than eighteen or nineteen.

"Everyone, please meet Darcy. She said she'd give baking bread a try today." Resting her arm around Darcy's shoulders, Edna softened her voice. "Darcy, this is Kayla, Sean and Wayne. Kayla and Wayne only recently started helping out here, but Sean's been making bread for almost a year now.

They are all very nice and will be glad to help you learn the craft."

"Thank you, ma'am."

"You're very welcome, honey." Turning to Sean, she said, "Let me know if you need help with the ingredients or anything. I have time—it's been pretty quiet out front."

"I will. Thanks."

As Edna turned away, Darcy said, "What should I do first? I've made bread before, but it's been a minute."

"I can help with that," Kayla said. "Everyone needs to head to the sink and wash up."

"And while you two do that, I'll bring over everything you need, Darcy," Sean said.

"Thanks." Darcy smiled at him before following Kayla to the sink. "So, wash up?"

"Yep. Make sure you wash your hands and forearms well. Anything that might touch either the food or your workspace. Then put on your apron, a hairnet and gloves. When you finish, come meet me back at your space. Between us all, you'll be getting the hang of things in no time."

"Thanks," she said softly.

As Kayla left Darcy, she realized that she felt almost like a veteran, even though it was only her third time volunteering. Yet, she already felt comfortable here. So comfortable that she knew if Edna told her they had to cut back on volunteers and she wasn't needed anymore, she would be sad.

"She's a sweet little thing, isn't she?" Wayne said.

The older man with twinkling eyes was working across from her. Since Edna had walked in to check on him more than once, it was apparent that the two of them were friends.

"She sure is." After checking to see Darcy was still out of earshot, she murmured, "I wonder how old she is."

"I don't think she's seen her twentieth birthday yet, do you?" Wayne asked.

"No," Kayla said.

"Here's everything," Sean said as he approached with a tray just as Darcy returned. "Ready for this?"

She held up her gloved hands. "As ready as I'll ever be."

"Okay. First things first. Here's the recipe, but I'll go over it, too." Lowering his voice, he said, "Can you read it okay? The font is kind of small."

"I can read it just fine."

"Great." As he continued, Kayla felt a warmth flow through her from the way Sean easily explained the directions and showed Darcy what to do. She also came to realize that he'd mentioned the directions and the font not because the words were hard to read, but so she could have a way to learn the directions without having to admit to strangers that she might have difficulty reading.

Kayla was impressed. And humbled. She hoped

she'd one day be able to instruct a newcomer with such grace and dignity.

At last, Darcy was stirring her ingredients and seemed perfectly at ease.

Sean returned to his spot and punched the dough in the bowl before pulling it out and kneading as well.

"You're doing a real fine job, Darcy," Wayne said.

"Thanks." She smiled at him. "I'm glad I said yes when Edna asked if I'd like to join y'all today."

"Y'all?" Wayne raised his eyebrows. "That doesn't sound like you're from Medina."

"I'm not. I'm from Tennessee."

"That's a ways from home."

Her dark eyes clouded. "Yeah. It is."

Though Kayla was curious about her story, she didn't dare pry. "I'm from a town just about twenty miles from here. Sean is, too."

"Oh, are you a couple?" Kayla asked.

"No. Just friends," she said quickly.

Sean smiled at Kayla. "We went to high school together but just reconnected. We actually saw each other again for the first time in years right here."

"Isn't that something?" Wayne asked.

"That's nice," Darcy said. "I...well... I'm kind of embarrassed, but I had to come here for food. One of the reasons I said yes to volunteering was so I could take home this bread. It smelled amazing."

"There's nothing to be embarrassed about at all," Sean said quickly. "And you're right. The smell of homemade bread is amazing. It gets me every time."

"Do you have a place to sleep tonight, honey?" Wayne asked in an easy, nonthreatening tone. "If you don't, Edna or I can put you in contact with someone. Even if it's one of my cousins." He lowered his voice. "I promise, they're not creepy. You'd have a lock on your door and everything."

Darcy looked shocked. "You'd do that?"

"Of course." Looking down at the loaf of bread he'd just placed in a pan, he continued, "Think on it, okay? I'm not trying to pry, but there's no way I'm going to be able to sleep tonight if I'm worried you're in a car or a shelter or something."

"I've got a place. It's just a room in some woman's house, but it's okay. She just… It's expensive." With a wry look in her eye, she said, "Or maybe it's that everything is expensive to me now."

"I'll ask around," Wayne said easily. "If I find a place that you might like better, I'll tell Edna. She can fill you in next time you come in for food."

"I'll do the same," Sean said.

Darcy blinked. Blinked again. "I don't know what to say. I mean, other than thank you."

"There's nothing else you need to say," Sean replied in a gruff voice. "I'm glad you shared. Now we can all look out for you."

A feeling of warmth filled Kayla's heart as she

gazed at Sean. He really was the whole package. Not only was he handsome and athletic, he was kind, too.

Realizing that she'd been gazing at him, she turned to Darcy. "Things will get better now," she said. "I'm sure of it."

"I sure hope so. They couldn't have gotten much worse."

"I promise, coming through the doors of Loaves of Love was the right thing to do." She knew that from experience.

Twin spots of color formed on Darcy's cheeks as she smiled. "I'm starting to think you might be right."

When the conversation moved on to Wayne's children and grandchildren, Kayla allowed herself to reflect on what had just happened. The moment Darcy had shared her circumstances, all Sean and Wayne had done was try to help. Not once had they asked prying questions.

Neither one had even asked if Darcy had a job. Or worse, asked how she could have let herself get in such a situation.

Then, instead of appearing more self-conscious and embarrassed, Darcy's expression had eased. She hadn't let her pride get in the way.

How could this much younger woman be so much braver than herself?

"You sure are quiet today, Kayla," Sean said when Wayne walked Darcy to the back of the room. There, a volunteer manned the ovens. She was smiling at Darcy and speaking with her and Wayne. "What's going on with your job?"

"Nothing good." She tried to smile, even though there was nothing pleasant about her work situation at all. "The latest is that instead of firing me on Thursday, Tamera acted as if it was my idea to quit."

A line formed in between his brows. "But I thought you leaving was her idea."

"Oh, it was." Looking down at her twin loaves of bread that were now rising, she added, "Susan, a friend of mine there, thinks that when Tamera told the owner about her decision, the owner told her the employment contract states that Tamera can't fire anyone without giving them notice."

"She's covering her backside."

"Yep." She shrugged. "But I'm not going to deal with her anymore. So, I'm looking for another job."

"Any luck yet?"

"I have an interview at the candle company and at two other retail shops." She shrugged. "I might try waitressing. I haven't done it for a while— I wasn't a very good waitress, I'm afraid—but maybe someone might hire me on the weekends, too."

"Things are that tight?" Sean asked in a low tone.

Taking a cue from Darcy, she nodded. "They are. But I'll be okay." That wasn't a lie, either. Kayla knew she would be okay. Somehow or someway. She smiled, hoping that would ease his mind.

It didn't seem to. Still looking concerned, Sean added, "Didn't your ex give you anything?"

"Not really. I had to give a lot of it to my lawyer, too. And don't say I should've gotten a better lawyer. My self-esteem was so low when we were going through the proceedings, if I hadn't had him, I probably would've ended up not getting any money at all."

"If you need anything, let me know, okay?"

"I will. Thanks."

The door opened and Edna peeked in. When she turned her way, Kayla knew that was an indication that it was a good time to go back to the food bank shelves.

"I'll be right back," she said. As she walked toward the director, Kayla was ashamed that the first thoughts that entered her mind centered around how quickly she could peruse the shelves, gather the items and stash them in her vehicle before Sean wondered where she was.

She hung her head. What was wrong with her?

"Whatever's going through your head needs to stop right there, dear," Edna said as she escorted her toward the back hallway.

"There is no 'right' way to accept assistance. I've seen some of the toughest-looking guys in the world send in their kids or their wives for food. Accepting help isn't easy."

"Thank you for saying that. And thank you for—"

"You're welcome. Now, I decided to do something different for you. I put together a couple of sacks while you were making bread. I thought that might make things easier."

"You're so kind. I want to be you when I grow up."

Edna smiled. "How about you just be you? I happen to think that the world would be a pretty bad place without you in it. Now, come on. Let's get this done."

Edna's words ringing through her head, Kayla stepped forward and picked up a sack.

CHAPTER FIFTEEN

SEAN RARELY ATE in the teachers' lounge. Between his work with his two history blocks and the many responsibilities he had with the football team, he didn't have time to sit around and talk. Not when he wanted to give Jackson as much of his attention as he could when they were home.

However, his Monday had been going so smoothly that he felt foolish sitting in his classroom. Taking his lunch into the large, comfortable area, he took a seat next to a couple of freshman English teachers. They were talking about recent shows they'd been streaming, none of which he'd seen. But perhaps it was time to start watching one.

Half listening while he ate his turkey sandwich, he noticed Marissa, the high school's Spanish teacher, at the end of the table flipping through a stack of job postings. When she stopped to take a picture of one of them, he got curious.

"What's going on, Marissa? Are you looking for another school?"

"Not a chance. I'd have to go to the junior high

and there's no way I want to deal with thirteen-year-olds every day."

One of the English teachers grinned at her. "Same."

"Me, too," Sean said. "So…what's going on?"

"My sister's husband asked me to look into some of the support positions in the elementary school. My sister just got a big promotion. The money's great but the hours are going to be tough. Jeff knows some of these positions pay pretty good by the hour and some of them are only twenty to twenty-five hours per week. He's thinking about doing that so one of them can be home for the kids."

"Hey, that's great."

"Yeah. I'm proud of both of them." Flipping over the last page, she said, "Hopefully, something might come of this. Right now they're having to ask family to help them watch their twins."

"Does it say how much some of these positions pay?" Sean asked.

"Sure it does. It lists the requirements for applicants to apply, too."

It felt like an answer to a prayer. He wasn't sure that the job would interest Kayla but, based on how well she got along with Jackson, Sean believed she'd do really well. "Pass that over when you're done."

"I'm done now." Handing the stack to him, Marissa said, "You know someone looking for a job, too?"

"I do. A friend of mine was just let go from her

job at a retail store. She needs something steady and that pays well."

"She should look into the para positions, if you think she might be a good fit. They pay well and she won't have to work evenings or weekends."

"Or holidays," one of the English teachers said.

Selfishly, Sean liked that a lot. If Kayla had off the same days that he did, they could spend some time together. "It sounds a lot better than what she was dealing with. Her manager was ridiculous."

"Good luck to her," Marissa said. "If she does decide to apply for one of these jobs, tell her to not wait. HR will be anxious to fill them."

"I'll do that. Thanks."

After finishing his sandwich, he pulled out his phone and did the same thing Marissa had done. He took a picture of five of the listings, as well as the phone numbers and email addresses.

Remembering how guarded Kayla had seemed, he decided to add a little bit of encouragement, too.

I think you'd be great at any of these positions listed. I hope you'll give them a call and apply

Almost immediately, he saw the telltale line of dots appear on the screen. Are you sure I don't need to have a college degree?

Positive. I think you should call and speak to someone

After a pause, she replied, Okay. Maybe I'll email them.

Sean knew he should leave it alone. Kayla was

a grown woman and sure didn't need another man in her life telling her what to do.

However, he couldn't seem to shake the feeling that she needed a break and more than a little bit of encouragement.

I heard they're anxious to fill some of these spots. You'll have better luck if you call.

Feeling like he was being pushy, he added, It's up to you, of course. Good luck.

LATER THAT NIGHT, after he got Jackson into bed and took a long, hot shower, Sean sat in front of his fireplace in an old T-shirt and a worn pair of plaid pajamas his mother had put in his stocking years ago.

When his brother, Jack, called, they talked football. Both about his Medina kids and the Browns. Then he said, "Did I hear right that Kayla Harding watched Jackson the other day?"

Half annoyed that his family's rumor mill was focusing on Kayla, he bit out, "Who did you hear about Kayla from?"

"Mom. You must have told Meg."

He tried to think...then remembered he'd mentioned something to their dad. "I told Dad. I can't believe he remembered Kayla's name, let alone told Mom about it."

"Stop sounding so annoyed."

"It's hard not to be."

"Come on, Sean. She's a woman who you trust enough to meet Jackson. It's a big deal."

"Jackson really likes her."

"Kayla Harding was always easy to get along with back in high school. Glad she's still the same."

"How did you know her?"

"One of my buddies took her to his junior prom. We all hung out together that night."

"I can't believe I didn't know that."

"You weren't too interested in much outside of sports," he replied with a laugh. "Anyway, I'm glad you connected with her. I heard she married a jerk and got divorced."

"She told me that, too."

"That's a shame, isn't it? A girl like that? Well, I hate to think she ended up with a guy who didn't appreciate her."

"Me, too, though she hasn't shared too much about her ex."

"Well, if you two are becoming close, I think that would be a good thing."

"We're just friends, Jack."

"Okay."

"Seriously. That's it."

"I hear you. But if, say, things happened to progress between you and Kayla, the four of us should get together. We'll go out to dinner. I bet Kayla and Kim would get along great."

"You're right. I think she and Kim would get along well. But, like I said, the two of us aren't dating."

Though, why was he starting to think that taking her out wouldn't be a terrible thing?

"Gotcha. No time limit on the invitation. Now, on to more important things... I got the opportunity to buy four tickets to the Browns first week in January. You and Jackson want to go?"

"Of course. Give me the date and the prices. I'll Venmo you."

"No need. They're from my boss. He gave me a big discount."

"Fine. Then I'll buy you a beer at the game."

"I'll count on it."

After talking a few minutes more, they hung up. He'd just picked up the remote to start looking at some of those shows the English teachers had been talking about when his phone chimed.

Looking down, he saw that Kayla had sent him a text.

Sean, I took your advice and called.

Well, don't keep me in suspense, he teased. What happened?

I couldn't believe it. I spoke to an assistant, told her a little bit about myself and now I have an interview!

I'm so proud of you. Congratulations.

It's just an interview. NOT a job offer, but it's a step in the right direction. I'm excited! Even better, it's on Wednesday!

Smiling at how different and upbeat she sounded, even in a simple text, he quickly responded. Wednesday's great. I'm excited, too.

After they exchanged a few more words, she told him good-night.

An hour later, long after he'd turned off the TV and gone to bed, Sean was still smiling. He was so proud of Kayla and happy that she now had something to look forward to.

On the heels of that thought was his conversation with Jack. His brother had been a little pushy, but now Sean could admit to himself that he did want to see more of her.

He didn't want to just be her friend and he really didn't want to see another guy take her out. He didn't want to see that at all.

Dwelling on those feelings, he got out of bed and opened up the hall closet. He looked at a trio of boxes stacked on the floor. Feeling brave, he pulled out the top one and set it on the coffee table.

Inside was an assortment of Dannette's things that Meg had boxed up to donate. He'd told his sister that he'd drop them off, but had hidden them away instead. All this time, he'd never had the courage to inspect the contents.

Taking off the lid, Sean waited for a rush of sadness. Instead, all he felt was dismay. Inside was a raincoat. A couple of coffee cups. Two old tote bags that she'd lugged library books around in. A purse that her aunt had given her for Christmas one year that she'd never used.

None of them had meant much to Dannette. If she'd still been around, she would have donated them years ago. He'd been so intent on missing her that he hadn't recognized that none of the items would give him comfort.

They were just stuff.

Closing his eyes, Sean could practically hear Dannette reminding him to stop grieving and start living. To start going out and doing things. To start keeping his promises to her.

Taking the box out to the garage, Sean set it on the ground next to his vehicle. In the morning, he'd take it to the donation site.

And then he was going to finally move on. It was time.

CHAPTER SIXTEEN

KAYLA'S FIRST IMPRESSION of the elementary school was that it was adorable. There were vibrant bulletin boards decorating the hallways, and a low hum of chatter punctuated by childish laughter flowed from each classroom.

After briefly visiting with the principal in the office, Kayla met Patrice Redmond. She was the woman in charge of the paraprofessionals in the school. Patrice was both lovely and intimidating. Even dressed in black pants, black tennis shoes and a floral sweater, the fortysomething lady looked like she could run the world. She had an air of confidence that Kayla had always admired in others.

Maybe it was the fact that she seemed to know every single person's name in the whole school. Teachers, aides and students.

Or maybe it was her manner that was impressive. She had a direct way of looking at Kayla when she spoke. It almost felt as if Patrice was committing each word that Kayla said to memory. And that, of course, had made Kayla's already ramped-up nerves climb higher. She was as nervous as all get-out and probably babbling a bunch of nonsense.

Reminding herself that she could only do her best, Kayla tried to at least look calm and collected when they sat down. She listened intently as Patrice continued to describe the work she would be doing if she got the job.

"So, that about sums it up, Kayla. You'll work with three teachers in the fifth-grade wing and assist in the classroom. You'll also need to monitor one of the lunches in the cafeteria or be on the playground once a day. Most of my people alternate days on that. Do you have any questions?"

"What are some of the things I'll be doing in the classrooms? I mean, will I be helping kids or grading papers?"

"You will be working with children."

Which told her nothing. "I'm sorry. I'm not exactly sure what that entails. Would you mind giving me some examples?"

After studying her for a long moment, Patrice stood up. "I can do better than that. I'll introduce you to some of the teachers the new paraprofessional will be working with."

She was on her feet and walking down the hall before her words completely sank in. As Kayla hurried to catch up, she allowed herself to feel a thread of hope. Patrice wouldn't introduce her to the teachers if she didn't think Kayla had a shot, would she?

Hating that she felt so unsure and was over-thinking just about everything Patrice was saying, she focused on the school's design. "Every wing is off to itself, isn't it?"

Looking pleased that Kayla had noticed, she said, "It is. Every wing has a classroom for each teacher, a small workspace for the teachers and paraprofessionals, and a space where the entire class can sit together." She pointed to her left. "Every grade also has its own set of bathrooms for the students."

It was a large school. Beautiful and modern. "I don't remember my school being like this."

"That's probably because it wasn't," Patrice said with a smile. "Not every elementary is blessed to have so much space. Everyone appreciates it—kids and adults. And...here we are," she said as she stopped in front of a closed door with a small rectangular window in the center of it. "First up is Mrs. Kuhn." Lowering her voice, she added, "Mrs. Kuhn is in the middle of a lesson, so she probably won't say a word to us. But we will get a chance to see Hilary. She's one of the paras working in here." Smiling at Kayla, she added, "Hilary knows that you're visiting today. She's friendly and kind. You'll like her."

"Okay."

Her hand on the door handle, Patrice met her eyes. "Ready?"

"Yes."

"All right, then." She opened the door and walked quietly toward the back.

Just like she'd warned Kayla minutes before, Mrs. Kuhn didn't stop speaking. She was presenting a PowerPoint on her computer and writing things on a whiteboard as well.

Barely pausing, she smiled and nodded in their direction before continuing her lesson on cells.

To Kayla's surprise, few of the students even looked her way. Most were taking notes. Some were doodling on their paper, though they tried to look more interested in what was on the screen when Patrice walked by.

And then she noticed Hilary. She was sitting next to a little girl who had cochlear implants in her ears. When they stepped closer, Hilary whispered something to the little girl and then joined them at the back of the class.

"Hi," she said. "I'm Hilary."

"I'm Kayla. It's nice to meet you."

"Same," Hilary replied with a warm smile.

"Could you join us in the workroom for five minutes?" Patrice asked.

Glancing at the lesson as well as the little girl's progress, Hilary nodded. "I can. Willow is doing well. I've been mainly offering her encouragement today."

Patrice opened another door and closed it after the three of them were inside. "Hilary, Kayla's interviewing for Jason's position today. She's hoping to start as soon as possible. Any advice?"

Hilary grinned down at Kayla's low-heeled pumps. "Wear tennis shoes and eat a good breakfast."

Kayla thought that was cute, but was far more worried about the job. "I've never worked in a school setting before. I guess I'm worried about doing something wrong without realizing it."

"A lot of the paras we hire have never worked in a school setting before. If you're willing to learn, you'll be just fine. Mrs. Kuhn, Mrs. Vera and Mr. Chambers are great teachers and super easy to get along with. Most of the time, you'll be doing what I'm doing, which is sitting with one of the kids and helping them listen or understand what the teacher's talking about."

"So, not a lot of lesson prep?"

"Sometimes I do make copies on Friday afternoons or gather supplies or something for the following day. I don't mind that, though."

"I won't mind that, either."

"We'll all help you, too. So don't worry about needing to know everything on the first day." After a pause, she added, "Most of the teachers just expect you to lend a helping hand. We have a great and supportive staff. I hope that helps?"

"It does. Thanks for filling me in."

"Good luck. But… I better get back."

"Thanks for visiting with us, Hilary," Patrice said.

"Sure thing." Smiling at Kayla, she said, "See you soon," before she opened the door and slipped back into the classroom.

"What do you think?" Patrice asked. "I hope she alleviated your worries a bit?"

"She did. I feel a lot better."

"Good. Let's hit the other two classrooms."

Mrs. Vera's room and Mr. Chambers's room looked about the same as Mrs. Kuhn's, though Mrs. Vera was able to walk over and say hello and Mr. Chambers's class was taking a vocabulary test. Mr. Chambers had a paraprofessional sitting at a circular table off to the side, but Mrs. Vera didn't have anyone.

As they walked out to the hall, Patrice said, "Like I mentioned in the workroom, you'll be taking Jason's spot."

"Was he usually in Mrs. Vera's classroom?"

"For the most part, yes. But Hilary, Ed and you will likely be in all three classrooms. It depends on the needs of the kids and what's going on in the classroom. For example, if all the kids in Mrs. Vera's room are working on a project but Mrs. Kuhn is having a science lab, two of you might be in one classroom. Or, if the kids are watching a movie, you might be in the workroom cutting out letters for a bulletin board or even on lunch duty for third graders."

"Wow. So I'll need to be flexible."

Patrice nodded. "Flexible is the key, for sure. The motto around here is that we do whatever it takes to help our students. But our unofficial motto is that we also do whatever it takes to help each other."

"That's nice." She liked that a lot. It sounded like the opposite of her life at Tami's Cards.

"I think it's a great motto, too. A lot of people in our profession get burned-out. Dealing with test scores and educational expectations is hard. But we're also dealing with people, right? Some of our children have difficult home lives or learning disabilities. Or behavioral issues that they're working on. And, sometimes some of the folks who work here are going through difficult times, too."

"So everyone is human."

"Exactly," Patrice agreed with a smile. "If we don't remember that, everyone suffers."

"I think you're right."

"I'm glad you understand," she said as they walked back to the conference room where they'd begun the interview. "So, what do you think?"

She thought she really wanted to work there! Because that was the wrong thing to say, Kayla said, "I think it sounds like a lovely place to work."

"Well, I think you'd fit right in. As soon as I saw you smile at the children in the hall, I knew you were going to work out fine."

"Thank you."

"Do you have any questions? I believe Mr. Alexander discussed the background check and the salary with you when he called?"

"He did."

"All you have to do now is stop by HR and complete the final paperwork. As soon as we get the background check back, you'll be all set."

All set? "Wait. Does this mean I have the job?"

Patrice chuckled. "Yes, honey. Unless something unforeseen pops up, you may consider yourself hired. When can you start?"

"Whenever you need me to." She was proud of herself for not telling Patrice that she could start right that minute.

"Where are you working?"

"I'm not working at the moment. I was working at Tami's Cards but I was recently let go."

"Do you have to finish your two weeks?"

"No…she didn't want me to do that."

Patrice looked taken aback. "What happened? I'm curious, but you don't need to answer. You already have the job."

Feeling like it would be best to be completely honest, Kayla said, "I was fired because I needed to leave on time. I promised a friend that I'd be at his house when his little boy got off the bus."

Patrice stared at her for a long moment before releasing a breath of air. "Man, sometimes it's hard just to catch a break, isn't it now?"

"It sure feels that way."

"Well, welcome to our school." Standing up, she

said, "You're going to need to go to the administration building next and fill out some paperwork and get fingerprinted. I'll call them and say you're on your way."

"Okay. Thank you."

"On your first day, just go to the office and one of the secretaries will tell you where to go. Hilary or Ed will meet you and you can shadow one of them the first day."

"That sounds great."

"I have a feeling you're going to like working with us, Kayla." She covered Kayla's hand when they shook. "Have a good afternoon."

"Thanks, you too, Patrice."

When she walked back to her car, Kayla glanced at her phone and saw that Sean had texted her three times.

Thinking about you.

Well, how is it?

Call me when you can. I can't wait to hear about how it went.

All smiles, she quickly texted back. I'll call tonight but I'm on my way to the admin building now. I got the job!

When she pulled into the parking lot of the

admin building, her phone buzzed again. That's awesome! We need to celebrate! So proud of you.

Thanks!

She was proud of herself, too.

CHAPTER SEVENTEEN

SINCE IT WAS the first of the month, Edna was in the food pantry checking expiration dates on the latest donations. She was ready for a break when Wayne wandered in.

Surprised—and, yes, pleased—to see him, she put the can of pumpkin puree she was holding on the counter. "Hi. What brings you here?" She glanced at his hands, but he wasn't carrying a container of food to drop off.

"Believe it or not, I'm here to see you. You are a hard lady to track down."

"Not really." If anything, she thought, she was very easy to find. She was always at Loaves of Love or home.

Wayne leaned against the wall and folded his arms across his chest. Not for the first time, she allowed herself to admire his looks. Unlike a lot of men their age, he hadn't allowed himself to fall apart. The Henley shirt he was wearing skimmed over an impressive set of muscles.

Horrified that he was watching her eye him like he was a forbidden snack, she turned her head.

And tried to focus on what they were talking about. Ah, yes. The fact that he seemed to think she was hard to get ahold of. "I'm sorry you had to come to Loaves of Love to talk to me. Did you need something?"

One of his eyebrows lifted. "Ah, yeah."

Worry filled her. "What?"

"How about giving me a reason why you haven't picked up the phone any time I've called."

She tried to remember the last time he had. "I was working with a client when the phone rang. I could've sworn I called you back." She wasn't lying, either.

"And the time before?"

She honestly didn't remember when he'd called the time before. Embarrassed about that, and feeling a little bit defensive, too, she said, "I don't know what to say. Things have been busy here. So busy I sometimes forget everything else in my life."

"That's kind of a shame, don't you think?"

Yes. Yes, it was. But did she want Wayne to sashay in here and start telling her what to do? No, she did not. "Wayne, forgive me, but what is your point?" When his eyes flared, she regretted her snippiness.

But she wasn't in a mood to back down, either. She folded her arms over her chest.

He groaned. "Edna, my point is that when I delivered meat and we talked a couple of weeks ago, I thought there might be something special between us." He held up his hand before she could interrupt. "And, yeah. I know I sound presumptuous. But, I truly thought you were also interested in us getting to know each other better."

"I am."

"Edna, if you are, then why have you been ignoring my calls and never responding when I text if you want to get together?"

"The reason I don't respond is because I can't. I'm busy here." Feeling her cheeks heat, she forced herself to apologize. "However, you are absolutely right. It was rude of me to never respond. If you had treated me that way, I would've been hurt. I'm sorry."

"Apology accepted."

Pleased, she picked up another can and looked at the label. "I'm glad you came in, Wayne."

"Hold on a minute. How many hours do you volunteer here?"

"It's not just a volunteer job. I own this space."

"Okay. How many hours do you work here?"

Too many to admit. "A lot," she said grudgingly.

"Edna."

"Okay, a whole lot."

"That still isn't an answer."

"I'm not answering because I don't keep track of them. Even though this place is a food bank, I also rent the space out to other groups in order to fund the kitchen. So sometimes I'm here for that."

"How many hours do you spend in this building, Edna?"

"I don't know."

"Guess. Forty?" His voice was sharper.

She didn't like the way he was gazing at her. Like she was doing something wrong by helping other people. And she wasn't doing anything wrong! Feeling a little bit justified, she cleared her throat. "More," she bit out.

"Fifty?"

"Probably more than that." When he just stared, she said, "Fine. Usually between sixty and seventy hours a week."

"Edna."

He sounded both irritated and amused. She didn't like either reaction. "Why did you say my name like that? What is that supposed to mean?"

"It means that I don't think you have much of a life."

"Well, you're wrong." Putting the can she was holding back on the shelf, she added, "I'll have you know that my life is great. It's fulfilling, too. I help people."

"Good for you."

He sounded sarcastic! "Wayne, I don't know what made you think you could show up here and start putting down my life, but I sure don't appreciate it. If you don't like the way I am, I suggest you go find someone else to bother."

Wayne's lips pursed. She could practically feel the irritation wafting off him. Then, to her surprise, he started laughing. "Edna, you get under my skin like nobody's business."

That didn't sound good. "I don't mean to." When he started laughing harder, she felt like throwing up her hands. "No, I'm just confused! I don't know what you are expecting me to say."

"Maybe try to work a little bit less? Or, if you can't do that, maybe carve out an hour or two for us to spend time together?" Before she could respond, he added slowly, "Or, you could look me in the eye and tell me that I'm wasting my time because you aren't interested in spending more time together."

He was giving her an ultimatum. It was unfair and she felt pushed into a corner.

She felt like letting him know that, too. Who did he think he was?

But then, right on the heels of that thought, Edna realized that he was simply putting his feelings out there. He was being brave and bold and honest.

And…hadn't it crossed her mind more than once that she needed to delegate more often? "You're right," she said on a sigh. "I think I do need to start giving some people more responsibility around here. It would be good for them."

"And maybe good for you, too?"

She nodded slowly. Because, what else could she do?

Wayne's voice softened. "I know this place is special. I want to help you out, too. But I'm not sure spending almost every waking hour here is a good thing. Don't get mad, but one day you might regret it. Like you were trying to make it a replacement for living a full life."

"I agree." Her mind started spinning. "Maybe I could ask some volunteers to do things like check expiration dates."

"I think that's a good start. Now, what about the front desk?"

"I'd only trust someone I paid to do that. Even if I couldn't pay that person much, I would need him or her to take it seriously. People who walk through these doors need to feel welcomed. But more importantly, they must be treated well according to their needs. I wouldn't feel comfortable having a string of volunteers do this."

"I see your point."

Still thinking aloud, she added, "But, I couldn't afford to give that person very much or very many hours. At least, not at first. Like, only four hours a week. I don't know who would want to do that, though."

"I have someone in mind."

"Who?"

"Kayla."

"Kayla, the volunteer?" She was also in need of food still.

He nodded. "She mentioned the other day that she was having trouble with her job. I think she's struggling more than she's letting on."

Edna knew she was. But...was she the right fit? "She's a nice girl..."

"Why don't you give her a call and talk to her about it? Feel her out. Or, maybe you could think about some of the other volunteers who come in. A lot of them are retired and have time on their hands."

"You're right. A lot of the volunteers would happily work here. I'll think about all of that."

"Good." Wayne smiled at her. "I'm going to take off."

That was it? After making her rethink her life, he was just going to walk out the door? Panicking, her voice rose. "Are you sure you have to leave this minute?" Realizing she was somehow holding that stupid can of pumpkin puree yet again, she slammed it on the shelf.

Then she told herself to get a grip.

Taking a deep breath, she added, "How about we do something now? Do you have time to grab a cup of coffee?"

Wayne's eyes warmed. "I can make time. Can you?"

She knew right then and there that if she said no, he wouldn't ask again. Not because he wanted to prove a point, but because a relationship could only last if both people were making an effort.

Just as importantly, Edna knew that if she passed up this opportunity, she was going to regret it. He'd been right, too. Practically living at Loaves of Love didn't replace a full life. "I can."

When Wayne smiled again, his eyes were warm with approval. "Let's go grab a doughnut and a coffee. My treat."

"No, this time it's my treat. I owe you one."

"Edna. You don't owe me for anything."

"I mean, I owe you for this pep talk. It was sorely needed. I really appreciate it, too."

"In that case, I'm going to give in gracefully."

Chuckling, she walked toward him. "Let's go before one of us changes their mind."

Later that afternoon, she skimmed through her listing of volunteer names and numbers. When she found Kayla's name, she gave her a call. And, after an awkward minute or two, talked about her four-hour-a-week job and how she thought Kayla might be just the sort of person that Edna could trust.

Kayla sounded surprised and excited, though she did share that she was about to start a job at the elementary school and wasn't sure that she would need to work on Saturdays, too.

After they decided that Kayla could try it out before making a decision, Edna decided to call Nancy, too. Nancy was one of her longtime volunteers, and always asked if there was anything else she could do. She made plans for both ladies to shadow her on a future Saturday.

Thinking about the conversation, Edna knew that Wayne had been right on the money. Other people were happy to get more involved. Plus, she didn't need to work on Friday nights. She could start closing the doors to Loaves of Love early on Friday afternoons.

Kayla was not only going to be kind and patient with folks who came in, but she would also appreciate the additional income. Nancy was delighted to be needed and excited to help out as much as possible.

And even better, Edna was about to have one evening and half a Saturday free.

Before she lost her nerve, she picked up the phone and called Wayne to tell him about it.

He answered on the very first ring. "I was hoping you'd call," he said the moment he picked up.

She was glad he couldn't see the blush that was no doubt staining her cheeks.

CHAPTER EIGHTEEN

LOOKING AT THE CAKE, the flowers and the small, wrapped gift resting on the kitchen table, Sean started feeling a little uneasy. "What do you think, Jackson? Did we go overboard at the grocery store?"

His son wrinkled his nose. "What do you mean?"

"Well, you remember how I told you that Miss Harding was coming over for dinner because she got a job at your elementary school?"

"Uh-huh. What about it?"

"See, I wanted to show Miss Harding that we're happy and excited for her, but maybe it's too much?"

"What is?" Jackson was looking around the room like he was missing something.

"I don't know. Maybe she doesn't need us to give her all three things."

"But I like it all, Dad."

"You do, huh?" He couldn't resist smiling. His kid was six. *Of course* he was going to think that giving Kayla a cake, flowers and a gift was the right thing to do. "You know what? Maybe I should give her the present another time."

"Dad, it's just a holder for her school ID card. She'll like it. Don't you think so?"

"I do."

Jackson smiled. "Then it's going to be great. I like Miss Harding a lot. I'm glad she's going to be at my school."

Only then did he realize that Jackson didn't just like Kayla, he liked her *a lot*. As in a whole lot. "She's pretty special, isn't she?"

"Yeah. She's pretty, too." Jackson paused, studying his face. "Don't you think so?"

"I absolutely do."

Jackson smiled up at him before walking into the kitchen. "I sure hope she likes Chinese food."

"Me, too, buddy." After he'd picked up Jackson, they'd gone straight to the mall. In addition to getting Kayla's present, he'd gotten Jackson a new pair of shoes, jeans and pajamas, since he was in the middle of a growth spurt.

Right after that, they headed to the grocery store to get the cake, flowers and food for the next couple of days. Because he had Jackson by his side, they also had to examine all the cereal boxes and look at ice cream and whatever other brightly colored object caught the boy's eye.

Almost an hour later, he was pushing a cart full of food and paper goods to his vehicle. By the time they got home and put everything away, Jackson only wanted to play with his trains and Sean had no interest in attempting to make something to eat.

All of that was why ordering Chinese food was sounding like a great idea.

"She's here!" Jackson called out from the window next to the front door. "Can I go get her?"

"Sure, buddy." Watching Jackson hurry down the front walkway to Kayla's vehicle was pretty cute. So was the smile she greeted him with.

By the time they'd walked inside, Sean was just as eager to be by her side. Especially since she was beaming when their eyes met—and he once again felt that warm rush of attraction. "Hi," he said.

"Hi, Sean." In a soft voice, she added, "Thank you for inviting me over again."

"She likes Chinese food, too, Dad," Jackson chirped as he walked inside and closed the front door behind him. "Isn't that great?"

"Very great. I'm relieved to hear it." Reaching out, he said, "Here, let me help you with your coat."

"Thank you." Shrugging out of the black wool coat, she looked almost shy as it slipped down her arms.

If he wasn't so transfixed by the way her blond hair looked against the dark wool, he probably would've had a hard time not staring at the way her cranberry-colored sweater seemed to hug every curve. "I'll, uh, hang it on the hook by the door."

"Okay—oh," she said with a gasp. "You've got a cake and a present out! Is it your birthday, Jackson? I wish I would've known. I would have gotten you something."

Jackson giggled. "It's not my birthday, silly. The cake is for you."

"For me?" She turned to face Sean. "What's that for?"

Unable to help himself, he leaned closer and kissed her brow. "We're celebrating your new job, Kayla."

Grabbing her hand, Jackson pulled her to the table. "See, we bought you flowers and everything. And Dad even asked the lady behind the counter at the bakery to write *congratulations* on the top! I thought of pink icing because you're a girl."

She put her hands over her mouth, but her eyes were filled with tears.

Worried that he'd done too much and maybe pushed too hard, he stepped forward. "Kayla?"

"Do you not like pink?" Jackson's voice was filled with panic.

"No. I mean, I love pink," she said. Resting a hand on the top of his head, Kayla added, "I'm sorry for the tears. It's just—well, everything you two have done is so sweet and unexpected. I love it. So much."

"You sure?" Jackson asked.

"I'm sure," she whispered to Jackson. When she turned to Sean, her voice was a little husky. "Sean Copeland, you are full of surprises."

"We wanted to make you smile. Besides, I think we're almost as excited as you are."

"That's so sweet of you to say." She swiped at a tear on her cheek.

"Come here, Kayla," he murmured as he pulled her close into a hug. When she wrapped her arms around his waist and pressed her cheek to his chest, Sean felt his insides give a little jump. She felt good in his arms. Right.

"I'm sorry for the tears. It's…well, it's been a long couple of months," she confided in a soft tone. "My ex, he never went out of his way to make me feel good."

He ached to tell her that she was better off without him, but it wasn't the right time. So, instead, he ran a hand down her back. "Cry all you want."

She chuckled. "Don't say that. I might take you up on it one day."

"Anytime you're ready, I'll be willing and able to hold you tight."

"Dad?"

"Yeah?"

"Can Miss Harding open her present now? Or can we go play trains?"

Dropping his arms, Sean forced himself to give her space, but even with the foot of air now separating them, he felt like something had changed between them.

Maybe all three of them.

There was a new, sweet connection there that

felt real and solid. He knew right then and there that he'd do a lot to keep that connection strong.

He hoped that was possible.

CHAPTER NINETEEN

KAYLA HAD NEVER imagined she'd have so many good reasons to cry. Or, maybe that wasn't fair. Perhaps it was more accurate to think that she'd forgotten that it was possible to be so happy that tears were the only way her body was able to convey such an overwhelming emotion.

Whatever the reason, she sure wished she could stop. Poor Jackson was staring at her like she was a creature from another planet.

"Dad, you've got to do something," he whispered to Sean as she dabbed her eyes. Yet again. "She's gone through two whole Kleenexes."

Sean patted his son's back. "I have no idea how to stop them, buddy. I think we're just going to have to go with it."

"Really?"

Jackson sounded so dismayed and his words so adorable, Kayla giggled. Then she took a deep breath and got a grip on herself.

At long last.

"I'm sorry for all the waterworks, Jackson," she

said. "It's…well, it's just been a while since anyone got me a cake or gave me flowers."

He wrinkled his nose. "How come?"

Well, that was the million-dollar question, wasn't it? "I don't know."

"Do your parents not like cake?"

"They do. Maybe it's just that after a person gets to be a certain age, they start believing they don't need to celebrate little things anymore."

"Only the big things?"

She had to think about it. Unfortunately, she couldn't remember the last time Jared had bought a cake or flowers for any occasion. Or her parents, for that matter. She knew her parents loved her. But they were more likely to hand her a check than a bunch of balloons.

Which, now that she thought about it, was kind of too bad.

"For anything. They, um, aren't too into celebrating."

"Oh." He looked up at his dad again.

"That's okay," Sean said. "Every family is different, right?"

"Yeah." But Jackson didn't look like he believed a word of that.

"I like the cake and the flowers very much," she reassured him. "The flowers are beautiful and the cake looks yummy. I promise, I'm really, *really* happy. I, ah, sometimes cry when I'm like that."

Jackson wrinkled his nose. "Do you think we've got to get used to Kayla crying, Dad?"

"I reckon so, Jackson." Smiling at her, he added, "I think our new friend Kayla comes with an occasional bout of tears."

"I'm afraid you're right about that," Kayla said. "Sean, you don't mind?" she asked.

"Nope. Not even a little bit," Sean said. His voice was warm, too. Tender.

Eyeing him more carefully, Kayla realized that Sean didn't look upset about her tears. Only amused by her antics. "Let me guess. Did Dannette not cry when you got her a cake?" she blurted—right before realizing that she probably shouldn't have mentioned his deceased wife.

"I can't remember a cake ever setting her off like this." Sean paused, as if he needed to think about it for a moment. "But she wasn't a crier by nature."

"I'll try to be better."

After exchanging a look with Jackson, Sean said, "Don't go changing on our account. I think it's kind of cute."

Cute. "Great."

Jackson smirked. "You're really girly, Miss Harding. You have bouncy hair and everything. It's funny."

"Bouncy hair?"

He waved a hand in the air. "You know, it's long and has curls."

"That's from a curling iron." And why she told a six-year-old little boy that, she didn't know.

"See. It's bouncy." He grinned.

Sean winked. "Don't worry about a thing. We'll get used to the tears and the bouncy hair in no time at all. Right, buddy?"

"Yeah. So can she open her present now?"

"You got me a present?"

"Uh, yeah," Sean said, sounding like he was worried that she was going to dissolve into a mess of tears all over again. "That's what that wrapped package is."

Picking up the small, slim box, she said, "Which one of you boys wrapped it?"

"Neither," Sean said.

"The lady at the store wrapped it up," Jackson announced. "Go on. Open it."

It still felt like too much, but it wasn't like she had a choice. "Okay, then." Carefully, she removed the ribbon, then pulled open the paper and at last lifted the box's lid.

And there, nestled in a little velvet pouch was a bright red leather ID holder. "What's this for?"

"Your school ID. Everyone has one," Sean explained. "Half the women at the high school wear theirs on lanyards around their necks. They're key cards, required to open some of the doors. I figured with you being a para, an ID holder on a lanyard is going to save you a lot of grief."

"I think you're right. I didn't think too much

about it, but Patrice and Hilary both wore lanyards around their necks."

"Do you have your ID yet?"

"I do. It's in my purse."

"Let's put it together!" Jackson exclaimed.

Loving his excitement, she grinned at him. "That's a great idea. Would you go get it for me, Jackson?"

"Sure."

While he went to retrieve her purse, Sean reached for her hand and squeezed her fingers. "You okay?" he mouthed.

"Yeah. Better than okay."

"Here you go!" Jackson called out.

Then, next thing she knew, they were all giggling about her goofy picture and then slipping it into its new fancy leather case.

After Sean attached the black rubber lanyard, she put it around her neck. It was so silly, but she was kind of proud of the thing. "Well, gentlemen, what do you think?" she asked as she playfully struck a model-like pose.

"I like it," Sean said.

"Yeah, Miss Harding. You look just like all the other teachers now."

And…there came the tears again.

"Oh, no! There she goes again, Dad."

"It's okay. I've got this. You go hang out for a minute so Miss Harding can pull herself together."

Jackson didn't wait another second before running to his room.

"I think my tears scared him off."

"Maybe so. But that's okay."

"You sure about that?"

"Positive," Sean said as he stood up. "Come here, Kayla."

When he held out his arms, she walked right into his embrace. Immediately, she was struck by how much bigger he was. Taller, stronger, more muscular. And so tender, like he didn't want to bruise her skin—or her heart.

"This is nice. I think I really like your hugs."

"Glad to hear it."

Still feeling chatty, she said, "Until you hugged me the other night, I hadn't been hugged in a while. I mean, my mom and dad do, but not like this." Horrified that she'd been chattering about nothing, she tilted her chin up so she could meet his eyes. "Ignore everything I just said. What I mean to say is that this—"

"Is so much better," he murmured. Right as he cupped her jaw and kissed her. Firmly and with passion.

As if he was afraid to let her go.

She hoped that was truly how he felt, because she didn't want to be let free anytime soon.

CHAPTER TWENTY

"I'm SORRY IT's been so long since I've come over, Mom," Kayla said as she walked with her mom around her parents' neighborhood on Sunday afternoon. The sky was a pale blue and the cold snap they'd been experiencing had drifted toward the east. In its place were warmer temperatures with just a lingering bite in the air. It was a picture-perfect, crisp fall day. An excellent excuse to get outside and take her parents' dog for a walk. Just like they used to do when she was a teenager.

"You call me and Dad quite a bit, dear. There's no reason for you to spend what little free time you have driving over here. What with the traffic and all, our houses are now almost forty-five minutes apart."

Her mom had a valid point. Kayla hadn't had a lot of time and she'd had even less money. Filling up her car's gas tank was something she dreaded.

But those weren't good excuses. Not when her father was still recovering from forty days of radiation and her mother was spending all her extra time caring for him. "I'll try to do better."

"Dad and I are fine." Bending down, her mother rubbed Roscoe's head. "Plus, we have this guy keeping us company." Looking at her dog with a fond expression, she added, "He's turned into such a good dog."

Roscoe, a two-year-old pit bull mix, looked like he understood every word her mother said. He was positively preening.

Reaching over to pet Roscoe, too, Kayla couldn't deny that he was a super dog. He was affectionate and kept her parents active. And, judging from the way he had picked up his leash and brought it to her mother when she'd said the word *walk*, he was smart, too.

"When you first said you and Dad were going to adopt this guy, I wanted to tell you both not to do it."

"We knew you weren't a fan of the idea, but I had a good feeling about him. Plus, he needed a good home. I thought he would be happy here."

"I know. It's just that that breed can have a bad reputation."

"Oh, who cares? Pit bulls aren't mean dogs, Kayla. They're just big and strong dogs. And they need training."

"Which you did."

"Boy, did we! The three of us went to pet school and we graduated with flying colors. I think your father was more excited about the certificate than Roscoe here."

"I can see that." Her father had never encountered a goal he didn't try his best to achieve.

Looking down at Roscoe, her mom added, "He's a wonderful dog and now he has a home. I feel good about that."

Bending down, Kayla patted Roscoe on the head again. "Me, too. I'm glad I was wrong about him."

They turned a corner and continued down the sidewalk, her mother waving hello to every car and walker they passed. Her friendly nature was nothing new. Her mom might look like an older version of Kayla, but she'd always been far more open than her daughter.

Sometimes, Kayla wondered where she'd gotten her reticence from. Had she been born that way? Or, had it been something she'd picked up over the years?

When they stopped so Roscoe could sniff yet another bush, her mother looked her in the eye. "Kayla, dear, we've now discussed the weather, Roscoe, your father's radiation for his prostate and my volunteer job at the animal shelter. When are you going to tell me something about yourself?"

"There's not much to tell." Of course, the opposite was true, but every facet of her life currently felt like a land mine. The last thing she wanted to do was make either of her parents worry about her—or share too much.

"Come now. You can do better than that." Her mother's tone had taken on an impatient thread, reminding Kayla that she might be friendly and outgoing, but her mother had never been a pushover.

"Fine. I do have some news. Good news, too. I got a new job," Kayla said as they continued their walk.

Her mom frowned. "When did this happen?"

"This past week. I filled out the online application, spoke to several people on the phone and then did a visit. I'm excited."

"Hold on. I think we need to backtrack a couple of steps. Why did you get a new job? I thought you liked working at the card store. It really is the cutest place."

"It is a cute store. I liked the job and enjoyed the customers, but my manager wasn't very nice."

"Maybe she was just demanding, dear."

Kayla knew her mother didn't mean that in a bad way, but it did feel like criticism. "Tamera was demanding, but in the worst ways. Plus, she kept cutting my hours."

"Well, that isn't good."

"It absolutely wasn't." Which, of course, was a big understatement.

"Well, tell me what you decided to do. Where are you going to work now?"

"I got a job at the elementary school as an aide." She cleared her throat. "They call my position a paraprofessional. I'm going to be helping in the classrooms as well as monitoring the lunchroom and playground."

"You'll be doing all sorts of things."

"Yes. It's going to be challenging, but I'm excited about it. All the teachers I met were nice and the kids were, too."

"I can see you being up for a challenge. You've always been a hard worker. But, working in an elementary school? That doesn't sound like you."

"Why not?"

"Well, besides the fact that you always seemed to like quiet things, you're going to have to be with children all the time. I didn't think you enjoyed kids."

There was yet another jab. "Mom, Jared and I weren't ready to have kids," she said slowly. "We wanted to wait a few years. Thank goodness we did, too."

"Maybe you weren't ready, but Jared told me more than once that he was anxious to start a family."

Hating that she was having to defend herself, Kayla said, "Jared was also a jerk, Mom. And a bad husband. He cheated on me, then left me for another woman."

"He turned out to be awful. He was so selfish and a liar. Which is too bad." Her mom's voice had a lilting tone, though. Like, sure, Jared was a jerk, but maybe Kayla could have done something to turn their relationship around.

Realizing that this wasn't the first time she'd gotten the feeling that her parents hadn't exactly understood her point of view, Kayla sighed. This was why she didn't hang out with her mom and dad too much anymore. Though they'd given her the money to put a deposit on her apartment, they hadn't exactly sounded happy for her.

Or, maybe they hadn't understood her choices because she hadn't been completely forthcoming with them. She bit her lip. If she'd been more open, would they have been more supportive?

"Anyway, I start on Tuesday. I think it's a good step forward for me. There's even some room to advance. That's something that was never an option at Tami's Cards."

Her mother smiled at her. "You'll have to call us Tuesday night. Your father and I will be eager to hear how your first day goes."

"I will."

"So, anything else new?"

"Yes. I reconnected with Sean Copeland. You might not remember him, but he and I were in the same class in high school."

"Oh, honey, I remember Sean. I see his mother all the time."

"You do?"

"Alice and I get our hair done at the same salon." Looking pleased, she asked, "How did you two find each other?"

"We met while we were volunteering at a place called Loaves of Love."

"And what is that?" she asked as Roscoe stopped to smell a grouping of shrubs.

"It's a food bank in downtown Medina. A lady named Edna runs it. It's a great place. Not only does it help people in need, but everyone there bakes bread, too. Both people who are being served and the volunteers."

"I don't understand. What do you do with the bread? Does the organization sell it to pay for the food that's given away?"

"Oh, no. People who come in for food always get to take home a fresh loaf of bread. Volunteers do, too."

"Giving out loaves of freshly made bread is certainly nice for those people."

"Those people?"

Her mother rolled her eyes. "You know who I'm talking about. People down on their luck."

"Ah." Of course, all she could think was that she was currently one of "those people."

"You certainly are full of news today. I'm very proud of you, Kayla."

"For what?"

"You not only are doing something besides working and sitting in your apartment, but you're volunteering and making friends. And even making homemade bread. That's good." Looking pleased, she added, "I think you've finally landed back on your feet. You must be so happy."

"Yes." Of course, she'd lost a job, had become one of "those people" and the guy she was becoming friends with didn't realize that she'd been lying to him.

Other than that, she was doing great.

As they paused so Roscoe could sniff more flowers, her mother chuckled. "And to think Dad and I were going to try to convince you to move back home."

"You were?"

"Dad was worried that maybe Jared didn't take very good care of you in the divorce."

"Mom, you know he didn't."

"Yes, but Dad and I thought that you were close to being at loose ends." She let out a small laugh. "Believe it or not, one evening we were even worried about you being able to afford your groceries!"

"Wow." She wasn't sure if she was surprised that they'd think that or surprised that she hadn't known they would help her out if she had just asked.

Most of all, she was mentally kicking herself because she still wasn't ready to simply tell her mom the truth.

Completely oblivious to Kayla's musings, her mom continued, "Isn't it something how the mind works? Before you know it, a person can go from worrying about A and B to suddenly worrying about U, V and W!"

It took Kayla a second to figure out what her mother was getting at, but she couldn't deny that she'd made a good point. "Jumping to conclusions is exhausting. That's true."

"Well, don't you never mind that. It sounds like you are doing just fine. Now, all we have to do is hope that you like this job."

"Yes. Let's hope that happens," she said in a dry tone.

"I'm sure you will do a decent job. Who knows? Maybe one day you'll even be interested in going back to school." She continued, completely oblivious to the fact that Kayla had always been interested in going to college—she'd just never been able to afford it, "Maybe you'll want to be a real teacher instead of someone who just helps them. That would be so nice, wouldn't it? You could have your own classroom."

Her throat felt a little tight as she realized that her mom still believed that she was still trying to grow up. She wasn't going to see value in being a paraprofessional when she could be a "real teacher" instead. "We'll see what happens, Mom."

"I'm proud of you, dear. And let's not forget Sean Copeland."

"What about him?"

"Well, after playing for OU, Sean is a football coach at the high school. Now that you two have reconnected, maybe he has a friend who might ask you out."

Kayla swallowed the pain that shot through her. Reminded herself that her mother didn't mean to sound judgmental. Or to imply Kayla wasn't all that date-worthy at the moment. "One thing at a time, Mom."

"That's what I always say." Looking down at her dog, she said, "Right, Roscoe?"

When Roscoe barked, her mother seemed even more pleased. Like they'd just solved all the world's problems in one cozy conversation.

Somehow, her mother's happiness made her feel even more ill at ease.

It was probably time to head on home to her little place in Medina. Her apartment wasn't perfect and her life was a disaster. But at least within her four walls she could be honest with herself.

That was a good thing.

CHAPTER TWENTY-ONE

JACKSON WAS A good kid. He was thoughtful and kind. He enjoyed playing with other children, had no problem sharing and was meeting or exceeding all his teachers' goals for him in first grade. Sean should feel proud about that.

With Mrs. White's glowing words still ringing in his ears, Sean walked down the brightly decorated elementary school's halls to the gymnasium. There, a couple of high school kids were earning volunteer hours so parents could attend parent-teacher conferences without worrying about childcare.

Not for the first time, he wondered how his mother had done it. Somehow, she'd managed to always pick them up from their sports activities, make it to all three of her children's conferences and still have a homemade dinner ready that evening. His dad, of course, had been around, but he'd spent the majority of his days at the office and all his household chores had centered around the lawn.

Now that Sean was a single parent, he had a whole new respect for his mother. One day, he was going to ask her how she'd been able to do so much while making it all look so easy.

When he walked into the gym, Mandy, one of his freshman history students, hurried over to him. "Hi, Mr. Copeland!"

"Hi, Mandy. How are things going?"

"Good. I'm used to babysitting so getting credit for hanging out with first and second graders is easy. Are you all done?"

"I am." Scanning the area, he found Jackson sitting on one of the bleachers by himself. "How did Jackson do while I was gone?"

Mandy picked up the clipboard so he could sign out his son. "All right, but he's been kind of quiet. When I talked with him a little bit, he seemed okay, though."

Concerned, Sean glanced at Jackson again. "He didn't want to play with any of the other kids?"

"Not really." She shrugged. "Maybe he's tired."

"Maybe so." That didn't seem right, though. "I'll go get him, Mandy."

"You sure? I don't mind, Coach."

"I appreciate that, but you've got more parents coming in," he said as a couple approached. "See you tomorrow."

"See ya. I'm going to ace that test."

"Good." He grinned at her before walking across the floorboards to where Jackson was still seated and looking down at his kicking feet. Growing more concerned, he picked up the pace. "Hey, Jackson."

Jackson popped his head up. When he spied him, a look of relief crossed his features before he covered it up again. Alarm bells went off inside of Sean. Jackson was just six years old. When had he gotten so good at covering up his feelings?

Grabbing his backpack, Jackson hopped to his feet and then shrugged the backpack over his shoulders. "Are you all done talking to Mrs. White?"

"I am. And, I'm ready to get out of here. What about you?"

"Yep."

"Let's go get some supper. You hungry?"

Jackson shrugged.

Growing more worried, Sean pressed his hand to Jackson's forehead. It didn't feel warm, but maybe he had a stomach bug or something? A kid didn't have to have a fever to be sick.

"Stop, Dad."

Realizing that even first graders could get embarrassed about being fussed over, Sean said, "Hold on a sec. I thought you might have a fever." Bending down slightly, he studied his boy's eyes. Looking for something wrong, though he didn't know what. "Do you feel bad? Does something hurt?"

Those eyes rolled. "No. Can we leave now?"

"Sure. I thought that burgers from Freddy's sounded good. What do you think?"

"Yeah, all right." Jackson fell into step by his side.

As they walked out, a couple of kids called out

his name. Jackson waved to one of them but ignored the rest. "Are we going to go through the drive-through?"

"I thought so. Is that good with you?"

"Yeah. I just want to go home."

When they got to the car, Sean helped him get settled and started the ignition. It was a cold night; the temperatures were likely in the low thirties. The leather seats were freezing and the heater was taking its time to warm up and blow out hot air.

"Mrs. White had lots of good things to say about you, Jackson. She said you're doing real well and that she likes you a lot."

"I like Mrs. White, too."

"She said you got along with everyone and were even good at sharing. And that your reading is coming along, too."

"Really?"

"Yep," he said as he pulled out of the parking lot. "In fact, you got such a glowing report, I think you deserve a treat. I'll get you a shake to go with your burger and fries. Whatever kind you want, too."

"Thanks, Dad."

Thanks, Dad? Jackson loved asking for candy or cookies to get mixed in with his shake. Sean rarely let him get away with that because he'd fill up on the treat before he ate half the burger.

There was no denying it any longer. Something was going on with his boy. Stopping at a red light, Sean decided to push a little bit more. "You're not yourself tonight, Jackson. Since we've determined that you're not sick, I figure you're upset about something. What's bothering you?"

"Nothing."

"Jackson, I'm tired. You probably are, too. I'm not going to give up on this until you tell me what's on your mind." Just as the light turned green, he allowed his gaze to meet his son's eyes in the rearview mirror before he continued down the road. "I can't help you if you don't tell me what's wrong."

"It doesn't matter. You can't help me with this."

As he drove through another intersection, Sean racked his brain, but couldn't think of a thing that could put such a damper on Jackson's spirits that he couldn't fix. "You don't know if I can or can't help you yet. That's why you've gotta go ahead and tell me what's on your mind."

"Oh, all right," Jackson said as Sean pulled into the fast-food parking lot and entered the drive-through line. "It's—"

"Oh. Hold on," he interrupted. "We're next. I've got to tell them what we want. You want your usual?"

"Yeah."

"What kind of shake?"

"Strawberry with Oreos."

"Got it." Sure enough, he was able to pull up and call out his order thirty seconds later.

Then, of course, it was time to pay, and then time to get their food. By the time they were once again on the road, the interior of the car smelled like fresh-cooked burgers and fries and the atmosphere between him and his little boy seemed to have changed again.

Jackson was now irritated with him.

"Sorry about that," Sean tried to joke. "No way did we want to wait another second for food, though. Right?"

When Jackson only shrugged, Sean inwardly sighed. "What's bothering you?"

"It doesn't matter."

It was hard to be patient when it seemed like Jackson was shutting him down again, but Sean did his best. "It does, son, and you know it."

"Mom wouldn't have done that."

The mention of Dannette felt like a lightning bolt had come out of nowhere and struck him in the center of his chest. It took a couple of seconds, but at last he was able to speak normally. "Mom wouldn't have done what?"

"Asked me something and then told me to wait."

"She would've if she was in the Freddy's drive-through line. It's always been crowded or moves like lightning."

Jackson's eyes flashed. "Mom didn't even like Freddy's. She wouldn't have come here after a conference, anyway."

"Sorry, but she did. Your mother cooked like a dream but she liked burgers and fries as much as anyone."

"Maybe."

Sean would give anything to already be home and get to take a ten-minute break. Anything to come up with the right words.

But that wasn't an option.

"Jackson, what do Mom and Freddy's have to do with how you were feeling when I walked into the gym? Even Mandy said you were quiet tonight."

"All the other kids had their moms there." He frowned. "No, a lot of the other kids got to stay home with their dads while their moms came up to school."

"That may be true, but I wasn't the only dad. I saw lots of other dads there."

"Yeah, but they came with their wives."

Finally, he understood.

Why was he so blockheaded sometimes?

"Sorry, buddy. Sometimes I'm a little slow. You've been missing your mom today, haven't you?"

"Yeah."

A lump formed in Sean's throat as he was once again reminded that no matter what he did, he could never fill the gap Dannette's death had left in Jackson's life.

Though he knew that it wasn't possible to bring Dannette back or try to completely fill that void, Sean did allow himself to wish that he could do better.

"That's okay," he finally responded. Hating that his voice sounded hoarse. Clearing his throat, he continued, "Do you remember what the counselor told us during our last visit? You know, how it was okay to be happy and not think about Mom for a while but then think about her all the time. It's normal."

Jackson wrinkled his nose. "Avery said that lots of kids didn't have their dads but I was the only person she knew who didn't have a mom."

Well, Avery sounded like a twit. Since he couldn't say that, he settled for a noncommittal grunt. "Hmm."

"What do you think about that?" Jack asked.

"Nothing, really. It doesn't matter to me who Avery knows or what she thinks. Don't you let that bother you, either. As much as I would love for you to still have Mom, and we both miss her a lot, I'm glad I'm still here to be your dad."

"Yeah. I guess so."

Ouch. That was faint praise, but whatever. "Let's go home, get showers and call it a day, okay?"

Releasing a ragged sigh, Jackson nodded. "Okay, Dad." Then, miraculously, he smiled.

And just like that, everything inside of Sean resituated yet again. He was far from perfect, but he wasn't ruining everything for his son. That would do.

CHAPTER TWENTY-TWO

BY TWO O'CLOCK on Tuesday afternoon, Kayla was wishing she could go back in time and thank every teacher and aide who'd helped her when she was in elementary school. She'd had no idea just how hard they all worked!

Since that wasn't possible, she decided to simply focus on her job. Which, at the moment, was making copies for one of the fifth-grade teachers.

Thank goodness she and the copy machine were getting along so well. So far, she hadn't had a single jam. She also hadn't messed up any of the instructions that the teachers had left for her. Even when she'd had a question, no one had gotten impatient. While she didn't expect every teacher was always going to be so forgiving, she sure appreciated it on her first day of work.

"How's it going, Kayla?" Hilary asked as she walked into the workroom. "Are you hanging in there?"

"I am. I only have two more sets of copies to make for Mr. Chambers."

Hilary smiled. "That's good news. He's kind of demanding, but he always gives people plenty of time to get things done. Not everyone is that way."

"I didn't expect it."

"And no problems with the machine?"

"Not so far." She crossed her fingers. "Let's just hope I don't jinx anything."

"If you've gotten this far without a major mess-up, you and the copy machine are going to get along just fine." Looking at the monster copier with a look of distaste, Hilary muttered, "It hates me."

Kayla grinned. "I hope you're right that me and this thing will get along."

"There you go."

Enjoying Hilary's sense of humor—and the way she'd checked on her almost every hour, Kayla said, "When I'm finished with the copies, what would you like me to do next?"

"Call it a day."

"Really?" There was still another forty-five minutes of school left.

"Really. Jean, the secretary, let me know that you worked an extra recess, so you didn't get an afternoon break. You deserve to take off fifteen minutes early."

"I didn't mind working that recess," she said as she pushed the copier button to run the last set of copies.

"I'm sure it was appreciated, but we try to have

each other's backs around here." She wagged a finger. "And don't you dare try to argue. Tomorrow, something else might come up and you might have to jump in to help in the lunchroom or in a first-grade class. There's no reason to overdo it."

"All right, then. Thank you."

"No, thank you, Kayla. I don't know what made you decide to apply for this position, but we're all really glad you did. Everyone loves you already. You're going to be a great part of the team."

"I hope so."

Hilary was prevented from saying anything else when her phone beeped. "Oops, I've got to go help Mr. Martinez. Have a good night and see you tomorrow. Remember, Rosanne will be your mentor for most of the day."

She'd been introduced to Rosanne, who'd worked at the school for two years, about an hour ago. "I'll remember. Have a good night, too."

When she was alone again, Kayla finished running the last set of copies, paper clipped them and then placed them in Mr. Chambers's tray. After making sure that everything was in order, she headed to the staff lounge. In the back of the spacious room was a set of lockers that employees could use if they didn't have a space in one of the classrooms. Though one of the teachers had invited Kayla to store her things in her classroom, Kayla had liked being able to look at her phone or get into her purse without having to interrupt a teacher.

After collecting her things, she stopped by the office just to make sure that she didn't need to do anything else before she left.

Jean looked a little more frazzled than she had when Kayla had arrived but still had a smile for her. "Did you survive your first day here?"

"I did, and it wasn't even surviving. I had a good time. I wanted to double-check to see if you need anything before I head out. Hilary told me to go ahead and leave."

"Your paperwork is all in order. I even made sure that you'd get paid on Friday."

"Really? I thought I'd have to wait two weeks."

"The support staff gets paid weekly. This week, you'll receive a check from me," the secretary said. "By next week, your direct deposit will be set up in your account."

"Thank you. That will come in handy."

"See you tomorrow."

As she walked out, Kayla realized that things might be finally getting better for her. She sure hoped so. Just before she pulled out of the parking lot, she glanced at her phone again. Edna had texted to see if she was still up for helping her on Saturday.

I'm planning on it, she texted back, though she was now pretty sure that she didn't want the paid position.

If everything went as well as her first day had gone, she would soon just be a volunteer at Loaves of Love. It would be amazing to only go there to bake bread instead of also getting a sack of food. Just as she parked in front of her apartment building, Sean called. "Hi," she said. "You have perfect timing. I just got home."

"That's great. I've got to head out to the field in a minute, but I was hoping to catch you and figured I would leave a message if I didn't. So, how did it go today?"

"It was wonderful." She had a feeling she was probably grinning like a fool, but she didn't care. Not only had she had a good day, but Sean had cared enough to check on her before he went to football practice.

"Wonderful, huh?" His voice warmed. "I can't wait to hear all about it."

"When you have time, I'll fill you in."

"What about tonight?"

She frowned. "You want me to call you tonight?"

"No, silly. Come over for dinner. Jackson would love to see you. I would, too."

"I'd love to see you both. What can I bring?"

"Nothing. We're not going to be eating fancy. It's just grilled chicken, baked potatoes and broccoli."

"It sounds delicious. I'll bring some bread or rolls. Or dessert." Maybe she had enough things to make sugar cookies?

"If you want to make something, any of those things would be great. But if you just want to relax, that's fine, too. We're celebrating your first day of work."

"What time should I come over?"

"Five?"

She had a little over two hours. "I'll be there."

"See you then."

"Yeah, see you."

After she hung up, she called her mom and briefly filled her in. Then she took care of her lunch bag and started a load of laundry.

Finally she opened up her cabinets and took stock of what was inside. She vaguely remembered that Edna had given her a box of brownie mix the second time she'd visited. Kayla had stuffed it in the back of a cabinet because she hadn't wanted to waste an egg or her small supply of oil on brownies.

But now that she was going to get paid on Friday and could look forward to getting a small sum on Saturday after helping Edna at the reception desk, Kayla figured a pan of brownies was in order.

Thinking how much Jackson would like those, she pulled out a bowl and got to work.

Her day just kept getting better and better.

CHAPTER TWENTY-THREE

"She's here!" Jackson called from his perch in front of the window. "She's getting out. Oh! And she's holding a bag. Dad, do you think she brought us something?"

Wiping his hands on a dish towel, Sean smiled. "I guess you'll have to find out. Go out and offer to help her, son."

As he'd suspected, Jackson hadn't needed any further encouragement. He hurried to the front door, pulled it open and scampered down the front steps to greet Kayla.

Sean knew Jackson had done all that because he'd been watching from the window. And…he'd also glanced out the window a time or two during the last twenty minutes.

He could admit it. His son wasn't the only one who'd been looking forward to seeing Kayla.

When he watched Kayla bend down to listen to whatever Jackson was excitedly talking about, Sean felt the now-familiar lump that formed whenever he saw her and Jackson together.

After the tough conversation he'd had with Jackson about him missing his mom, Sean was thankful that he was becoming friends with Kayla, too. There was something so peaceful and kind about her. Simply put, she was easy to be around. Easy to talk to, easy to plan things with.

Even though he was starting to have feelings for Kayla, he doubted she felt the same. She was good company, but sometimes he still felt as if she was keeping her guard up around him.

And maybe she was.

If that was the case, it would be hard to move forward if she wasn't willing to give a relationship a real try.

He hoped she would, though. Unlike most other women he knew, Kayla seemed to appreciate every little thing he did and expected nothing from him. Remembering how pleased she'd sounded just because he'd taken the time to call her that afternoon, he shook his head in wonder. She was so easy to please. Maybe too easy. Her jerk of an ex-husband must have been even worse than he'd thought since it was obvious that she wasn't used to being looked after.

It made him want to do even more for her. Even if it was simply inviting her over for dinner.

"Dad. Dad!" Jackson called out as he threw open the front door. "Miss Harding's here!"

"Kind of figured that, Jackson. You know, since I'm standing right in front of you."

"Oh, yeah. Sorry for yelling."

Sean noticed then that Jackson had grabbed Kayla's hand with one hand and was holding a paper gift bag in his other. He didn't seem in any hurry to let go of that hand, either.

Meeting Kayla's eyes, Sean said, "I'm glad you could make it."

"Me, too." Her pretty brown eyes warmed as they exchanged a look before glancing back down at Jackson. "If I get a greeting like that every time I show up, you just might see me over here once a week."

"That's okay. You could even come over more than that," Jackson said. "I mean, if you wanted to."

"You're the nicest guy, Jackson." A lovely blush stained her cheeks as she dropped his hand. "Jackson, would you mind putting that bag in the kitchen? I need to take off my coat."

"Sure."

Sean figured that his boy couldn't be the only guy showing off good manners. "Here. Let me help you." When he rested his hands on her shoulders, he was sure he felt her lean toward him before she shrugged out of the coat.

But maybe he had imagined it.

"How was the drive over?" he asked.

"Fine. No traffic to speak of."

"Guess what? Kayla made brownies, Dad," Jackson called out from the kitchen.

Looking apologetic, she said, "They're just from a box. They are pretty good, though."

"We haven't made brownies...ever," he said with a grin. "I'm sure they're great. Thanks."

"How can I help with supper?"

"You can sit down in front of the fireplace and relax. What would you like to drink? I bought a bottle of wine. I've got soda, too."

"Just water for me."

He walked to the kitchen, filled a glass with ice and water then handed it to her. "As soon as the grill is finished heating up, I'll put the chicken on."

"That sounds great. I'll just sit here in front of your fireplace and be lazy."

"I'll sit with her," Jackson said.

"No, you will set the table."

After a small pause, Jackson walked into the kitchen and pulled open a drawer.

Sean shared a smile with Kayla before turning to his boy. "Thanks, son."

After putting on some music, Sean spent the next twenty minutes cooking chicken, checking potatoes, herding his son and steaming broccoli. For her part, Kayla looked like she would have happily joined them or even taken over the meal prep. But he didn't want her to remember his celebratory dinner being yet another meal she had to cook.

Plus, he was starting to realize that he liked looking after her. He liked it a lot. Dannette had been wonderful but she'd been constantly busy.

Every time he'd tried to do something for her, she would get irritated. Kayla's acceptance and appreciation of his efforts made him feel good.

When the three of them were sitting down together at last, Kayla complimented the meal like it was something right out of one of Julia Child's cookbooks. Even though he knew she did it for Jackson's benefit, Sean couldn't deny that the praise felt good.

"I told my teacher you were going to be at our school, but I didn't see you," Jackson said.

"I looked for you, too, but I was mainly with the older kids today," Kayla said as she carefully cut a bite-size piece of chicken on her plate.

"What about tomorrow?" Jackson asked.

"I hope I'll get to see you, but I'm not sure where I'll be. I have to go wherever I'm told to go." Turning to Sean, she explained, "I'm what they call a floating aide."

"That means Kayla goes somewhere different every day, Jackson," Sean explained. "You know, like you can float around in a pool."

"That's it exactly," Kayla said with a smile.

"Well, I hope you float into first grade real soon," Jackson said.

"Me, too," she replied. "I'll cross my fingers."

Jackson's eyes lit up as he crossed his fingers. "I'll do that, too."

Sean only smiled but a part of him felt like crossing his fingers, too. Whatever was happening between Jackson and Kayla was a good thing. Jackson seemed to gain a little bit more confidence every time he was around her. And Kayla? Well, he might be wrong, but it was starting to be obvious that she would be a great mother. He wondered if she wanted children one day.

Right on the heels of that thought, Sean wondered how he would feel about having more kids. He wouldn't mind that one bit, he decided.

Later, after Jackson took a shower and was looking at books on his own, Sean made Kayla a cup of hot tea and joined her on the couch. "I'm glad you didn't decide to leave immediately."

"I probably should, but to be honest, all that's waiting for me back at my apartment is the mail and a couple of chores to get ready for tomorrow." Her eyes widened. "And... I just realized that was a pretty rude thing to say."

"What? You think I'm going to be offended that my company ranks higher than looking at bills and magazines or making a lunch?"

"You definitely rank higher than that...but I could've said that in a nicer way."

"Everything you said was fine with me. And, for the record, I'd rather sit with you instead of going through the mail or packing tomorrow's lunches, too."

"That's something we can agree on."

"I think it's one of many things."

Her eyes widened, but she only smiled as she took another sip of the hot beverage.

"You know, I realized that we've talked some about high school and growing up, but not a lot about after," he said.

For the first time all evening, a guarded expression filled her gaze. "There isn't a lot to say for me. I mean, not beyond what I've already told you."

"I know you didn't go to college."

"You're right. I didn't. My family didn't have the money for that. And unlike you, I'm afraid I didn't have a lot of scholarship opportunities." She waved a hand. "I was one of those in-the-middle people in school. I made B's, not tons of A's. I was in the choir, but not all that gifted or passionate about it."

He understood her explanation, but it still seemed like she was leaving out something. "You didn't want to take a couple of classes at the community college or take out some loans?"

"No." She'd been trying so hard to be the wife Jared had wanted that she'd been afraid to not be available whenever he wanted her to be around.

"Oh. Okay."

"Sorry, I didn't mean to sound so abrupt. It's just that I don't enjoy talking about not going the college route." Before Sean could start another topic, Kayla continued. "I mean, I have thought about taking some classes, but it seemed like a waste of money." She bit her bottom lip. "When my parents suggested I just go get a job in retail for a year, that sounded like a great idea."

"So, you starting working at a card shop?"

"Oh, no. I worked at a department store down at the mall in Strongsville. It was fun and I was pretty good at it." Looking over his shoulder, she added, "I was even thinking about taking some classes in business and retail management when I met Jared."

"And then the rest is history."

"Yeah."

Sean knew they'd divorced. What he didn't know was anything about Jared. "Were you two happy for a while?" When she tensed, he held up a hand. "And feel free to tell me that your marriage is none of my business."

"No, I can talk about it. I... Well, your question made me realize that it's been a while since I've thought about how the two of us started out." After a pause, she said, "Yes, I guess you could say that we were happy for a while."

"I see."

She chuckled softly. "I'm sure you don't. And if you don't, that's fair because that was a pretty bad answer." After taking another sip of tea, she said, "Looking back, it's now obvious that we were never very happy together, but we wanted to be. And, there's a difference, you know?"

He nodded. He thought about his life one year after Dannette's death. He'd wanted to be far happier than he was or was pretending to be. "Almost a year after Dannette died, I got tired of always being seen as the grieving widower. So, you know, I kind of started faking it."

The compassion shining in her eyes told him that she understood completely. "Smiling in public."

"Yeah. I made myself take my family up on their offers to watch Jackson and went on a couple of weekend trips with the guys. Golf games, fishing, you know. It was okay, but the whole time I felt like hitting something. Like yelling at everyone that I wasn't okay and I could care less about playing eighteen holes on a championship-level course."

"Because all you wanted to do was sit and mourn."

"Yeah, or just *be*. So, I get what you're saying to some extent."

"Jared was older than me by a few years and had opinions about everything. At first I thought it was kind of cute but then it grated on me. We used to argue quite a bit."

"Did it help?"

Her smile was strained. "Not even a little bit." She sighed. "Eventually, we stopped arguing. Then stopped talking. Then we even went to some horrible couples weekend that was supposed to make us learn to communicate." She rolled her eyes.

He smiled at her expression. "What happened?"

"Oh, we communicated, all right. We talked about all the topics we were given. And realized that we had never really learned too much about each other from the start." She sighed. "So, we started going out on Saturday night dates and I started trying harder."

"To talk?"

"No. To be, you know, more attractive and interesting." She chuckled. "Sexier."

"Sorry, but Jared sounds like an idiot. I hope he appreciated everything you did." Especially since he didn't think Kayla had to do anything to be better. She was already all three of those things.

"Eight months after that, he told me he'd been having an affair." Bitterness filled her voice. "While I was focusing on being the wife Jared wanted and getting dolled up on Saturday nights, Jared's weekly late-night teleconference call with Asia every Thursday was his other date night."

"What a snake." Sean was feeling pretty proud of himself for not calling the guy anything worse.

"He was a snake." Looking almost amused, she added, "Some might call him something worse than that." Taking a deep breath, she added, "But I could've been more perceptive. I was kind of an idiot."

"No way should you be taking responsibility for his weaknesses, Kayla."

"Well, I could've been a lot smarter. When he told me that he could only take those calls at the office, I believed him." Averting her eyes, Kayla continued, "After that, even though Jared was once again calling the shots, all I wanted was to get out. So, we did a fast-track divorce." Lowering her voice, she said, "I should've been smarter about that, too."

He remembered what she'd said about barely getting anything. "I'm so sorry, but he took advantage of you."

There was a new bleakness in her eyes that made him want to pull her into his arms and hold her close. Whisper that no matter what happened, she was better off now. He was sure of it.

But she looked too fragile. Like, if he pushed too hard, she might break.

Kayla ran a hand over her face. "And… I have just told you way too much about my marriage."

"Don't say that. I'm the one who asked all the questions. I knew it was going to be uncomfortable for you, but I still pushed…because I wanted to know more about you."

"Well, you did get that," she joked.

He didn't return her smile because he wanted Kayla to know that he was being completely sincere. "I'm glad you shared so much with me. Don't regret sharing what happened, or your feelings. It's all safe with me." He was glad she'd been so honest. Now that he realized how hard she'd been on herself, he was going to make it his goal to build up her self-esteem.

"All right. I won't, then." She stood up. "But I do need to go."

"Leave your cup. I'll pick it up after I walk you out to your car."

"All right."

After he helped her on with her coat and she gathered her purse, he threw on a jacket and followed her outside. Thankfully, the night was clear, if cold.

"Want to warm up your car a minute?"

"All right." He stood as she got in, tossed her purse on the passenger seat and turned on the ignition. Then she got back out. "Thanks again for dinner. I love spending time with you and Jackson."

"Thanks for coming over. We like spending time with you, too."

"I hope I see Jackson tomorrow."

"If you do, I know that will be the first thing he tells me."

Kayla smiled. She seemed about to say something, but held her tongue. Instead, she pulled in her lip yet again. Bit.

Unable to stop himself, Sean pressed his thumb on her bottom lip. Gently, he freed it from her teeth. "Careful, now. You're going to hurt yourself one day." And then, for good measure, he ran his thumb across her cheek. As he'd remembered, her skin was soft and smooth. Perfect.

He kept his hand there.

Her eyes widened, then it was as if she'd mentally come to terms with what was happening between them.

Because she leaned in and tilted her chin up.

A burst of nerves hit him hard. Or maybe it was adrenaline?

Desire? Anticipation?

Whatever it was, Sean knew what to do. He closed the gap and kissed her lightly on the lips. When her hands gripped his arms, that was all the incentive he needed to kiss her again, this time deepening the kiss enough to make him remember that kissing Kayla was a perfect experience. She was reserved yet passionate. Sweet but not saccharine.

When they broke apart, he smiled. Then he kissed her cheek before stepping away. "Text me when you get home."

"Okay."

He stood on his porch while she got in the car, buckled up, adjusted a couple of knobs then finally drove out of sight.

Closing the door behind him, Sean thought about their conversation about being happy and faking it.

And he decided that right at that moment, he was genuinely happy. He wasn't faking a thing. Happy and already thinking about kissing Kayla again.

It couldn't be soon enough.

CHAPTER TWENTY-FOUR

"KAYLA!" AN EXCITED, little boy voice called out. "I mean, Miss Harding! Hey!"

Kayla turned around just in time to see his teacher remind Jackson to neither call out to adults in the hallway nor call them by their first names.

"Sorry about that," Mrs. White said to her after Jackson apologized.

"Don't be," Kayla replied as she walked closer. "Even though I've been here two weeks, it still feels like I'm the new girl. It's nice to see a familiar face." Lowering her voice, she added, "It's good to see you, too, Jackson."

He beamed. *Beamed*. "Uh-huh." He opened his mouth to say more, but stayed silent when his teacher raised an eyebrow.

His smiling face made her day. It was also a good reminder of how much better her life was. Not only was she getting to spend time with Sean, who was kind, thoughtful and so handsome, but she was becoming close to Jackson. He already had her heart.

Just as she was about to tell him goodbye, Jackson blurted, "Are you coming to my classroom today, Miss Harding?"

She glanced quickly at Mrs. White, who looked like she was barely refraining from ending the conversation, but nodded. Kayla replied, "I'm sorry, but I'm with second graders today."

"I wish you were going to be with us."

"Me, too, but maybe another day." Unable to help herself, she rested her hand on the top of his head. "I've got to go, but you have a good day, now."

"Okay. Maybe I'll see you again soon."

"I'm sure you will."

Looking at his teacher, Kayla mouthed that she was sorry for disturbing their quiet line before hurrying back down the hall.

She was quickly learning which teachers were easygoing and which ones were all business—at least with the paraprofessionals. Though she'd never worked in Mrs. White's classroom, she'd heard that the fifty-year-old lady was a bit exacting.

Kayla hoped Mrs. White wasn't that way with her first graders, or at least not all the time. Jackson needed love and support, not a bunch of rules he was expected to follow.

Just as quickly, Kayla reminded herself that she was neither the boy's mother nor a teacher. She shouldn't start believing she had a right to have opinions about what was best for Jackson or how a first-grade classroom should be run. All she did know was that she wanted to see more smiles on his face.

"Kayla, have you had lunch yet?" Patrice asked when she walked into the workroom.

She'd soon realized that her supervisor Patrice could give Mrs. White a run for her money. Patrice was also exacting and liked keeping tabs on everyone at all times.

Luckily, she was also fair and easy to get along with. As long as Patrice knew that Kayla was doing the best she could—and putting the children's needs first—she was super supportive. After Tamera's crazy behavior, she'd take rule-following Patrice any day. "No, I haven't," she finally answered.

"Go ahead and take a break now. You're going to need the sustenance since you're on double recess duty. Sorry about that. Rosanne is out sick."

"It's not so bad, but I'll be happy to go to lunch now."

"Take the full thirty minutes." Glancing at her watch, Patrice added, "But then go right out on the playground."

"Sounds good." Pleased to be working with Jazmine, since she seemed to know almost every kid's name in the school, and to have a short break, Kayla went into the staff room, found her lunch in the back of the refrigerator and sat down to enjoy it. Today's meal included some peanut butter crackers she'd gotten from Loaves of Love as well as an apple and a carton of yogurt that she'd bought herself. In a previous life, she knew she wouldn't have ever thought she could feel pride for buying her own meal, but she was used to dealing with her new reality by now.

After visiting with some of the teachers and other paras, she filled her water bottle to sip on while she did the same thing about half of the table was doing—scanning her phone and answering text messages or emails.

To her delight, she discovered two texts from Sean.

Still thinking about last night. Hope you're having a good day.

She'd met them at a local pizza parlor that was running a special on a salad and pizza bar. Their "date" hadn't lasted long, but it had included a hug from Jackson and a light kiss from Sean before she'd gone home.

Still feeling a glow from that, she replied to Sean's text right away. I am. And guess what? I finally saw Jackson in the hallway, and we got to say hi. He looks happy.

While he was replying, she noticed that he'd sent an additional text.

Jackson and I are going to a family birthday party on Saturday afternoon. Want to join us?

A family party sounded like they were getting more serious. She was happy about that, but was also starting to feel guilty that she was keeping a secret from him. He was still under the impression that she'd shown up out of the blue at Loaves of Love that first day.

Though she had a feeling he wouldn't care that she'd gone there for food, she was pretty sure that he wouldn't like that she'd kept it from him.

Or…was she making a mountain out of a molehill? It was a family birthday party, not some big romantic night out.

Let me look at my schedule, she typed. I'll let you know by tomorrow. While she'd been debating, he'd written two more notes.

Glad you saw Jackson.

Sounds good. And don't worry. My family is good people. You'll like them and they'll like you.

She gave him a smile emoji back but she wasn't so sure about his family being happy if she showed up at a family party by his side.

Maybe it was Jared's toxic betrayal sneaking hurt into her head, but Kayla had a feeling that she was never going to measure up to Dannette's memory. Especially since she was nothing like the successful pharmacist Dannette had been before Jackson was born. The woman hadn't liked to cry, and here Kayla had gone and cried about a cake and flowers.

Even though Sean seemed to like her just the way she was, Kayla had a feeling his family might have different opinions. If their positions were reversed, she sure would.

Unable to help herself, her mind flashed back to the visits with Jared's family. Though they'd been polite, Jared had told her many times that his parents thought he could've done better.

Most of the time, she'd thought Jared said that because Sandy, her former mother-in-law, had been the opposite of delightful. She hadn't even been all that pleasant to her son. His father and sisters had always seemed to like her, though.

But from the moment Jared had left, she'd never heard another thing from his family. It was almost like they'd been glad she was out of their lives and any relationship she'd developed with them had been erased.

Hating that old doubts and bitter memories were ruining her mood, she closed her phone and threw away her trash.

"You done already, Kayla?" Jazmine asked.

"Almost. I need to get my sunglasses out and put on my coat. I've got recess duty in a few."

"Have fun."

"I'll let you know if I need help," she teased, since it was a running joke that Jazmine would rather do just about anything besides recess duty.

When everyone in the lounge chuckled or grinned, Kayla's mood lifted again. Sure, she might still have a lot to figure out with her relationships, but here at work, things were going well. She needed to focus on the positive.

She liked her job and was good at it. That was a very good thing.

CHAPTER TWENTY-FIVE

KAYLA HAD REGRETTED saying yes to Sean's invitation from practically the moment she'd agreed to go. It felt like too big a step forward when they were still just getting to know each other. And when she was still learning to trust herself. She was also pretty sure that although the focus would be on Sean's brother-in-law's celebration, she and Sean were also going to be a matter of interest. How could they not be when no one in the family had seen Sean date since Dannette had passed away.

So, she had a lot of very good reasons to feel worried.

It was too bad that those weren't the real reasons Kayla wished she was staying home on Saturday night.

The big problem was that the Copeland family was too close to her own—and she was worried sick that she was going to somehow say something about running out of money. Or gas. Or food.

Her fears were illogical. She knew that. First of all, no one gave a date the third degree unless either they or the date seemed off-kilter. Neither she nor anyone in Sean's family was like that.

Secondly, no one there would suspect that she would have gotten into such dire financial difficulties. Not because Kayla was so smart and capable, but because she'd married a fairly successful guy and most women made sure to receive something when their husband cheated on them and asked for a divorce. Jared's infidelity and impatience to move on wasn't a secret, either. He'd never been shy about admitting that he'd found someone better and her parents had been just as vocal about how upset they were with his infidelity and entitled attitude.

So, pretty much everyone in their circle around Avon Lake knew what had happened.

Finally, the Copelands knew her parents. Sean's mom, Alice, knew her mom and they were friends. No one in their right mind would ever imagine her parents letting her go without food. And they wouldn't have…if she'd been honest with them.

But now she simply felt like she was living a lie. Both with her family and with Sean. It didn't feel good, but she also wasn't ready to admit everything that she'd been going through. No one wanted to be a subject of pity…even more than she already was.

So, Kayla knew that her secret was safe, but she could still let something slip. Now that things were getting easier and she was enjoying the time spent at Loaves of Love so much, it felt almost natural to forget the fact that she wasn't just a volunteer, but she'd been a recipient, too.

But not yet.

Kayla wasn't proud of herself about any of this. Sure, the fact that she'd been so broke she'd ended up at a food bank was unfortunate, but it wasn't something to be ashamed of. She knew that plenty of people in far better circumstances than her had ended up destitute.

What was embarrassing was that she'd let her life spiral out of control the way it had. She was reasonably smart and she had never been afraid to work. Shouldn't she have been able to feed herself at the very least?

Of course, on the heels of that humiliation was the fact that she was keeping what had happened a secret. She would never shame a person for seeking help. Why was her pride making her presume to be different?

The one time she'd volunteered at the reception desk, the women she'd helped with food had been proud. They'd also been embarrassed to be there and grateful for the help, just as she had been.

But somehow, Kayla hadn't had big enough britches to own her problems. She hated that.

Of course, as soon as she arrived, Kayla discovered that she'd been worried for no reason. Sean's parents were kind, his brother and sister and their families were friendly, and the other close family members polite.

After a few awkward moments, she'd relaxed enough to make small talk. When Sean had been cornered by a couple of men talking football, she'd decided to make herself useful in the kitchen.

"Hey," Sean said when he found her washing dishes. "I was looking everywhere for you."

Turning off the faucet, she smiled up at him. "You found me."

"I'm glad about that. But not glad that you're in here by yourself washing a casserole dish." He frowned. "What's going on?"

"Nothing that exciting. I was helping your mom get a couple of people drinks and happened to notice a sink filled with dirty dishes. I thought I'd help her out."

Before she knew what he had planned, Sean was folding her into his arms and kissing the nape of her neck. "You are absolutely the sweetest girl I've ever met."

She loved his affection but knew she wasn't doing anything special. "Sean, it's just dishes."

"Yeah, but it's more than that. You're helping to make everyone's life easier, all in that quiet, unassuming way of yours. Just like you did a load of laundry in my house the first time you helped out with Jackson."

She smiled up at him, enjoying his praise, though thinking it was a bit effusive. "You're making too much of this. It's just a couple of dishes. I really don't mind being in here."

"Or, perhaps, being alone for a few minutes?"

Feeling her cheeks heat, she shrugged. "Maybe."

His voice lowered. "Do you know why I was looking for you?"

"Nope. Why?"

"Because Jackson is spending the night here. He wants to have a sleepover with MeMe and Pop. That means that you and I can be alone tonight. Just like a real dating couple."

Unbidden, her stomach clenched. Sure, they'd gotten pizza and shared meals, but it had always been with Jackson. Almost as if they were firmly in the friend zone. But what he was suggesting was something else.

She hoped she was ready for it. "Just like one of those, hmm?" she teased, though she was pretty sure her voice sounded flat.

"What do you say we get out of here?"

Sean's body was tense, but he was gazing at her like he couldn't wait to get her alone. Sexy, handsome, former football star Sean Copeland. She couldn't help but feel a little charge of desire run through her. "I say that's a great idea."

"Thank goodness." Handing her a dish towel to wipe her damp hands, he said, "Where's your purse?"

"In the guest bedroom."

"Okay. Here's the plan. You're going to sneak in and get it and I'm going to wait for you by the back door."

She giggled. "Sean, what?"

"We're sneaking out of here."

"I can't do that. I have to thank your parents for having me."

"They know you're thankful."

"And Jackson. I can't just leave and not tell him goodbye."

"You can. I promise." When she continued to stare at him, not quite getting why he wanted to sneak out, he said, "If we make a big thing about leaving now, everyone's going to have something to say. We'll be here another thirty minutes at least, all while telling everyone what we plan to do tonight. Then Jackson will suddenly decide that he wants to be with us, too."

"I think you're jumping to conclusions," she teased, though she'd certainly been guilty of doing the same thing that evening. "No one's going to do that."

"Believe me, it's best for Jackson to keep busy. He's not going to miss me unless he senses that he's supposed to."

"Out of sight and out of mind," she murmured. "All right. I'll give you that."

"As for the others, I know my brother. And my brother-in-law. And my cousin Mark. I promise, once we let it be known that we're thinking about getting more serious, everyone in my family is going to get involved in our business. I don't know about you, but I'm not ready for that."

"I'm not ready, either."

"So, will you trust me on this?"

Sean looked adorable. Almost like a naughty kid, excited about doing something that he shouldn't. Though Kayla wouldn't call wanting to spend some time together without a six-year-old nearby scandalous, she did appreciate Sean wanting to avoid a thirty-minute goodbye and speculation session.

"I trust you and I'll meet you at the back door."

He kissed her quickly. "Good luck. I'll grab our coats."

Kayla was sure her cheeks were red as she quietly avoided groups of people, went into the guest room for her purse, and then walked toward the back of the house.

When she reached the back door, Sean's coat was already on. After helping her with hers, he held out a hand. "Ready?"

"Ready," she said with a smile.

Striding out to his SUV, she couldn't resist teasing him. "This was a whole new side of you, Sean. Sneaky and devious."

He laughed. "There's a whole lot about me that you don't know—get ready to be amazed and impressed."

"I'll do my best."

"Good, because I intend to feel the same way about you when you share some of your secrets with me, too."

And...just like that, all the excitement about

their quasi-clandestine mission dissipated. In its place was the realization that she could either tell him just how bad things had gotten with Jared during their separation and divorce…or gloss over it.

If she told him the truth, there was a very good chance he might hesitate taking things to the next level with her. After all, it wasn't just himself he was thinking about, it was Jackson. And his former wife had been assertive, smart, well-educated and had a good job. She'd been everything Kayla wasn't.

And right then and there, Kayla made her decision. She was going to persuade Sean to do most of the talking and evade talking about herself as much as she could.

At least for a little bit longer.

Just until she was sure that he wouldn't look at her with pity or distaste.

Or place her firmly back in the friend zone.

If that happened tonight, Kayla didn't know if she would be able to handle it.

CHAPTER TWENTY-SIX

SEAN WASN'T SUAVE. Not by any stretch of the imagination. He knew some women loved the high life. They expected to be taken to the most expensive and exclusive restaurants in downtown Cleveland. Or to the symphony. Or to Playhouse Square, with the giant chandelier hanging above the theater district.

Spending a couple of hundred dollars eating food he couldn't pronounce had never interested him and he'd rather do about a dozen other things than sit through any symphony, no matter how famous the orchestra or composer was.

He'd always been a pizza-and-burger guy. Or salads and grilled chicken. A couple of beers or sodas every now and then. If there was any kind of game on TV, whether it was football or curling, he was in. If he was dressed in gym shorts or sweats, even better.

But now that he was sitting next to Kayla in front of a roaring fire in his living room, Sean wished he had a bit more polish. She expected so little from him that he found himself wanting to go above and beyond to make her happy.

That was why he'd opened a bottle of cabernet that Meg had gotten for him a couple of months ago. She'd said it was an exceptional vintage and to enjoy it with someone special.

Though Kayla had taken a few sips, she didn't seem too impressed by it. Maybe it wasn't a good wine, after all. Did a bottle of cabernet go bad if it sat on the shelf for a while? He didn't think so, but what did he know? Maybe wines like that were supposed to be drunk immediately.

"Sean?" Kayla murmured, interrupting his thoughts. "Are you okay?"

"Of course. Why?"

"You keep frowning at your wineglass. Do you not like it?"

He did not. But how could he say that since he'd brought it out? "Do you?"

"I think so." Her expression appeared perfectly blank.

Kayla had taken off her shoes and had her feet curled up underneath her. She looked comfortable and gorgeous and maybe just a little bit awkward, too? "Are you not a wine girl?"

"Not really. To be honest, I'm not much of a drinker. Like at all. I'm sure this is good, though."

"How come you don't drink? I mean, I don't care if you drink or not. I just wondered if there was a reason." If there was a religious reason or she knew someone with a drinking problem, he didn't want to make her uncomfortable.

She shrugged. "It's just never interested me. Plus, the expense has never been part of my budget."

"Not even when you were married to Jared?" Sean had heard they'd had a nice house.

She looked down at her hands. "That was yet another way we disagreed, I guess. He liked to have cocktails. I know a lot of gals who enjoy one from time to time, too. So, I'm not being judgmental. It's just not my thing." Her eyes widened. "But that doesn't mean we can't sip this wine."

He got to his feet. "Kayla, I was just sitting here wondering why I wasn't enjoying this stuff at all."

Her eyes crinkled with a smile. She also looked like she was trying not to laugh. "Oh, no."

"Yeah. Meg acted like I was going to think it was amazing."

She giggled. "Maybe she should have given it to someone else."

Liking the way she was finding humor in the awkwardness, he stood up and reached out for her glass. "Come on. Let's go find something else to drink."

After handing him her glass, Kayla followed him into the kitchen.

"What do you think? Water, soda? Tea? I don't have decaf…"

"A glass of water is fine. I'm not all that thirsty, Sean."

Turning to face her, he reached for her hands. "So far I don't think I'm going to win any prizes for treating you to a romantic night."

"Why is that?"

"Family party, sneaking out, sipping fancy wine that neither of us liked…"

"Actually, I think that tonight has been really fun."

"Kayla, I found you washing dishes alone in my mother's kitchen. That was not *really fun* for you."

"Honestly, it was. I was glad to get a little break. Plus, it was nice to do something instead of following you around." When he tried to interrupt, she added, "And I was in the kitchen only about thirty minutes. Not two hours."

Leading her back to the couch, he sat down in the middle. She moved to settle right against him. He wrapped his arm around her shoulders and she snuggled closer, eventually resting her head against his chest. For a few moments, neither of them spoke.

Sean watched the flames jump in the fire and enjoyed how perfect she felt in his arms. Kayla was slim and soft. She favored a light floral scent. He didn't know if it was perfume or her shampoo or lotion, but it was appealing. So feminine. Just like her blond curls. Or the way she was so tender with Jackson and teary-eyed whenever Sean did something nice for her.

He loved that she appreciated little things.

"This is nice," he said at last.

"I was just thinking the same thing."

Shifting so he could see her expression, he said, "Next time we spend time completely alone, I'll take you out to eat or something."

"There's no need. I like sitting here."

"You're too easy to please, Kay."

"Since all I want right now is to spend time with you, I guess I am."

And there she went again. Sliding in deeper into his heart and making him dream of a future together. Holding that dream close, he gazed into her brown eyes.

When he spied the same emotions there that he was feeling, he shifted and pulled her closer. And kissed her.

And then, there they were, maybe doing what each of them had wanted for most of the night. Kissing on the couch by firelight.

All too soon, they had to stop before things went too far. After he helped Kayla into his truck, drove her home and walked her safely to her door, Sean drove home. He sat back down on the couch to watch the last of the smoldering fire burn.

And smiled.

There would always be a part of his heart that belonged to Dannette, but the majority of it was Kayla's now. He was falling in love again.

CHAPTER TWENTY-SEVEN

SEVEN DAYS HAD passed since he and Kayla had escaped the family gathering, gone to his house and spent time together.

Which meant Sean had now had seven days to try to figure out what he'd done wrong.

Every time he reviewed the last two hours of their date, he came up with no answers. Yes, they'd talked more about their marriages and he'd told her about some of his darkest days after Dannette's death.

He'd also held her close. Kissed her. One kiss led to a couple more. They'd ended up making out a little bit. It hadn't been too heated or crazy, but experiencing passion again had been great. He'd been sure Kayla had felt the same way.

She'd been sweet and responsive. Made him feel like she was on the same page as he was.

But then, when he'd called her on Sunday, she'd been quiet and distant. Like he'd said or done something wrong. He had no idea what it could have been.

Ever since, she'd been too busy to see him and had kept every conversation short. It was really frustrating, especially since his Dannette had been nothing if not assertive.

Sometimes, he realized, to a fault.

He'd let himself forget some of the difficulties they'd experienced from time to time. Dannette had been brilliant and, before they'd had Jackson, she'd easily made double what he did.

Every once in a while, he'd gotten the feeling that she thought her higher salary meant she should get her way when they disagreed.

He hadn't wanted to think anything negative about Dannette. He'd loved her deeply and she was Jackson's mom. But now, as time passed, Sean was able to admit that his wife hadn't been perfect and that their relationship had sometimes been a little rocky.

He'd hadn't liked how much Dannette loved to analyze things—because she'd believed in sharing every complaint or problem with him.

He also hadn't liked that her need for perfection meant that she often looked for faults. More than once, he'd suggested she focus on the positive. And that advice, predictably, had never gone over well.

All of that was on his mind when he walked into Loaves of Love and headed to the kitchen on Saturday afternoon. To his surprise, Edna was wearing an apron.

"Are you baking today?"

"I sure am. Nancy has started manning the welcome desk. Today's the first day she'll be completely on her own, but I didn't want to be too far away, just in case she needed help. Plus, I could sure use a day of baking. It's been a hectic week."

"I feel the same way."

More volunteers arrived during the next fifteen minutes. It was a smaller group than usual, but Sean was happy to see that he knew a lot of them. He enjoyed meeting new folks, but this crew had been making bread as long as he had. Today, there wouldn't be a lot of explanation and coaching—just simple conversation.

And, of course, a lot of kneading.

After saying hello to the two women who would be working with him and Edna, Sean got to work, measuring and stirring, flouring surfaces and kneading dough. Almost working in sync, his table of bakers finished at the same time. Together, he and one of the women placed the loaf pans on the large baking sheet and slid them into the commercial oven.

When he went back to his station, he noticed that the two women had left and Edna was in the front speaking to Nancy.

Deciding to go ahead and get started on the next batch, he pulled out more ingredients and began measuring them into his stainless steel bowl.

He was just about to start kneading when Edna came in. "I'm on my way, Sean. Could you put the ingredients in my bowl? I've got to wash my hands again."

"On it." Pulling out the measuring cups, he got to work. By the time she walked to his side, all she had to do was stir the ingredients together.

"Sorry about that," Edna said. "We had a rush of new clients. Nancy looked nervous for a moment, but then as soon as I offered to help, she was able to calm one of the ladies down."

"Calm her down?"

"Poor thing was near tears. Walking in here the first time can be a traumatic experience, you know."

"No, I didn't. Why would you call it traumatic? I mean, everyone tries to go out of their way to be nice."

"No one is worried about the volunteers, Sean. Instead, they're thinking about everything that brought them to this point. Not being able to provide for one's family is a difficult pill to swallow. So is not being able to even provide for oneself."

"Sorry. My comment was insensitive."

"No apology necessary. We're friends here." She pulled out the dough, expertly sprinkled it with flour, divided it in half and then began to knead. "I am so proud of Nancy. She's doing a great job."

"She was a client at one time, right?"

Edna nodded. "I don't ask anyone to man the front desk who hasn't been in the clients' shoes. Time and again, they prove to me that their experience and empathy can help the most agitated or nervous newcomer."

Sean was in midnod when he remembered a past phone conversation he and Kayla had shared. She'd said she'd been asked by Edna to man the front desk and had even given it a try one Saturday. Later, she said she decided to pass on it because she didn't want to work on the weekend.

"You do ask other people though, too. Right?"

"No. I honestly don't. The best people to man the reception desk are those who have been in the recipients' shoes." Then, as if noticing the tension that had to be emanating off him, her body stilled. "Why do you ask?"

"No reason. I was just thinking about someone who said she was considering volunteering…"

"Who is that?"

"Kayla."

"Ah."

And then, nothing. Edna went back to kneading.

But Sean's head had connected the dots. And come up with the surprise of his life. "Kayla was a client, wasn't she?"

"I'm not going to discuss clients, Sean."

So she was. Or she had been.

He was shocked.

No, stunned. And wondered what he should do with this knowledge. Part of him felt a little betrayed. He'd thought they'd gotten close. He'd sure shared a lot of painful stories about his journey after Dannette had passed away.

Why hadn't she felt comfortable enough to tell him that she'd gone hungry? Had he somehow made her feel like he wouldn't be sympathetic?

After placing one of his balls of dough into the pan, he attacked the next with renewed vigor.

Edna interrupted his thoughts. "Sean, I need to apologize to you and ask you a favor." Looking frustrated with herself, she continued, "I shouldn't have mentioned anything about the volunteers' requirements. To be honest, I hadn't even thought about how close you and Kayla had become."

"Or maybe you're as surprised as I am that I didn't know she'd come here for help before?" What had he done wrong with her? Why did she feel like she couldn't trust him? Her omission really hurt.

Appearing even more troubled, Edna added, "Sean, I don't want to put you in a position to lie to her, but perhaps you'll try to understand that she had her reasons for not sharing her situation."

"I understand. I'm surprised, that's all. And, please don't apologize."

"I'm not going to tell you what or what not to do. That's your decision. But I will ask if you could at least think about it before you bring it up?"

"I will."

"Thank you. Trust and confidentiality are important around here." The line that had been playing hide and seek in between her eyebrows settled in deep. "I knew that, but I still spoke out of turn. I feel terrible."

He sympathized with her but had trouble keeping his voice—and probably his expression—neutral. "Or maybe you're just human," Sean said. "I know you didn't mean to betray anyone's confidence."

"Thanks." Her smile was full of gratitude.

The door opened and Nancy stuck her head in. "Edna, I'm sorry to bother you again, but a family just buzzed in. I'd help them but I have to go get my kid from day care."

"I'll be right there," Edna said as she untied her apron strings. "Thanks for everything, dear. You did a great job."

"I sure enjoyed it. Not only did I like helping, but it was a lot of fun."

With a look of apology, Edna turned to him. "I've got to go. I'm afraid I'm going to put the rest of my station in your hands."

"Hand me your apron. I'll put it away and clean up everything after I get our loaves in the oven."

"I appreciate it, Sean." She hurried toward the door, obviously ready to help the family in need.

Sean hadn't worked at the welcome desk, but he had made bread with at least a dozen recipients of the food pantry over the years. More than one of them had quietly confided that they'd gone without for several weeks before finally deciding to get some help.

Just imagining Kayla going without something she needed made the center of his chest hurt. And then, like a pesky fly, on the heels of that heartache were the memories of the hours they'd talked on the phone or been in deep conversation over a cup of coffee. The way she'd listened to him describe his pain and grief after Dannette's passing.

How he'd confided to her that at times he'd even felt angry with God and, inconceivably, with Dannette. He'd told her so much that he'd never told another soul.

He'd shared things with her about his grief that he'd never even had the guts to tell himself.

Instead of making him feel guilty and ashamed, she'd only listened and said she understood.

She'd said she understood.

Should he have thought about what could have happened for her to understand something so raw? Had he been so self-absorbed that it hadn't even occurred to him to spare a thought for her?

Looking down at his hands, he realized that he'd been kneading Edna's bread dough by rote. Quickly, he placed the first loaf in a pan and moved to the second.

That small break freed another set of emotions. Hurt and irritation. Maybe even betrayal. Kayla had heard all his stories, absorbed all his pain, but had never felt close enough to share what she'd been going through.

She'd been hungry when they first met.

Thinking back to the first time she'd come over for a meal, he remembered she'd acted as if their simple meal had been gourmet. She'd savored each bite.

Because she'd been hungry.

He would've taken her to the store and gladly bought her a couple of hundred dollars of groceries. He would have done it more than once.

Shoot, he would have asked his uncle, who was an attorney, to visit with Kayla and see if there was anything that could be done to force her scumbag ex-husband to give her alimony.

But she'd never said a word. Essentially suffered in silence. At least, she'd been silent around him.

Realizing that the last of the bread dough was ready, he placed it in the pan, then carried all four loaf pans to the back where they would rise for thirty minutes before baking.

"Thanks, Sean," said George, one of the older senior citizens who came to help out once a month. "Four loaves today? You've been busy."

"Not so much. Edna got called out to the front so I helped with her station."

George nodded in understanding. "That's what we all do here, isn't it? Help out in a pinch."

"I wish the rest of the world was like that."

"You and me both, buddy." George cocked his

head to the side. "Of course, I've got to admit that we have more kind people around here than most places."

"I agree." Pulling off his gloves, Sean said, "I'm going to clean up then get out of here."

"See you next time. Have a good evening."

"You, too, George."

It took no time to wash the bowls, measuring cups and spoons. Wiping down two surfaces was just as easy as one.

When he walked out the door, he was startled to see that it was snowing pretty heavily.

Well, it was November. That went with the territory, he figured. Jackson would be thrilled.

But instead of thinking about that, all he could seem to focus on was the fact that it was going to be even harder to ask Kayla to come over. He couldn't ask her to drive in this. Not when the roads were going to be even worse later on.

So, he was going to have to wait a bit to say something to her. Which, he reasoned, was probably a good thing. He needed to get control of his emotions.

He wondered if that was going to be possible.

CHAPTER TWENTY-EIGHT

IT HAD TAKEN a little while to tell Wayne her story about inadvertently revealing Kayla's secret, but Edna did. All the while, Wayne had quietly listened on the bench they were sharing. He didn't fidget, sip from his water bottle or glance at the few people who had walked by. Instead, he focused on her completely.

So few people did that anymore, she appreciated it. She also found Wayne's intent way of listening refreshing.

Unfortunately, Edna didn't believe that telling her story to him had done any good. She still felt the burden of her mistake weighing down her shoulders.

When she stopped at last, Wayne waited a full beat before saying a word. "That it?"

That was all he had to say? Feeling a little bummed, she nodded. "Yes. I mean, that's everything that happened."

"Okay, then." He stood up. "Want to start walking again?"

"All right." She took his hand when he held it out to her, though she didn't need any help getting to her feet, and started walking by his side.

But did she feel better? No. But, maybe he didn't understand how upset she was. "Wayne, what I'm trying to tell you is that I really messed up. Like, royally."

"Uh-huh. I got that."

"Well…what do you think I should do?" Edna asked as they turned right.

They were in the middle of their usual two-mile walk up and down the streets of downtown Medina. When each had admitted that they weren't fans of sitting around and talking, Wayne had mentioned that he liked to take walks. That had been all the encouragement Edna had needed to buy a new pair of walking shoes and start meeting Wayne outside Blue Door Coffee Shop.

From there, they would walk the two-mile course that Wayne had mapped out and then end up either back at the coffee shop for some much-needed caffeine or at a nearby wine bar for a soothing glass of red wine and a couple of appetizers from the revolving menu.

Usually, they didn't speak about anything too serious. Sometimes they mentioned cute phone calls from grandchildren, or they'd comment on a house's new landscaping or the vibrant colors of the leaves. Other times, they didn't talk much at all.

But Edna knew that if she kept all her guilty

feelings to herself, she'd never be able to sleep. And she really needed to sleep because there was too much on her plate to be at half-mast in the morning.

So, she'd taken a chance and told Wayne her story. To her relief, he didn't interrupt once.

She'd appreciated that, too. Until he decided to take his time answering her. A million doubts settled in. Maybe she'd shared too much?

Maybe he was so shocked that he didn't know what to say without hurting her feelings?

"Wayne, I would like to hear your thoughts," she prompted, again. "Do you have any ideas about what I should do?"

"I know you're waiting, but you've got to give me a sec."

"Why?"

"I'm thinking on it."

They stopped at a corner so the cars at the four-way stop could make their way through. "And?"

"And...I'm still thinking."

Phil had never stayed silent for so long. He'd had an opinion about everything. Sometimes, she'd even wished he'd kept those opinions to himself. But this...well, Wayne's silence was maddening! "Wayne, come on. Say something."

"It's only been a minute, Edna. Settle down."

He was grinning, so she knew he was teasing but it was still a bit of a jolt to hear him speak to her that way. Phil had never been snippy with her.

Which sounded unbelievable. He'd been no saint and neither had she. They'd had more than their share of squabbles and disagreements over the years. She needed to remember that.

"Okay, I'm ready now."

She would've smiled if she hadn't been so eager to hear what he had to say. "Yes?"

"I think you are blowing things out of proportion."

"That's what you have to tell me?" He'd made her wait all this time for that?

"Obviously. I just voiced my thoughts."

She gritted her teeth. She increased her pace. "Sorry, but your thoughts didn't help."

"Maybe I'm not trying to help you as much as commenting."

"Commenting?"

"You know, sharing my opinion." He grunted. "Which you asked for, by the way."

"I've now heard it. And, just for the record, next time you want to tell me that you think I'm blowing things out of proportion? Thanks, but no thanks." And yes, she knew she sounded peeved, but couldn't he have tried a bit harder to come up with something to make her feel better? Couldn't he have…tried to read her mind?

Feeling ridiculous, she moved her arms with more oomph.

"Edna. Come on." Before she knew what he was

about, Wayne reached for her hand. He linked his fingers through hers and held on tight.

Maybe that felt nice...but she wasn't going to admit it! "We're holding hands now?"

"Yep. And before you start chewing on me again, listen for a spell. And think about what happened."

"It's all I've been doing!"

"Hush and think for a sec. Think about that conversation. You weren't gossiping. You didn't tell Sean about Kayla. He put two and two together. You couldn't have known that he would. Also, all you were talking about was Nancy and what a good job she's doing because she can relate to the folks coming in. There is nothing wrong with telling someone why a person is qualified."

"I guess that's true."

He tugged her hand so they were walking a little closer together. "Now, what do you think is the worst thing that could happen, now that Sean knows about Kayla?"

"Well, I don't know." She swallowed. "I thought they were seeing each other, but maybe I read it all wrong." Feeling worse by the second, she muttered, "To tell you the truth, I have no idea how close they are."

He almost smiled. "Which is yet another reason you didn't know he'd put two and two together. Now, do you think Sean is suddenly going to look down on Kayla?"

"Of course not. He's not that kind of man."

"Do you think he's going to start asking you for names of other volunteers who've also needed food?"

Was he making fun of her? "No."

"Now take a deep breath."

They were now standing under a streetlight that had just popped on. The faint glow it emitted seemed to shine directly on them.

Or maybe it was her imagination.

But whatever the reality was, Edna knew that the warmth she was seeing in his expression had nothing to do with amusement or criticism or anything else that was petty. Instead, she instinctively knew that it was approval. And, maybe, pride.

He was proud of her for being willing to listen.

"Deep breath, Edna," he whispered.

What could she do? She obediently inhaled. Exhaled. "Now what?"

"Do it again."

"Wayne, I don't need—" Seeing the determined expression on his face, she exhaled. "Oh, all right. Fine." Dutifully, Edna inhaled then exhaled again.

"Happy?"

"It depends."

"On what?" He was infuriating.

"How do you feel?"

She practically gaped at him. "Feel?"

"Yeah, Edna." He leaned closer, and even though they'd been walking at a pretty good pace, he somehow still managed to smell delicious. "How do you feel?"

How she felt was…better. Giving him a sheepish smile, she shared the truth. "Better."

"Good." He nodded, like he was pleased.

"Hey, thanks for listening to me. And thank you for being patient even though I was being difficult."

"You weren't being difficult."

"But still, it's appreciated." She continued as they started walking again. And yes, they were still holding hands like teenage sweethearts. "You really helped."

"I'm glad," he said simply. And then he lifted their linked hands and he kissed her fingers, all while walking by her side.

She was self-conscious enough to look around, just to see if anyone saw.

But whether they did or they didn't, it didn't seem to matter much.

All that did was the new feeling in her insides. It was a fluttering of expectation and happiness.

Giddiness.

Hmm. It seemed romance was in the air.

CHAPTER TWENTY-NINE

SEVERAL DAYS HAD passed since Kayla had seen Sean. It felt longer, especially since she'd seen Jackson almost every day at school. Every time their paths crossed, he smiled, waved or said hello. Then, there was yesterday.

Yesterday, she'd been on first-grade duty on the playground, and he'd stopped playing basketball in order to chat. It had been adorable and had made her feel good. She'd missed him.

The truth was that she was growing to love this little boy and knew if one day he was a permanent part of her life, she'd mother him as if he were her own. Not that she and Sean were anywhere near that point, but if they had been…she'd love to be a mom to this special boy.

Jackson's happy chatter had made her day. Even the other aides and Mrs. White had commented about how animated Jackson had been with her. One of the aides had mentioned that Jackson had kept to himself a lot when he was in kindergarten.

But their interaction had been bittersweet, too,

since he seemed just as confused as she was about why the three of them hadn't gotten together all week.

Of course, there were likely a dozen reasons why Sean hadn't invited her over. He had work, was tired, had family obligations…or even laundry to do. Now that she was working full time Monday to Friday, Kayla knew that household duties got woefully neglected and she didn't even have a child at home.

So, sure, there were a lot of reasons for Sean to need some distance.

But that didn't seem quite right. He'd gone from texting her several times a day to only once or twice. The tone seemed different, too. Instead of slightly flirty, they were fairly generic and flat.

Especially the lone text he'd sent the night before, which was in response to her somewhat desperate text at eight o'clock at night.

She'd written, Hey! I saw Jackson again at school today. I love seeing him so much! It made my day. Hope you had a good day, too.

His tepid response had pinched a bit. All good here. Busy. Have a good night.

He'd been busy? Have a good night?

Sent at a quarter after eight in the evening?

Actually, his text had more than pinched. It had upset her. Especially because she might have been blindsided by Jared's affair, but she hadn't lived under a rock all her life. Sean's text had been a firm message that he was not interested in either continuing to text or speaking to her on the phone.

So, something was off. Sure, he could be busy, and it was the end of football season. But after the way they'd kissed last weekend and then he'd later shared his feelings about losing Dannette, Kayla had been pretty sure that their relationship was heading somewhere serious.

So, whether it was obvious, or her sixth sense was sending out a message loud and clear, she knew that something was going on with him.

Of course, every time she thought something like that, Kayla remembered that her sixth sense had absolutely malfunctioned when Jared was having an affair. She'd been clueless about that.

And then, before she could stop herself, she'd exaggerated Sean's chilly-sounding texts and jumped to the conclusion that he'd found someone else. Maybe someone else Sean liked a lot better.

She hated reaching that conclusion, but Jared's actions and words had hurt deeply.

She was still stewing over Sean's distance on Saturday afternoon, which was too bad because she had something pretty amazing to celebrate. She was going to be able to pay for her groceries. A full run, too. Not just a handful of items to get her through.

She was going to be able to buy enough food to have a full refrigerator and extra snacks in her cupboards.

After she'd gotten paid on Friday, she'd placed the check on the kitchen table, pulled out her bills and prioritized her expenses. To her surprise, nothing was due for another two weeks, which meant she would have another two weeks of paychecks to take care of those bills.

And so, for the first time in months, she'd gotten out some of her favorite cookbooks and decided to make something. Like a real meal. And maybe a cake because she really did need to celebrate.

Oh, she wasn't going to go crazy and buy steaks and out-of-season fruit. But she definitely was going to buy some items to make her favorite casserole. It had chicken and broccoli and cheese. And crumbled crackers on top. Smiling, she decided that Jackson would probably eat it right up without a complaint. And Sean might not think it was special, but she was pretty sure he would like the filling meal.

If she dared to let down her guard and ask him over for supper. Looking around her apartment, she knew it was a far cry from his comfortable home, but it wasn't terrible. It was clean and bright. Definitely good enough to have Sean and Jackson over. If she stopped imagining the worst and pulled herself together.

"Oh, you are overthinking this way too much. Text him an invitation!" she said out loud. "What's the worst thing that could happen? That he tells you he's busy?"

Wishing she felt confident enough to give him a call, she sent a simple text.

Hey! I'm cooking tonight. Would you and Jackson like to come over for dinner? I'm even going to make a cake.

She was just about to put down her phone when she spied the tell-tale collection of dots appear on the screen. And then Sean's reply appeared.

No need to go to so much trouble.

It's no trouble, she typed. I like to cook

Still, it's too much. Plus, Jackson and I have plans already. After another second passed, Sean sent another text. Sorry.

It's too much? What was too much? Dinner together? The cake? Her enthusiasm?

All of it?

Rereading their messages, Kayla's stomach churned. She started to feel slightly sick. Which meant that she was overthinking everything waaaayyy too much.

So, why was her heart breaking?

When her phone rang, breaking the sudden stream of self-doubts, she felt a burst of optimism. Followed by a fierce plummet when she saw that the caller was her mother. "Hey, Mom."

"Hi. What are you up to today?"

"Nothing much. I was just writing down a list for the grocery store."

"Oh, good. That will give us something to do."

"What are you talking about?"

"I decided to drive down your way. I miss you."

It was like her mother had known Kayla needed her. "I miss you, too, Mom."

"You aren't busy, are you?"

Swallowing past the lump in her throat, she said, "Nope. I'm glad you're coming over."

"Me, too. Hey, you sound a little off. Are you sure you're okay?"

"Positive." She tried to interject a bit of pep. "I was, um, just looking at recipes."

"Oh. That makes sense. Well, I'll be there in about an hour. How about we go out to lunch before we hit the store? Otherwise, we'll put everything that looks halfway yummy into the buggy."

Though she knew she wouldn't be overloading any shopping cart in the near future, Kayla had to smile. Her mother had used two words she rarely heard anyone use: *yummy* and *buggy* for the shopping cart.

"That sounds good. Thanks."

"Yay! See you soon."

After they disconnected, Kayla pulled out a dishcloth and some spray cleaner to wipe down her bathroom counter. It probably wasn't needed, but a mother's visit was still a mother's visit. No way was she going to have spotty countertops when Mom arrived.

A countertop wipe-down led to some light dusting. She was contemplating how much better her apartment's worn carpet would look with a fresh vacuuming when her mother knocked on the door.

"You got here just in time," she teased. "I was about to start vacuuming."

"Why on earth would you do that?"

"Obviously, because my mother was coming over," she said, grinning. Looking at her mom, Kayla privately thought that her cleaning burst had been justified. Her mom had a way about her that was flawlessly put together. Even dressed as she was in jeans, loafers and a cream-colored sweater, she still looked ready for just about anywhere. Of course, her designer plaid blazer and freshly styled bob probably had something to do with it.

"Oh, pshaw." She held out her arms. "Hi, sweetie. It's good to see you."

"It's good to see you, too," she replied after they hugged. "Would you like a cup of coffee or a glass of water?"

"Water sounds good."

"I'll get it."

Mom tossed her bag on the kitchen table and looked around as Kayla pulled out a glass and filled it. "Everything looks nice, Kay."

"Thank you."

"I think we have a lot to talk about. First your job and next the new man in your life!"

"I'll be happy to talk about my new job. I like it a lot," she said as she handed her mother the glass. "There's not much to say about the man, though."

"No? But I heard Sean and you were getting along like bread and butter. And I heard that from Sean's mother, by the way."

"I thought we were, too." She paused, then added, "Maybe I was imagining things, though, because he's been acting kind of distant this week."

"Could be that he's just busy with work or his son."

"No, I think it's something more than that. I think he's changed his mind about me." And she had no idea what she'd done.

Her mother sat down at the kitchen table. "What do you think could have happened?"

"I don't know. I thought everything was going really well, but now he seems distant." She rubbed the center of her chest. She hated to make the comparison, but Sean's sudden distance felt a lot like Jared's. Only this time, she couldn't call Sean a snake. He was one of the best men she'd ever met. What could she have done or said?

"Maybe it has nothing to do with you. You know, your father never did learn how to compartmentalize his job."

"Perhaps." She didn't feel that was the case,

though. "It could be that he isn't ready to get in a serious relationship."

When her mother's eyes widened, she hastily added, "I mean, we're not anything close to serious, but if he thought we might be headed that way, it could have made him want to put on the brakes."

Her mother nodded slowly. "That's a very good point. Some of my lady friends who've recently started dating have shared that the idea of seeing someone new is a lot different than actually becoming involved."

Tired of dwelling on Sean, Kayla stood up. "I have my grocery list ready. Shall we go?"

"Yes, but let me see what you have in the refrigerator first."

"Mom, that isn't necessary."

"Don't be silly. What are you worried about? Have you not wiped down the..." Her voice drifted off as she stared at Kayla's near-empty refrigerator. "Kayla, where's all your food?"

"I need some. That's why I was going to the store, remember?"

"No, this is different," she said as she opened up the freezer drawer, closed it, then moved to her cabinets. Her mother's posture stiffened as she took in the embarrassing sight of a no-name box of crackers, a small bag of sugar and a can of pumpkin. All three items had come from the food pantry.

Kayla could practically hear her heart beating as

her mother quietly closed each cabinet door. She stood for a moment, then turned to face Kayla.

"What's going on?" she asked in a new tone of voice. It was the one she'd used all the time when Kayla was fifteen. "And the truth, if you please."

There was no way she could lie. "Until I got this new job, I was having a difficult time buying groceries."

Her mom shook her head. "Difficult time means that you don't get extras. This is something else."

Shame clogged Kayla's throat as her eyes filled with tears. "When I started losing hours at the card shop, I couldn't afford to pay for my rent, gas and food."

"So you went hungry?" Her mother sounded as if she was choking.

Yes, she had. But no way was she going to share that. "No. I...um...I went to the food bank."

"You went to the food bank," her mother uttered, each word sounding as if she was choking on them. "You went to strangers instead of letting your father and me know you needed help."

Somehow, Kayla now felt even more embarrassed. She'd been trying to do the right thing and live independently. But had she only been fooling herself? Had she been more concerned with her pride than her parents' feelings?

No. No, she'd been trying to do the right thing. "Dad's radiation treatments are bleeding you dry, Mom. Plus, you both helped me with the deposit on this place. No way was I going to ask you for anything else. You did enough."

"The cancer treatments have been expensive, but that's what insurance is for. We would've helped you, Kayla."

"I didn't want to ask."

She popped a hand on her hip. "You know what? It just occurred to me that if I hadn't opened that refrigerator and those cabinets, you still wouldn't have admitted how bad your finances are."

Because her mother was right, Kayla made herself respond. "*Were*, Mom. Now that I have this new job, my finances are a lot better. I was going to go to the grocery store today. I'm not going to have to ask Loaves of Love for help again."

She frowned. "I thought that was where you were volunteering. Was that a lie, too?"

"No! I am volunteering there. And it's helped me so much. I've met a lot of people. It's been fun, too. But I, uh, also went there to get assistance."

Her mother's feelings were written all over her face. *Skepticism. Confusion. Hurt. Anger.*

"I swear, if I saw that ex-husband of yours right now, I'd slap his face. He not only treated you shamefully when you were married, but he screwed you over in the divorce."

Her proper mother spewing the word *screwed* was almost funny. It was certainly nothing she'd ever heard her say before.

So all Kayla did was say how she felt. "If Jared

was here and you slapped him…well, I'd probably clap."

Her mother chuckled. "It's probably good he's living far away then. I'd hate to do him harm." Picking up her purse, she said, "Let's go, dear. We have things to do."

"Are we still going to go to lunch?"

"Of course, but a quick one, I think. We've got several stores to hit before I head home." Shaking one manicured nail in her face, her mother added, "And Kayla Elizabeth, if you even think about protesting one single purchase, we are going to have words. More. Words. Do you hear me?"

"Yes, ma'am."

"Those words are music to my ears."

FOUR HOURS LATER, Kayla was wearing new tennis shoes and hugging her mother goodbye.

After her mom drove off, she walked into her apartment, dumped the contents of one of the sacks on her bed and then continued to put away all the purchases from Target.

Soon, she had a drawerful of toothpaste, shampoo, moisturizer and makeup. Under the sink was more bathroom cleaner, toilet paper and tissue than she could probably use in a year.

And her kitchen cabinets, refrigerator and freezer were completely stocked. Maybe on another day, she'd feel embarrassed, but at the moment she was still riding the wave of her mother's good spirits.

There was no denying it. Her mom had gotten a kick out of their shopping expedition. More than once, she'd brought up the times when she'd taken Kayla clothes shopping for a new school year. Once she had realized that arguing and complaining wasn't going to do any good, Kayla had to admit that she'd felt like it was her birthday and Christmas all rolled into one.

Yes, she was stunned and grateful for all the food. But she was also excited to feel more like herself. She now had her regular shampoo and soap, body lotion and mascara. None of it was all that expensive. They were just purchases she'd normally made growing up in her parents' house.

And when she'd been married to Jared.

It was only recently that she'd changed all the brands for cheaper ones or done without.

So, all her mother's pampering was very much appreciated. She made a promise to herself to remember this feeling—and to one day pay it forward when she was able.

She had a feeling that, when that day came, she would be as giddy as her mother was during their outing. Making someone else's life easier was a gift that kept on giving.

CHAPTER THIRTY

SEAN HADN'T BEEN able to help at Loaves of Love for two weeks. After running tapes early last Saturday morning with the coaching staff and team after the loss on Friday night, he'd spent the day with Jackson at the park.

This Saturday, though, Jackson was still with his brother, Jack, and his family. Jack's wife, Kim, had picked him up at school on Friday afternoon. They'd taken him to the high school football game, then had him sleep over. Today, they were heading over to Vermillion to look at boats, go to a holiday arts and craft show, and likely eat a bunch of ice cream. After that, Jack and Kim were going to drop off Jackson at their parents', who were delighted to have him to themselves until Sunday afternoon.

Sean had the whole weekend to himself. He knew why, too—they thought he'd want some alone time with Kayla, and he hadn't told them differently.

Honestly, he didn't know how he was going to be

able to tell them that he wasn't sure what to think about Kayla anymore. His entire family had fallen in love with her. Almost every member of his family had taken a moment to either text or call him to voice their approval. They'd not only thought she was sweet and easy to be around, they'd all loved the way she and Jackson had gotten along.

At first, Sean had been a little dismayed by how easily they'd accepted him dating another woman. For some reason, he'd thought they'd be more loyal to Dannette. But then Jack had said something that resonated with him, which was that he thought it was possible to have enough love in one's heart to love both Dannette's memory and Kayla, too.

His brother's words had struck a chord. They would have felt really special if he hadn't still felt so betrayed by Kayla's silence.

Which he knew wasn't very fair. He knew he needed to get over his hurt feelings and move on. Unfortunately, it wasn't all that easy to do.

Walking into Loaves of Love on Saturday morning, Sean wondered if he should've tried to do something with some of his single friends. Go hiking. Hang out and watch a couple of college games.

That idea fled as soon as he realized that his single buddies' idea of fun was still barhopping all afternoon. That had never been his thing and he sure wasn't into that now.

He was much happier with his new friends at Loaves of Love.

"Sean, it's good to see you," Wayne called out when he walked inside. "It's been a minute."

"It has. Too long. Save me a spot while I go wash up." Ten minutes later, he was back in his usual spot, measuring flour and listening to Wayne grouse about the Browns. After spouting his own opinion about the defensive line, Sean realized that there was nowhere else he'd rather be.

Unless it was spending time with Kayla, a small voice reminded him.

His cool responses to her texts had done what he'd intended, kind of fizzled their relationship out. It had been almost a week since either of them had texted each other. He missed her. Missed her sweetness and the shy way she'd tell him about her interactions with all the teachers and kids at school.

By now he'd come to terms with his feelings of disappointment and resentment about her not sharing her circumstances. Everyone had their own story to live the best they could. It wasn't his place to judge. It certainly wasn't fair of him to feel betrayed because she hadn't trusted him enough to confide something that must have been painful.

Unfortunately, now he wasn't sure how to make things better. He didn't want to lie to Kayla and he sure didn't want her to lie to him.

So, he was at a standstill.

Until he saw her walk in the door.

"Kayla!" Wayne called out. "We have one space left at our table. Come join us!"

"Great. I will, Wayne," she said with a smile. And then it faltered as she caught sight of him. "You know, maybe I'll work over at this new table—"

"By yourself? No way."

When she still hesitated, Sean knew it was time to speak up. "Come join us, Kayla. Please."

"Um, all right," she said, though her eyes still looked wary. "I'll go get my gloves and apron."

As they watched her walk over to the sink to wash her hands, Wayne whispered, "I wonder what's going on with Kayla today. I've never seen her act so skittish. Do you think she's sick?"

No, he was pretty sure he'd acted like a jerk and scared her off. "I don't know, but I doubt she's sick. No one would be here baking bread if they thought they were contagious."

"I suppose that's true." Wayne frowned as they watched her quietly speak to a woman and show her where to get the measuring cups. "Well, I hope nothing's wrong. But if there is, that's what we're here for, right?"

Sean grinned at him. "For someone who only started volunteering here a few weeks ago, you've sure embraced this place."

"I could say that I owe it all to Edna, but I think it's more that this place gets under your skin. I feel good when I'm here, you know? Good about what we're doing. Good about the community." He chuckled. "Am I just waxing poetic, or does it make sense?"

"I think maybe a little bit of both," Sean teased.

"I'll take that."

"You'll take what, Wayne?" Kayla asked as she joined them.

"Nothing worthwhile. I was just spouting off some of my feelings about this place and realized that I might have overdone it."

"I don't think that's possible," she replied as she pulled over a canister and started measuring cups of flour into her large stainless steel bowl.

Sean noticed that she was taking care not to look at him, which made him feel even worse. He'd hurt her feelings and then had let his pride get in the way of good sense. He needed to fix things.

"How is school going?" he asked.

"It's going well. Thank you," she said as she added warm water to the mixture.

"Do you think it's going to be a good fit for you?"

"I do." The smile she sent his way looked both fake and forced. A terrible combination. "If I haven't thanked you enough—"

He cut her off right there. "You have. I was just curious. And interested. I wasn't looking for thanks."

"Ah." She didn't look at him again as she scooped up more flour and began mixing the dough with her hands.

Wayne raised his eyebrows at Sean. It was now obvious that he'd figured out that Sean had upset Kayla and she was hurting. This was bad. Really bad.

After another couple of awkward moments passed, Wayne said, "Hey, Kayla, did I ever tell you about the cute-as-all-get-out thing my grandson did the other day?"

Her voice brightened. "I don't know, but I doubt it. Trent seems to do cute things all the time."

"You're in for a treat, then." Taking a deep breath, Wayne launched into a long, convoluted story about his grandson, Trent, a neighborhood park and a beagle named Bob.

The whole thing sounded outlandish, but Sean was grateful for the man's tenacity and storytelling skills. If it wasn't for him, the three of them would have been working in awkward silence, which was exactly the opposite of every other group in the room.

For his part, Sean focused on kneading his two loaves. Then, while he was waiting for them to rise, he decided to go help the volunteer in the back of the room monitor the bread baking.

He rarely worked next to the commercial ovens, and was quickly reminded that it was hot work. Gratifying, too, as he was able to see the fruits of the group's labor.

After stopping briefly to punch down his dough and place it in the pans, he returned, thinking hard about how he could possibly make things right with Kayla.

Nothing sounded like it would help.

Then he realized that was because there was

only one right thing for him to do. He needed to come clean with her. And, since he didn't have Jackson back until tomorrow afternoon, he needed to do it today, and preferably in a place where she couldn't run off before he could find a way to explain himself without sounding like a total jerk.

When Kayla approached with her two loaves, ready for the oven, he took his chance.

"What are you doing after this?"

She set the loaves on the counter. "I'm probably just going home. Why?"

"Well, it's only midafternoon. Want to do something together?" Inwardly, he cringed. He'd heard freshmen use more finesse when they asked out girls.

Pure wariness shone in her eyes. "What do you want to do?"

"I don't know. Go for a walk?"

She blinked before answering. "It's a little cold for me, Sean. But thanks, anyway."

Belatedly, he realized that it was cloudy and forty degrees. Rain was also in the forecast. What was wrong with him? It was like he couldn't think clearly whenever she was around. "Wait," he blurted before she walked away. "Listen, I'm going to be honest with you. I want to speak to you about something, but it's made me nervous. That's why I'm currently acting like I've got rocks in my head."

"You're nervous about speaking to me?"

She sounded so incredulous, he had to smile.

Did she not have any idea about the way she affected him? "Well, yeah. So, um, what do you say? Since the weather's crummy, we could go to a coffee shop or a restaurant…"

"Would you like to come over to my apartment?"

"Yes."

She almost smiled, then suddenly looked worried. "I know you've seen where I live, but you haven't been inside. It's small."

"I don't care."

"I might not have put my cereal bowl in the dishwasher. Or, um, cleaned up yesterday's mail."

Man, he'd been such a jerk. She was standing there thinking that he'd find fault with her for not having a spotless apartment? "I don't care if you have this week's laundry scattered across the living room floor. I just want a chance to speak to you."

She nodded slowly. "I'll meet you there."

"Thanks, Kayla."

She didn't reply, just gave him a faint, almost distracted-looking smile, before going to the back to get one of the finished loaves of bread and retrieve her purse.

After she took off, he got his own loaf of bread and started mentally debating various ways to start their conversation.

"Hey, Sean?"

Turning, he watched Wayne approach. "Yeah?"

"Is Kayla going to finally give you some of her time?"

"Yeah. I guess it was pretty obvious that I was practically begging for it."

"Maybe not obvious to the entire room, but for someone who's done my share of groveling, it was easy to see the signs."

He chuckled. "You know, I think I did my share of groveling with Dannette, too."

Wayne stuffed his hands in the pockets of his baggy jeans. "If you don't mind, I'd like to give you one piece of unsolicited advice. I promise it won't take long."

"Okay…"

"I thought that after being married thirty years, I was pretty good at expressing myself and communicating. But I recently discovered that I had gotten good at doing those things with Georgia. Then I started seeing Edna and realized that she didn't need the same things as my wife had. She also approached things differently. In short, all the practice and skills I'd used with Georgia turned out to be unhelpful when it came to Edna."

"Because they're two different women."

"Yes, but they also had two different lives and sets of experiences. I had to adapt." He paused. "You might think about that before you and Kayla chat."

"Thanks. I… That's really good advice and something I needed to hear."

"I'll wish you good luck, then." Wayne reached out a hand.

Sean clasped it before picking up his loaf of bread and walking out the door.

Getting into his SUV, he realized that his shirt had raindrops on it. It had started to rain and he hadn't even realized it.

CHAPTER THIRTY-ONE

KAYLA WAS GLAD that Sean hadn't left Loaves of Love the minute she had. She needed a moment to gather herself together. Her insides felt chaotic and raw. She was pretty sure if Sean looked at her the wrong way, she'd dissolve into a mess of ugly tears.

No way did she want to embarrass herself by crying in front of Sean. She'd done that far too much with Jared and all it had done was drive him further away than he'd already strayed.

Instead, she needed to appear calm and collected. Friendly but distant. No matter what he had to say.

With that mantra replaying in her head, she hastily climbed the steps into her apartment, turned on a couple of lights and looked around. She knew what she needed to do.

Instead of taking care of her mail and cereal bowl, she went to her bathroom, looked at herself in the mirror, and decided to put on a little bit of lip gloss and a coat of mascara on her eyelashes. Then she pulled her hair out of the elastic and gave it a good brushing. When she was done, she glanced at herself again and realized that she felt okay. Maybe even a little bit better than that.

She'd gained a couple of pounds over the last month, and it suited her. Her cheekbones weren't quite so pronounced, and her figure had softened. Though she'd never have the kind of curves other women had, Kayla felt that she looked a little more feminine. She definitely looked and felt healthier.

More important than her looks was her state of mind, though. She felt better about herself and her future than she had in a very long time. Sure, she had a long way to go before she felt like she was firmly on two feet, but she didn't feel so beaten down by life anymore.

Sean was responsible for a lot of that. If not for him, she wouldn't have applied for her position at the school district. She wouldn't have even known about it. Chances were good that she would've applied at a couple of other retail stores and would be spending her evenings and weekends working.

If not for Sean, she would've still spent most of her evenings giving herself a hard time about how things had gone with her and Jared.

Now, days had gone by without her giving her ex-husband a single thought. That was huge.

So, no matter what he was going to say, she felt certain that she was going to be able to handle it. She might not be happy, but she wasn't going to fall apart.

Walking into her living room, she picked up the pile of mail and placed it in a white wicker basket. Just as she finished washing and drying her cereal bowl, Sean knocked at the door. Quickly, she put the bowl back in the cabinet.

Taking a deep breath, she opened the door to let him in. Whatever happened was meant to be, Kayla told herself. She'd survived much worse than a tough or uncomfortable conversation.

But all that coaching disappeared from her mind the moment she saw that he was soaked. "Sean, oh my gosh!"

He shook one of his arms out. "Yeah, it was like as soon as I got out of my car a monsoon hit."

"Come in, come in." After she closed the door, she got a better look. "I'll be right back. Let me grab you a towel."

"Thanks. Okay if I take off my shoes?"

"Of course," she called over her shoulder as she hurried to her linen closet and pulled out two bath towels. She wished she had an old shirt of Jared's so he could change, but of course she didn't.

"Here," she said, turning back to him.

Sean was still standing in the small, tiled entryway. "Thanks," he said as he grabbed the first one. "I was afraid to come any farther into your place." After rubbing the towel over his head, he bent down to dry his feet. Noticing the drops of water now decorating the tile, he groaned. "Sorry about this."

"Don't be. Want to use the bathroom to finish drying off?"

"Yeah."

"It's down the hall. You'll see it."

"Thanks."

He sounded distracted and uncomfortable. After lighting a fire in the fireplace, she decided that a pot of fresh coffee was in order and went about making it. The pot was half brewed by the time he joined her.

His hair was sticking up in all directions. Obviously, he'd tried to towel dry it some more and hadn't bothered to look at the results in the mirror before walking out. He looked younger. Almost boyish—and maybe a little bit more like Jackson than usual.

Seeing her expression, he paused. "You're smiling. Do I look like a wet rat?"

"No. Not at all." Unfortunately, her lips curved up. And how could they not? He didn't look like a wet rat, but he did look adorably rumpled.

"Boy, I don't know if my appearance is going to make things worse or better for me."

"Better," she said. That was true, too. If he'd come in looking perfect, she'd have been only worrying about the upcoming conversation.

He rested his elbows on the kitchen counter. "Yeah?"

"Yeah. Now, how would you like your coffee?"

"Hot and black."

"I've got that taken care of." She poured him a cup, then got herself a cup as well. "Let's go sit down."

"I would sit on the couch but I think I'm still too wet. Can we sit at the kitchen table?"

"Sure." Kayla was pretty sure he wasn't all that wet anymore, but maybe sitting a little more formally at the table would be better for whatever he was about to say. She cradled her own warm cup between her palms and waited for him to get started.

"Kayla, I have something to tell you, but I'm not sure how to begin. I don't want you to kick me out before I give you the whole story."

"Ever since you had said that you wanted to talk to me, I've been trying to guess what it could be about." She shook her head. "No, that's not true. I've been wondering what I did wrong at your parents' house."

"Nothing at all." Looking more troubled, he added, "Everyone loved you. You've been worrying about that this whole time?"

Kayla nodded slowly. "I sound like I'm overthinking everything, but your texts were short and abrupt. Plus, you didn't call. I know you're busy and you have Jackson, but I was pretty sure there was something else going on, too. It seemed like the complete opposite of how you were acting the week before."

"You weren't wrong. I was treating you differ-

278 THEIR SURPRISE REUNION

ently." After taking another sip of his coffee, he shook his head. "I messed things up."

That was the problem, though. She had no idea what he was taking about! "Just tell me, Sean."

"Okay. Fine. About two weeks ago, when I was volunteering at Loaves of Love, Edna said that the new receptionist had once been a client. You know, Nancy first visited Loaves of Love because she needed food." He stopped.

He was acting as if he'd told her something noteworthy, but she couldn't see it. "What does that have to do with me?"

"You had told me that Edna had asked you if you'd like to start working there."

"She did. It was just going to be four hours a week. I was thinking about it and even gave it a try one Saturday." Still not seeing why he would be upset, she folded her hands in her lap. "Why do you care?"

"Because Edna also mentioned that she liked having former clients working the reception desk because they could empathize with first-time clients. She said she *only* asked former clients to work the desk."

"Ah." A lump formed in her throat. "So you realized that I'd first visited Loaves of Love for a reason besides making bread."

"Yes."

She exhaled, half waiting to feel sheer embarrassment or shame. Instead, all Kayla felt was a surge of relief. Her big secret was out in the open. "So now you know that I couldn't afford groceries."

"Yeah." Leaning forward, he lowered his voice. "Kayla, why didn't you tell me?"

After a fortifying sip of coffee, she said, "There were a lot of reasons I didn't. I was embarrassed. I didn't want to talk about all that had happened to me after I learned about Jared's affair. I…well, I wasn't in a good place and you knew me before all this happened. I mean, we weren't close or anything, but you knew my family." She shrugged. "I didn't want you to know how different my life has been than yours."

"I get you not wanting to tell me right away. But why didn't you want to tell me later?"

"I didn't know how to do that." Frustrated with herself, she waved a hand. "It never seemed like the right time. But it would've been awkward. So… I kept thinking that I'd tell you soon. Or the next time we were together. Or when we both weren't tired. Or in a hurry…" Before he could comment on that, she said, "Sean, why are you making a big deal about this? Do you honestly think that much less of me because I was forced to visit the food bank?"

"Not at all."

"Are you sure?"

"Kayla, Of course I'm sure." Looking hurt, he added, "I would have never thought less of you."

"Then, why make a big deal out of it now? I'm

sorry I never got up the nerve, but surely you can see how humbling it was to admit to you that I was struggling with something so basic."

He shook his head. "I'm sure your confession would've pinched, but I would never have looked down on you. Honestly, if you'd told me, all I would have wanted to do was help you. I would've bought you some groceries."

"That would have made things worse. And I wouldn't have accepted the help."

"I see."

Kayla knew he didn't and that was on her. However, she was no longer hiding anything and that felt really good. "Even if you don't understand my point of view, I'm glad everything's out in the open."

"I am, too."

He didn't sound like it, though. "What's wrong?"

"Kayla, what I'm trying to get at is that while I get you were embarrassed about your circumstances, I thought we'd been getting close."

"I thought we were, too."

"I told you a lot of stuff about Dannette and me. I talked to you about grieving. About being lonely. About how hard it's been for me to move on. And you listened."

"I was glad to listen. I was glad you shared."

"But, don't you see the disconnect?" he asked impatiently. "I poured out some things to you that I had never told anyone else. I trusted you. But all this time you kept something as simple as you being hungry to yourself. It made me feel like I'd been reading things all wrong."

She slowly shook her head. "It wasn't simple."

"All right. But the fact of the matter is that while I trusted you with my pain, you didn't trust me with yours."

"It wasn't about trust, Sean."

He pressed his palms flat on the table. "Kayla, I've been falling in love with you."

"What?"

"You heard me. I'm falling in love. Heck, I'm probably already there. I want a relationship with you. I've allowed my son to get close to you. I'm all in."

She was stunned. She wanted to believe him, she really did. But what if he changed his mind like Jared had? Jared had always said he'd loved her... until he loved someone else.

If she told him how she was feeling, if she completely laid herself open to him...it would be so easy for him to stomp on her heart.

"Kayla?"

"I...I don't know what to say," she whispered.

And just like that, a shield covered his expression again. "That's the problem, don't you think?"

"Sean, you have to give me a second to catch up," she said in a rush. "I mean, this is all new to me."

He stood up. "I know. It was fast, right? And I

shouldn't have told you. But I guess that's the problem for us. I keep telling you too much and you keep yourself so guarded, I have no idea what you're thinking. And even after all the things we just said, you still have walls up."

She got to her feet as well. "You are making everything seem easy, but it isn't. Love and relationships and our pasts…it's complicated."

"But don't you see? That's why I've been trying to tell you. I don't think what's between us *is* complicated. I made some mistakes and I regret them. But I'm invested enough to bare my heart. I like you, you like me and Jackson…well, Jackson is happier than he's been in years. I thought we had a chance for a future together."

"We do have a future. And you know how I feel about Jackson."

He laughed under his breath. "That's the problem, Kayla. I'm not sure if I do," he said as he walked to her front door and slipped on his wet tennis shoes. "Look, I'm going to get out of here. I need to change clothes. I'm freezing."

"But the fireplace—maybe if you stand in front of it you could get warm?"

"Not warm enough, Kayla."

Ouch. She felt like everything he was saying had a double meaning. "I'll call you later. Is that okay?"

He sighed. "Yeah. Sure. Of course it is. I might not pick up at first. I'm…meeting a buddy for a burger later."

"All right. If I text and you don't reply right away I'll know why."

"But I'll respond later, okay?"

"Okay."

"Thanks for the coffee," he said before walking out the door and closing it gently behind him.

His towels were still on the ground. She should go pick them up and start a load of laundry. Clean up their coffee cups.

Figure out what she was going to eat for dinner. She didn't do any of that.

She felt frozen in place. Sean had been so hurt and irritated with her.

Did it feel unfair? Yes. But when he shared that he was falling in love with her and she could do nothing but gape at him? Well, that was unfair, too.

Because the truth was that she was feeling the same way. She just wasn't ready to tell him.

And, if she was being fair, she'd have to admit that she would've thought she could have told him the unvarnished truth about a lot of things by now.

So, she could kind of see his point.

What she couldn't see, however, was how she was going to make things right.

As the tears finally started falling—the tears she'd hoped he'd never see fall—Kayla felt like her world was falling apart yet again.

Since there was no longer a reason to pretend she had herself together, she sat down on the couch and cried.

CHAPTER THIRTY-TWO

FROM THE TIME they'd gotten home on Sunday afternoon, Jackson had talked nonstop. And complained. And asked for toys he didn't have, games he was too young to play and his very own iPhone. An iPhone! Like his six-year-old needed to text his friends.

After Sean had nipped that idea in the bud, Jackson brought up another thing on his new list of wants: a vacation.

That was the demand that had finally sent him over the edge. That was the problem with Jack and Kim's teenagers, he decided. Jack worked for an insurance company and Kim worked for a fancy interior decorating firm in Rocky River. Their two kids had a far different life than Jackson. Oh, he couldn't fault Brennan and Sophia. They were good kids, polite and did well in school. They also were very good to Jackson. Never had Sean seen them treat their little cousin with anything but patience. He loved them a lot. That said, Brennan and Sophia were spoiled. They had amazing Christmases, over-the-top birthday parties and spent their summers at the family's cottage on the lake.

Most of the time Sean was happy for them. Jack and Kim worked hard and spent their extra funds on things for the kids. They'd also had Jackson up to the cottage for a week every summer. That had been very generous.

The problem was that Jackson thought the teens were everything he should ever want to be. Especially thirteen-year-old Brennan.

Usually, Sean took all Jackson's stories about Brennan with a grain of salt. Jackson thought Brennan was perfect. He was especially jealous of how well his older cousin could play football. He wanted to be like Brennan one day.

Unfortunately, Sean's mood was pretty bad after going home in the rain and sitting in an empty house until it was time to pick up his son. He'd lied to Kayla about having plans with a buddy, which hadn't sat well with him, since he'd pretty much lectured her about how open and honest he could be.

All that was why he was on his last bit of patience with Jackson's questions about why they hadn't ever been on a cruise. "Dad, but it would be fun."

"I bet it would." Floating around on a boat in the sun sounded pretty great at the moment.

"Aunt Kim said that they'd love for us to come with them."

"That was nice of her to say."

"She was telling the truth, Dad. She meant it." He looked at him meaningfully.

"Maybe one day we'll get to go."

"That's it?" He scowled. "Don't you want to hear about when they're going?"

"No, because we can't go."

"But why?" Sean wasn't sure what had gotten into his usually agreeable son, but he was ready for him to get over it. "That's enough, Jackson."

Out went his bottom lip. "That's what you always say."

"You're lucky that's what I always say. I could be telling you that I don't appreciate you badgering me about things I can't change."

"I'm not doing that," he whined. Jackson crossed his arms over his chest, obviously gearing up to go to battle.

"It sure sounds like it." Regretting that he was playing into his son's argument, he sighed. "Come on now. Let's drop the subject. How about you go take a shower and then I'll put on one of your favorite movies? We'll eat dinner in front of the TV tonight."

"What movie?"

"I don't know. We could watch *The Avengers* or something."

"Did you know that Kayla has never seen that movie?"

The mention of her name caught him off guard.

Which caught him off guard, too. "That's not a surprise," he said slowly. "She doesn't exactly seem like the superhero type."

"Maybe she is and she doesn't know it."

"Maybe so. Now go shower."

"Wait. You should ask her to come over. She could eat grilled sandwiches with us."

"I don't think that's a good idea."

"Why not? She loves it when we invite her, and she always eats everything you make."

The mention of Kayla eating reminded him that she'd probably been hungry. Which made his grumpy mood plummet further. "Go shower, Jackson." Walking to the kitchen, he picked up a paper towel and some spray cleaner and started wiping down the countertop, even though it didn't need it.

"Why hasn't she come over lately?"

"Jackson, enough with the questions."

His boy didn't move. "Do you not like her anymore?"

Finally, he lost it. Dropping the paper towel and the bottle on the counter, he turned to glare at his son. "What did I just say, son?"

Jackson's eyes got big. "For me to stop asking you questions."

"I also asked you to go take a shower. But you haven't done either one. Now go do what I say."

"Fine." Jackson slumped as he walked away.

When he was out of sight, Sean blew out a burst of air he hadn't realized he'd been holding.

He stood there, telling himself to take a breath and relax for a moment. His son obviously missed Kayla. He did, too.

But he might have messed up everything with her. Why did he have to share how betrayed he'd felt for her not telling him about her troubles earlier? It was all in the past and couldn't be changed.

What he should've done when she'd told him about going hungry was pull her into his arms and reassure her that she wouldn't have to go through that again. That she was no longer alone.

Instead, he'd made things worse.

Ten minutes later, when he heard Jackson crying in the bathroom, he opened the door. Sean found his boy in flannel pajama bottoms with bare feet. He had his eyes covered.

"Jackson, you know I wasn't all that mad at you. Calm down, now."

"It's not that."

Leading the boy into his room, he sat beside him on his twin bed. "What is it, then? Do you really want to go on a cruise that bad?"

"No," he said around a loud sniffle. "I mean, it sounds like fun…but no."

"Then what is it?"

"Nothing."

"Come on. Help me out here. I'm listening."

He curved more into himself. Breaking Sean's heart. "I don't want to tell ya because you'll get mad."

SHELLEY SHEPARD GRAY 289

"I won't. Now talk to me so we can make things better. What's got you so upset?"

"I thought that you liked Kayla."

"I did. And I do. She's a nice lady."

"You know what I mean." Peeking at him out of the corner of his eye, Jackson said, "I thought she… I thought she was going to be special to you."

"You thought that maybe she'd be my girl-friend." His voice was hoarse. Was it because he'd made Jackson cry or because he'd wanted the same thing?

"Uh-huh. And maybe…maybe something more." He wrinkled his nose. "That's stupid, isn't it?"

"No. It wasn't stupid at all."

"Maybe I'm not supposed to ever have another mom." He swiped at his watery face with the side of a fist. "I mean, like a stepmom."

"Oh, Jackson." Sean felt tears well in his eyes, too. How could he have not seen this coming? Was this what he got for finally daring to fall in love again instead of only focusing on his son?

"Sorry."

"Nothing to be sorry about. I don't think any-one but God knows what's going to happen in the future. I do know that I miss your mom. I miss her a lot. But she would be the first person to tell me to not spend the rest of my life by myself. So, maybe one day." Bending down, he met Jackson's gaze. "Okay?"

"Yeah."

"Then give me a hug. I get sad whenever I see you cry, buddy."

His anxiety eased when Jackson leaned close and rested his face on Sean's chest.

Thinking about his days of being able to comfort little boy tears with a short conversation and a good hug, Sean relaxed and ran a hand down his back. Little by little, Jackson's breathing eased. Before he knew it, his son's body was heavy against him. At last he'd figured out why his boy had been so whiny and demanding. His two nights away had worn him out. He was exhausted.

Kissing his head, Sean elected to not try to get Jackson to eat. Instead, he got him settled in bed and turned off his lights. Then he handled the wet towel and dirty clothes scattered on the floor.

After that, he walked back to the living room and collapsed. The last hour had been hard. He didn't like making Jackson cry and he didn't like not having the right words or solution to make him happier.

"It's life, Sean," he told himself. "You can't lie or make things happen that aren't possible. If Kayla doesn't feel the same way as you, then you need to come to terms with it. And, yeah, Jackson needs to learn that, too."

Although Jackson had already learned this from losing his mother, he knew his son would have other painful reminders over his lifetime.

Sean had worked all his life on teams. In each

one, whether he'd been a player or a coach, the varying levels of talent and ability were evident. It was hard when players realized that their dreams weren't going to happen or that they wouldn't have the senior year or scholarship or NFL career that they'd yearned for.

Football players weren't the only ones who had to learn that all dreams didn't come true. Everyone had to come to terms with disappointment at some point in their lives.

So he understood Jackson being upset, but he instinctively knew that it was best not to get his hopes up.

Feeling better, he got a glass of water, picked up the remote, then noticed that he had five new messages on his phone. Two were from his sister-in-law, Kim. In one, she was reiterating how much she enjoyed Jackson. In the other, she apologized if her enthusiasm about their upcoming trip had made things uncomfortable for him and Jackson.

He quickly texted her his thanks and not to worry.

The third text was from one of the varsity players, saying that he had strep. That he had a note from the doc, but did Coach still want him to come to practice.

Sean hit a quick reply—a firm no. Infecting the rest of the team was a bad idea. So was not taking care of himself.

The fourth was from Zack. After Sean had started

bringing him food, the boy had repaid him by giving him updates about life at home.

Dad just got a promotion, Coach. And he got a bonus, too. He sent me out to the store for groceries.

That's great. Really great.

Clicking on the last message, he was prepared to discover it was from another student.

It was from Kayla.

His pulse sped up as he read it. I know I have a lot to work out but I'd still like to give us a try. Do you think you could ever give me another chance?

He didn't hesitate to answer. Of course. Thinking of the upcoming week, he added, This week is going to be tough for me. We have a Thursday night game. But on Friday night, my family is getting together again. This time it's a party for my parents' anniversary. Will you come with us?

She replied immediately. Yes. I'd love to attend. Unless you think it might be too awkward?

I think it will be just fine. Like I said, everyone really likes you.

Okay then.

Good. I'm glad

They texted a little bit more, then called it a night with him promising to fine-tune the details within a day or two.

Then he clicked on the remote, turned to a sports network and mindlessly watched the announcers share the latest scores. He knew if anyone asked what was discussed, he'd draw a blank.

He had something more important on his mind.

CHAPTER THIRTY-THREE

"KAYLA, WHEN SEAN told me you two were dating, I looked you up in the yearbook. It's not fair that your pretty, long hair looks exactly the same." Meg Brown, Sean's sister, said as she approached. "Honestly, I think you've gotten even prettier. I meant to tell you that at the last gathering, but I never got the chance."

Taking in Meg's outfit—a bright Hawaiian-print dress that somehow managed to look chic and elegant—she smiled. "I think I've changed a bit since high school, but I appreciate the compliment. It's so good to see you. Your dress is so cute. It's certainly putting my plastic lei to shame."

"I told everyone that having a luau in December was a silly idea. I was outvoted, though."

"I have to admit that it's kind of fun going somewhere that isn't football themed," Kayla said. Thinking that Sean might have a different opinion about that, she was glad he was talking with some friends of his parents.

"Put that way, you're right." Looking at her parents, Meg smiled. "To be honest, I think it's sweet that Mom and Dad are celebrating their anniversary with a nod to their honeymoon. All these years later, Mom still says Hawaii is her favorite place."

"How many years have they been married?"

"Thirty-five."

"That's a big one."

"I agree. Which is why my token complaint was easily overruled and I didn't put up a fight."

"You're a smart woman."

"I might be smart about luaus in December but I think my brother is the one with all the brains in the family right now."

"Do you mean Sean or Jack?"

"Sean, of course." Lowering her voice, she said, "Kayla, we're all ecstatic that the two of you are getting so close."

"I'm happy, too. He's a great guy." And so far, their evening had been good. After they got through the first couple of awkward minutes, she and Sean had settled back into their usual easy conversation. And, of course, Jackson had been very happy that the three of them were at the party together.

"Jackson talks about you all the time. Whenever I see him, he tells me all about you. He fills me in about which teachers you're helping, or what game you two played, or what meal you've made lately. Even what you're wearing."

"Goodness! I didn't know that."

"Believe me, he doesn't forget a thing about you. He said you're his favorite part about school."

"He said that?" When Meg nodded, Kayla felt tears form in her eyes. "Thank you for sharing that with me." Looking around the crowded basement rec room, she spied him with a teenager and his grandfather playing pool. "I have to admit that I feel the same way about Jackson. He's really special to me."

Meg's smile turned melancholy. "As you might imagine, Dannette's death hit Sean hard. It hit both of them hard, of course, but I think Sean had realized for a while that Dannette wasn't going to make a recovery. Jackson was barely more than a toddler."

"I respect all that they've gone through." Worrying that Meg was attempting to gently remind her of her place, Kayla added, "I don't intend to overstep."

"I get what you're saying, but that wasn't what I meant. I meant that you've been everything those two guys have needed."

"Oh!"

Meg smiled. "I think that all of us are in agreement that being in love looks good on Sean."

Her cheeks heated as she looked anywhere but at Meg. She didn't know what to say.

"Hey, I'm sorry," Meg said quickly. "I have a tendency to speak too honestly."

"No, no. You have nothing to apologize for. I,

um, have a problem with keeping too many things inside. I'm working on that."

"What are you working on?" Sean asked as he approached with a plastic cup of punch in his hand.

"Nothing that you need to know about, brother," Meg said. "Now, if you'll excuse me, I better go see how the kitchen's looking. It's probably a circus in there."

"Do you need some help?" Kayla asked.

"Thanks, but I think we've got it." After sharing a look with her brother, Meg added, "But if we do, I'll let you know."

When they were alone, Sean handed her a drink. "You two looked like you were in a deep discussion. I thought I'd try to get you out of it."

"It's appreciated, but I was fine. We were just getting to know each other."

"I also came over to see if you'd like to visit with my mom. Every time she tries to cross the room she gets stopped. She sent me over to bring you to her."

"This is her party. I can see that happening."

He held out his hand. "So, will you?"

"Of course." She slipped her hand in his. Then realized as they snaked around all the people that every single person in the room was staring at them.

Suddenly, she felt like she was sixteen again and holding her first boyfriend's hand in the hallway. Well, maybe it wasn't quite the same because she'd never felt even half for Matt what she did for Sean. Sean's palms also weren't sweaty, which was another plus.

He looked down at her. "You're wearing a funny expression. You all right?"

"Yeah. I...well, I was just thinking that holding your hand feels a lot more comfortable than Matt's back in high school."

"Matt? Matt who?"

"I don't remember," she murmured. No way did she want to start talking about someone from the past when she was about to sit next to his mother.

Sean raised his eyebrows but other than that only gripped her hand a little bit more firmly. "Mom, here Kayla is."

"Hi, Mrs. Copeland. Happy anniversary."

"Hi, dear. Thank you, but please, it's Alice."

"Yes, ma'am."

"Sorry I asked Sean to bring you over here, but we hardly got to talk at the last party."

"I'm glad you have time now."

"Me, too. You know, I told Sean that I don't remember seeing you much when you both were in high school."

"I'm not sure if you and I ever did meet, since Sean and I were in different groups."

Alice looked delighted. "You know what we should do? All of us should go out to dinner together."

"All of us?" Sean asked.

"Kayla's parents, you and Kayla, and Dad and me. Wouldn't that be fun?"

"Mom," Sean murmured. "Remember what we talked about?"

"I remember." Smiling at Kayla, she said, "My son reminded me that I can be pushy from time to time."

"I think we all can."

Her smile widened. "I knew I liked you." Pointing to a chair next to her, she said, "Have a seat, honey, while Sean gets you something to drink. We have everything. Champagne, wine, beer, soda…"

"A sparkling water?"

"On it," Sean said. "I'll be right back."

Loving how protective he was acting, even though there was no need for him to worry, she said, "Thank you for intervening."

Alice's expression softened. "You are good for him. Sean looks…well, more at ease than I've seen him in ages."

"I don't know if that's my doing, but I'm glad that he's relaxed."

"I'm fairly sure it's you, dear."

She hoped so, but she wasn't going to push things. Not after the last week. "Tell me about this party. Did you plan it?"

Her eyes lit up. "We did! The kids offered to set it up, of course, but Thomas and I knew what we wanted."

"I hope it turned out like you planned?"

"Better than that, since almost everyone we invited was able to be here. We'd been hoping for at least half the people to be free."

"Thirty-five years is an accomplishment."

"It is. We talk all the time about what a blessing it is! We're both in good health and we've stayed good friends, too."

"That is a blessing."

Looking stricken, Alice leaned toward her. "I hope I didn't just stick my foot in my mouth."

"Because Jared and I got divorced? Not at all. I'm better off without him."

"Since Sean shared a bit about what had happened, I'd say that was an understatement."

"I agree."

"I also heard that you're working at the elementary school?"

"Yes. I just started working as a teacher's aide."

"Jackson is very pleased about that."

"I like seeing him every day."

"Isn't it funny how fate has such a hand in our happiness? Here you and Sean are together, and Jackson loves you. To think just six months ago I wondered if Sean was destined to remain single."

She was beginning to feel more than slightly uncomfortable about the way Alice was so casually discussing her and Sean's relationship. Almost like it was a done deal. It felt like anything but that to her.

"I certainly couldn't have planned all that has

happened during the last few months," Kayla said after a small pause.

"Here you go, Kayla."

Tilting her chin up, she stared into Sean's concerned expression and immediately felt more at ease. "Thanks."

"Mom, I'm going to take Kayla over to visit with Jack and Kim."

"I understand. Have a good time tonight, dear. And thank you for coming."

"I'm so happy to be here."

"Look out for her tonight," she warned Sean.

"I will." After Kayla quickly hugged Alice, he handed her back her glass and guided her into a back hall. "How are you doing? Do you need a break from all the attention?"

"Are you offering one?"

"Yep. Come on." Reaching for her hand again, he led her up a set of stairs and then down a narrow hallway.

"Where are we going?"

"To my old room." He opened a door. "Here we are."

Inside was a double bed covered in a worn navy-and-gray comforter, a small desk and chair, a wide oak dresser, and about a dozen framed pictures of himself on one of the walls. On another wall was a grouping of his diplomas and various awards he received in high school and college.

"Wow," she said.

As if noticing all his pictures and such for the first time, he slapped a hand over his face. "Forget you're seeing this."

"Not a chance." Smiling, she walked to a grouping of his senior photos. "Look at you here. And this one! You look so tough." Unable to resist, she added, "I guess you were too cool to smile, huh?"

He groaned. "Probably. I thought I was a pretty big deal back then."

"I think you kind of were, Sean. Not too many seniors received a full athletic scholarship to play football."

"I know. I should've been more grateful."

"Come on. I know you were grateful."

"Yeah, but I felt relief more than anything." He shifted his shoulders, as if the memory still made him uncomfortable.

"I think you're being too hard on yourself." Pointing to a photo from the paper showing him scoring during a college bowl game, she said, "You earned that scholarship, Sean."

"I practiced a ton and did homework in the middle of the night. So yeah, I guess I did. It was worth it, though. I don't have any college loans to pay off."

"And you have your degree."

"Enough about me. My mom didn't give you the third degree, did she?"

"Nope."

"Sure?"

"Positive. I think all we talked about was what a blessing it was to have been married for thirty-five years."

"That is true."

Resting her palm on his chest, she said, "Stop worrying about me. I like your family and can handle a little bit of questioning. I'd be surprised if they didn't want to know more about me."

"I can't help it." His voice was gruff.

Confused by the sudden tension that seemed to emanate from him, she gazed into his eyes. She noticed that the muscles under her hand had tightened. "I guess you still work out."

"With the team a couple of times a week."

"I can tell." Still feeling the heat coming off him, she murmured, "I should work out some more, too."

"I don't think you have to worry about a thing."

"No?"

"You feel great to me."

This time, she was the one raising her eyebrows. Since he wasn't touching her at all.

"It's from memory," he said. "But, let me make sure..." And then, just as if she could have choreographed it herself, Sean pulled her close, wrapped his arms around her and kissed her senseless.

One kiss led to about five. Maybe more.

She didn't know because she lost count, only thinking about how good his arms felt holding her close, how good he smelled, like deep, expensive cologne and Sean. And yes, how good he tasted, like mint and the faint memory of the beer he'd sipped when they had first arrived at the party.

But she was even more aware of the way her body was responding—with an eagerness that she had forgotten she was capable of.

It was all lovely and shocking and reassuring.

"Uh, knock, knock." Meg stuck her head in the door.

Sean lifted his head. "What, Meg?"

"Sorry, but Jackson is looking for you. He told Dad. Luckily, I heard Dad tell Kim that he was going to come up here to see where you were at. I told him I had this."

"Thanks. We'll be right down."

"Yeah, that's probably best."

When they were alone again, Kayla pressed her hands to her cheeks. "Oh, my gosh. I can't believe your father almost walked in on us. That would've been terrible."

Sean chuckled. "Not for us. I would've had a lot to say to my dad, though."

"Sean."

"I'm a grown man in my thirties. You and I have both been married. All we're doing is kissing. My family has been after me for the last year to think about dating. No one is going to give me a hard time for falling in love."

"Falling in love," she repeated—because it really did sound good.

"Absolutely, positively." Worry filled his expression. "Listen, no pressure. I don't—"

"I'm falling in love, too," she blurted.

He froze. "You sure?"

She nodded, feeling light and free. Like she'd just unloaded the biggest burden off her shoulders. "I'm absolutely and positively sure I'm falling in love."

"Come here, Kayla. I've got to kiss you again."

Her hands were on his chest again, but she was pushing him away. "We can't. Everyone is looking for us."

"I have at least a dozen relatives who can look after Jackson. And now that Meg has likely told half of them what she saw, they know what we're doing. We'll be just fine here for a little while longer."

She might have been tempted to protest if his lips hadn't lowered again.

But then? Well, there was nothing left to do but wrap her arms around his neck and meet him halfway.

CHAPTER THIRTY-FOUR

IT HAD BEEN two weeks since Sean had first told Kayla he loved her. Almost a full week had passed since Kayla had admitted that she felt the same way.

And with those few short words, everything had changed.

Now, they texted each other as much as they could during the day. They talked to each other on the phone late into the evening. More than once, Sean had found himself being reluctant to tell her good-night. He would've felt embarrassed if he wasn't so glad that everything between them was so good.

Kayla had also come over to take care of Jackson a couple of evenings when he'd had late practices. She'd even sat with Jackson and his parents while they'd cheered for the Medina Bees the other day. Sean had never been the type of guy to want to look up into the stands during a game. When he'd been a player, he'd either been too focused or too afraid of a coach noticing that his head wasn't 100 percent in the game.

Later, he and Dannette hadn't had that kind of relationship. She'd either skipped his games or quietly sat somewhere out of the way. She had always said that she didn't want to be a distraction, but Sean had known that watching him coach wasn't really her thing.

After she'd passed away, he'd been in such a funk that it had taken everything he had to do his job as a coach.

Now? Well, he suddenly was feeling like a teenager in his first serious relationship. He wanted her to watch him and be proud of him. After that first game she'd attended, when she'd beamed and told him congratulations, he'd felt like the king of the world.

Yep, there was no doubt about it. He was head over heels in love with Kayla. And it was more than that, too. Knowing how badly she'd been treated by her ex-husband, and that she then had gone hungry, had made his dormant protective streak wake up.

Now, all he wanted to do was look out for Kayla. Make sure she was taken care of, that she ate, that she knew she wasn't alone in the world. Most of all, Sean tried to make sure Kayla knew she was vitally important to him. He wasn't shy about it, either. Not around his coworkers, his family or Jackson. He was constantly touching her, running a hand down her back, glancing her way. Texting and calling.

Sean had a feeling some of his friends and family were bemused about the change that had come over him. He didn't blame them. From the outside, it probably looked like he and Kayla barely knew each other. Even when he'd shared that they'd known each other in high school, his buddies' reactions had been varied.

A few had come right out and hinted that maybe Sean was moving a little too fast.

He knew he wasn't. All that mattered was that Kayla appreciated every little gesture, touch and kindness. Her eyes lit up or her expression softened when he'd cross the room during a get-together just to make sure she was okay. He knew the two of them were right.

Especially since Jackson seemed to completely approve.

Walking into their house after church on Sunday, Jackson said, "I wish Kayla had come with us."

"I know. It feels funny to not be with her, doesn't it?"

His boy nodded. "When she's not around I miss her."

"Me, too."

"Does she not go to church?"

"I think she has her own church, buddy. Besides, she's spending the morning with her parents, remember? They've probably been missing her because she's been with us a lot."

"I guess." Jackson' shrugged off his coat and

hung it on the hook by the door. "Is she coming over later this afternoon?"

"I think so. She said she'd call when she got home."

"Maybe we could go over there today."

"Maybe so."

"I wish Kayla lived here with us," Jackson mumbled. "Then we wouldn't have to wonder when we were going to see her again."

There it was. The opening he'd been looking for. "Let's sit down and talk for a second."

His boy frowned. "Why? What did I do?"

"Nothing. There's no reason for you to act so worried."

He frowned. "But you sound serious. Plus, the last time you said we needed to sit down on the couch and talk it was because I needed to pay more attention in school."

It had been far more serious than that. His preschool teacher had been worried that Jackson was sliding into a depression about eight months after Dannette had died.

Her worry had instigated an honest talk, which had revealed that Jackson had been keeping a lot of his feelings inside because he didn't want to upset his father.

After reassuring him that all his feelings were okay, Sean had phoned up the grief counselor Jackson had visited with right after Dannette's funeral. The two of them started appointments with him again. A couple of weeks later, his boy had returned to his regular self.

Thank goodness today's talk was about something far happier.

"Son, this is nothing bad. It's about Kayla."

He moved to sit next to him on the couch. "Is she sick, Dad?"

Hating that that was the first thing Jackson thought of, Sean answered quickly. "No."

When Jackson still looked worried, Sean reached for his hand and squeezed it tight. "I promise, she's fine. It's...well, I wanted to know what you thought about her. I mean, what you *really* thought of her."

He tilted his head to one side. "How come?"

"Because how you feel about Kayla matters to me." When Jackson still looked unsure, he added, "Jackson, try to trust me, okay?"

After a second's pause, he nodded. "Well... I like her." His eyes narrowed. "Don't you?"

"I do. I love her, Jackson."

He exhaled. "Well, that's good, because I saw you kissing her the other night."

"What? When?"

"When you walked Kayla out to her car but stayed outside forever."

His son was wearing a girls-are-gross kind of expression. "You shouldn't have been watching us."

"I guess, but you were outside for a really long time. *Really long.*"

"You were also supposed to be in bed."

"I know, but, Dad, you—"

"Don't say it again. I heard you." Feeling a little out of his depth, he said, "So, um, did seeing me kiss her upset you?"

"Yep."

"Yep?" Now what was he supposed to say?

Jackson patted his arm. "But it's okay, Dad. I was a lot better after I talked to MeMe."

"You called MeMe about seeing me and Kayla outside?" This conversation just kept getting worse and worse.

"Yep." He lifted his chin, like he was pleased with himself.

"When was this, Jackson?"

"When it looked like you weren't going to stop anytime soon."

"You called MeMe while I was outside kissing Kayla?" he asked slowly. Now he was feeling both embarrassed and a little betrayed.

"Yep, but MeMe didn't mind at all. She told me that I can call her anytime or when anything is bothering me. She doesn't even care if it's in the middle of the night."

"I see."

"Anyway," his boy continued, just as if they were talking about the latest snowfall, "MeMe said that you kissing Kayla is a good thing. And that Kayla must have liked it because she had her arms around you, too." Before Sean could comment on *that*, Jackson added, "That's what people do when they're in love, Dad."

His son sounded like he was forty years old. "Huh."

"So, it's okay. I mean it is if you love her a lot." Jackson took a deep breath. "So…do you?"

"Do I what?" He was still struggling over Jackson giving the play-by-play of him and Kayla to his mother.

How had he lost complete control of this conversation?

His son released a long, drawn-out sigh. "Love, Dad. Do you love Kayla a lot?"

"I do."

"Good. Because I love her a lot, too."

"I'm glad we talked." Feeling like a beer might be in order, he moved to stand up.

"Wait, Dad. Are you gonna ask her to marry you?"

"Don't you think you're jumping the gun?"

"I don't know what that means." He wrinkled his nose. "How do you jump a gun?"

"Jackson, the reason I wanted to talk to you was to see how you felt about Kayla."

"And we just talked about it. I love her, Dad. Just like you do. That means we gotta get married, right?"

"Well, yes. I mean, eventually."

"Why eventually?"

"These things take time. Plus, I don't even have a ring."

"Oh."

Feeling like he'd finally gotten the upper hand in the conversation, Sean smiled. "*Oh*, is right. I'm not going to get down on one knee and propose without a ring."

"Grandpa said you should use Great-Grandma's."

"He's involved in this, too?"

"Well, yeah. When Aunt Meg took me out for pizza, Grandma and Grandpa met us there. We all talked about it."

"The four of you talked about me and Kayla."

"Yep." Smiling, Jackson added, "Grandpa said Great-Grandma's ring is pretty and delicate. Like Kayla. And that it's just been sitting in a safe box waiting on her."

"It's waiting in their safe deposit box." He knew he sounded like a parrot but he couldn't believe how much his son had been talking with his parents. And Meg. He was almost afraid to ask who else Jackson had been chatting with.

"Uh-huh. Do you think Kayla would like that ring?"

"To be honest, I don't know. I barely remember it."

"We should go see it."

"You're right. We should. One day—"

Jackson hopped off the couch. "We could go now."

"Son, even if we wanted to see it, we couldn't. The safe deposit box is in a bank and it's closed today."

"I think they got it out, Dad. It's in a lockbox under their bed."

"Really?" He'd now given up all hope of doing anything but following his son's lead.

"Uh-huh. See, after Grandpa mentioned the ring, Grandma said they should get it out and clean it." He wrinkled his nose. "And take it to the jewelers to make sure the diamond wouldn't fall out. Because that would be awful," he explained.

"It sure would."

"So, we can go?"

"Let me give your grandparents a call and see if they did take it out of the deposit box."

"And if they did?"

"And if they did, I'll get back to you. Now, go get a snack or play with your trains or Legos or something. I need a minute."

"How come?"

"Because you, Jackson Copeland, have been full of surprises today and I need a second to catch up."

"Oh, fine. But I really think you should see Great-Grandma's ring."

"Thanks for the advice." After Jackson walked down the hall to his room, Sean pulled out his phone and called his parents. For once, he was glad they still had a landline, because otherwise he would have to figure out who to question about the many conversations that had been taking place between them and Jackson without his knowledge.

"Hello?"

"Hey, Dad."

"What's going on, Sean? You never call this line."

"Never mind that. I just had a pretty interesting conversation with your grandson."

"Is that a fact?"

"It turns out Jackson's been having quite a few conversations about me and Kayla with you and Mom. And Meg."

"Your boy had a lot of questions, Sean."

His father was definitely smiling. "Dad, I can't believe you and Mom have been talking to Jackson about me and Kayla but didn't let me know."

"Sorry, but I'm not sorry about that. The boy had concerns, especially since you were making out like a teenager in the driveway. You used to sneak off to the side of the house, son. There were no windows there."

"We were not making out." Okay, maybe they were. "Well, not like teenagers." Not quite.

"I don't doubt that, son. Hold on." Sean could practically see his father put the receiver against his chest. He'd done that for as long as he could remember. "Alice! Sean's on the phone and wants to talk about Jackson and Kayla."

"Dad."

"Hold on, son. Ah, here she is. Now, I've got the phone out so we can both hear you."

"Listen, I think we better do this in person. But, um, is Jackson right about you two getting Grandma's ring out of the safe deposit box?"

"We did. And you should see it, honey," his mother chirped. "The jewelers not only checked the mounting but cleaned it, too. It looks beautiful. It's perfect."

"Jackson and I are anxious to see it. Can we stop by today?"

"Of course," his mom said. "We'll have an early dinner."

"And then we'll take the boy to your house so he can get to bed at his regular time," his dad added.

"Why?"

"Well, you're gonna see Kayla, aren't you?" his mother asked.

"You can't very well propose on the phone, son," his dad added.

"Or in her driveway."

"I'm starting to think this relationship is out of my hands."

"No. It's always been in your hands, Sean. We all just happened to think that a little help might be a good idea. After all, Jackson has a lot of opinions about things."

They were right about that. "So, if Meg was in on this conversation...does that mean Jack knows about all this, too?"

His father let out a bark of laughter. "Son, when Jackson called us to give a play-by-play of you and Kayla kissing, Jack and Kim and their kids were over. Brennan and Sophia were in the basement but Jack and Kim heard every word."

"We put him on speaker," his mom added.

"I can't believe you did that."

"We couldn't help it. Jackson was concerned because you had her leaning against the side of her car for a *really long* time."

Just imagining the scene made his entire body burn bright red. He was sure of it. "Please. Stop. And promise that Kayla will never, ever find out about this."

"We'll try...but you know how it goes," his mom said. "See you soon, honey. We're so happy for you. Overjoyed."

"Thanks. And...thanks for everything."

"We love you. Don't forget that. Now come over."

"Yes, ma'am."

Standing up, he tried to get a handle on himself, but it was next to impossible.

Then he started wondering why he thought he needed to do that, anyway.

"Jackson?" he called out.

"Yeah, Dad?"

"Get ready. We're going to MeMe and Grandpa's house."

"They have the ring?"

"They do. I think it's time we went to see it."

Less than ten minutes later, they were on their way.

CHAPTER THIRTY-FIVE

NEVER AGAIN WOULD Kayla rent an apartment in a building that was a hundred years old. No matter how charming it was. Just like her grandmother used to say, looks weren't everything. It had been true for her...and, it seemed, this apartment.

The beautiful millwork around the windows did not make up for having no heat because of a temperamental boiler in the basement.

Her landlord's answer to the freezing wind slipping in through tiny gaps around the windows and the ice-cold temperature in her space had been to tell her to light a fire. Just like folks used to do a hundred years ago.

Kayla would do that, too...if she had any more firewood. Unfortunately, she did not. She'd used the last of her small supply when Sean had been soaked to the skin. She didn't regret that.

However, she might no longer need to go to Loaves of Love for food, but she sure wasn't solvent enough to spend twenty extra dollars on firewood.

To make matters worse, the snow that had kept

her from driving to Avon Lake to join her parents for church hadn't let up. Because of that, the snowplows were focusing on highways, not neighborhood side streets. Also because of that, even going two miles to get firewood was a scary undertaking, especially since her tires were nearly bald and had long since lost the ability to easily grip slippery roads.

After she'd complained to her landlord, he'd brought over a couple of logs. One of her neighbors had also taken pity on her and given her two small logs. So, that was a blessing. She knew they wouldn't last long, so she'd decided to wait until closer to evening to get them going.

That was why she was wearing jeans, a sweater, a down vest and thick socks when there was a knock at the door. She opened it to receive a pleasant surprise.

"Sean? What are you doing here?"

"When you texted that you were home, I decided to stop by."

"I wasn't planning to be. I was going to drive over to see my parents, but I didn't trust my tires to make it there and back." Realizing that she was keeping him out in the elements, she stepped aside. "Come on in."

"Thanks." After closing the door behind him, he toed off his boots and hung up his coat. And then he seemed to notice that she was bundled up like she was going for a hike. That was also probably about the same time he realized that it was under sixty degrees in her apartment.

"Kayla, honey, it's freezing in here."

"I know. I probably should have told you to keep on your coat." She smiled, trying to make a joke of the situation.

Sean didn't look amused. Like, not at all. "What's going on? Why isn't the heat working?"

"The ancient boiler down in the basement died. Since it's Sunday, everyone in the building is out of luck. They're supposedly coming tomorrow to fix it."

"It's twenty-eight degrees outside and it's going to get worse tonight."

"I heard."

Sean still looked like he was having a difficult time wrapping his head around how cold it was in her place. "Wait, I know the fireplace works. We need to light a fire."

"Don't," she said as he turned to do just that.

"Why? That's what the logs are for."

"Those are all I have. I'm going to save them for tonight and sleep on the couch."

Sean stilled. Stared at the small pile of logs. The couch. The windowpanes that were frosted. "When were you going to call me?"

"I don't know. Later?"

"That's your answer?"

Noticing that a muscle was twitching in his jaw, she tried to smooth things over—though she had no idea why he seemed irritated. "I didn't mean that I didn't want to talk to you today. It was... well, I knew you were going to go to church and to see your family. I'm sure I would've called you tonight."

"Tonight."

Becoming a little irritated, too, she folded her arms over her chest. "Sean, what's going on? Did you decide not to drive up to Avon Lake? And where's Jackson?"

"I did go see my parents. Jackson is with them. And what's going on is I came over because I wanted to ask you something."

"Oh! What do you need? I can help out with Jackson any evening this week."

"It's not about Jackson. I mean, not really." Looking increasingly frustrated, he said, "Kayla, I didn't come over to ask for a favor." A slight bemused look entered his expression. "I mean, not exactly."

"Am I supposed to get what you're talking about? Because I don't."

"No. I mean, I don't expect you to know. It's kind of a surprise." He drew in a deep breath. "Kayla, I wish you would've called me when your heat went out."

"Why? There's nothing you can do. I mean, not unless you have experience fixing boilers from around 1920."

"I want you to call me if you're cold. If you're

hungry. If you need something." Lowering his voice, he stepped closer. "I want you to call me if you're bored. Or if you hear a funny story or if you had a good day. I want to be that guy for you."

His words were sweet and tender and surprising and…and she didn't know what else. All she did know was that those words had left her kind of speechless.

Reaching for her hands, he tugged her closer. Threaded their fingers together. "Do you understand?"

She nodded. Where was her voice? Honestly, it was like it had taken a vacation—maybe gone someplace warmer without her?

Concern entered Sean's features. "Kayla, are you going to say anything?"

She chuckled. "Yes. I mean, of course. I guess my head went blank for a second. I'm back now." Mentally, she rolled her eyes. She couldn't sound sillier.

"So you understand that I care about you?"

"I do."

"And that I want to take care of you?"

"I do, though that's not necessary."

He stared intently at her. "You do know that I love you, right?"

"Of course. I love you, too." Whew. At least she'd gotten that right.

A second passed. Maybe two. Then, Sean Copeland seemed to come to a decision. Because he let go of her hands. Inhaled. Exhaled.

Then knelt down on one knee.

And...there went her voice again. Honestly, she could barely breathe.

"I want you now, Kayla. I want you for always. I want you to be mine. To be my wife." Then, he dug into his pocket and pulled out a ring. "Will you marry me?"

She stared at his handsome face. At the lovely, perfect diamond ring.

And found her voice again. At long last. "Yes." She smiled.

Sean stood up. Reached for her hand. Slid on the beautiful ring, a pear-shaped diamond nestled in a white gold filigreed setting. "Look at that. It fits perfectly."

"It's gorgeous. How did you know I would love a ring like this?"

"Believe it or not, it was my grandmother's ring. My parents thought it would be perfect for you. I agreed. And so did Jackson."

"They all knew you were going to ask me?"

Still holding her hand, he chuckled. "I think they're currently all staring at their phones, waiting to hear what you said."

"You think we should call them?"

"Yeah. After."

She raised her eyebrows.

"After you pack a bag, because you're spending the night in the guest room at my house. No way am I leaving you here to sleep on the couch in the cold."

Since she didn't want to stay in the cold apartment, either, she didn't argue. "Is that it?"

"Nope. First you have to kiss me."

She raised her hands. Slid them up his chest. Over his shoulders. Around his neck. Raised her face...and then finally kissed him.

Kissed her fiancé, Sean Copeland.

Sean, who'd entered her life at a moment when she'd thought she had nothing else...and then reminded her again and again that it was possible to have everything.

EPILOGUE

THEY WERE GOING to be late. After glancing at the time three times in the past two minutes, Sean knew he was going to have to take charge of the situation. Though what Kayla and Jackson were doing that could possibly take them so long was a mystery.

Walking down the hall to the master bedroom, he called out, "Jackson! Kayla! We've got to go!"

"We need five more minutes, Dad!"

"You needed five more minutes fifteen minutes ago." Shaking his head, he walked into the master bedroom, fully expecting to see Jackson lounging on the big, comfy chair Kayla had placed in the corner when she'd moved in—after a surprisingly big second wedding for both of them.

Smiling at the memory, he turned to the en suite bathroom. The door was firmly closed. His boy and his wife were whispering together. What in the world could they be doing? "Is everything okay in there?"

This time, Kayla was the one who answered. "Everything's good. Just a second, Sean."

"We're late, Kay. If we don't get a move on, the wedding is going to start without us."

"I know. It's just…just give me a moment. Okay?"

Her voice was off. He frowned as he realized what he was hearing. Tears. She was crying. With Jackson. Behind a closed door. And asking him to give her time.

None of this was like her. Not even a little bit.

That hint of worry that had been forming was now a full-fledged seed. No way was he going to stand around while she cried in the bathroom. He knocked on the door. "I think I need to come in."

"Dad, no!" Jackson said.

Once again, his mind started jumping to conclusions. Had Jackson upset her? Was he sick or did he have some injury that he didn't want Sean to see? An infected cut or something? He tried that idea on for size.

It sounded doubtful. Jackson had never been especially shy, plus Sean had been around scores of boys with injuries, rashes and assorted other ailments. Not much could surprise him anymore. His almost-seven-year-old knew that.

As the two of them continued to whisper, Sean stared hard at the closed door. Could they have gotten into a fight and didn't want him to find out? Or, maybe Jackson was suddenly missing Dannette and Kayla's warm heart had made tears start to flow?

That really felt like he was grasping at straws. Jackson had loved his mother dearly, but his memories of her were fading a little every day. In addition, Jackson was practically Kayla's shadow around the house and Kayla seemed to bend over backward to honor Dannette's memory while still showing Jackson that he was very loved.

So those ideas seemed off, too. But what could he do? His imagination seemed happy to adopt every worst-case scenario he could think of.

Unable to stop himself, he looked at the clock again. "Time's up, you two. We're now in danger of having to skip the wedding...and Kayla, Edna is not going to be happy about that."

The door flew open. "Sean, you're right. We better go," Kayla said, looking gorgeous in a pale gold dress that slid along her pretty figure and ended midcalf.

She hadn't let him see the dress, telling him that newlyweds needed a surprise every now and then.

That had to be why he was gaping at her. "You look stunning, Kay."

A smile played along her lips. "Thanks."

He reached her side and folded her into his arms. "No, I'm serious," he whispered into her ear. "I didn't think anything could come close to the way you looked on our wedding day, but you just proved me wrong."

"Thank you, Sean. I'm glad you like the dress."

He gently kissed her, then leaned back to see

her eyes better. And there were the tell-tale signs of her tears. "You have been crying."

"I'm better now." Pulling away from him, she looked behind her. "Jackson, are you ready?"

"Uh-huh." Trotting to Sean's side, he reached for his hand. "Come on, Dad. We're going to be late."

Jackson had a fishy expression on his face. And he wasn't going anywhere until he knew where Kayla's tears had come from.

"Why were you crying, Kayla?"

"I'll tell you later."

No way was he going to wait for another four or five hours to hear the explanation. "I think I need to know now."

"Sean, don't worry."

"Too late. Plus, I don't understand why Jackson was in the bathroom with you. Did you two get in a fight?"

"Dad!"

Kayla rested a palm on his chest. "Of course not. You're jumping to conclusions."

"I probably am, but it's got to be something big. Otherwise, you would've told me."

"Oh, it is, Dad. But it's something good."

Kayla gasped. "Jackson Andrew Copeland!"

"Sorry, Kayla, but I had to say something."

"Fine. But nothing else," she said in a firm tone. "Now, come on, Sean. Let's get going. Edna—"

"Is going to have to wait." He folded his arms over his chest and attempted to glare at his wife and his son like he did to squirrelly sophomores when they lied about why they didn't get their homework done.

"Uh-oh. He means business," Jackson said.

"I do."

Kayla slumped. "You aren't going to leave this alone, are you?"

"Nope."

After she stared at him for another few seconds, she said, "Jackson, do you want to go get it?"

"Yep!"

As Jackson tore into the bathroom, slammed the door, and then opened and shut a cabinet door with enough force to splinter wood, Sean gritted his teeth.

And then, there his boy was, bringing out a... ziplock bag? "Where did the bag come from?"

"The kitchen," Jackson said. "I went down and got it, 'cause Kayla said even though it's rinsed off, no one wants to touch it."

"Touch what?" he whispered, though he was starting to get a feeling he knew.

"Well, see, it was like this. I, um, noticed a couple of things that were different about me, so I went to the drugstore and got a test."

"A pregnancy test, Dad."

"And I had just taken it and was staring at the results when Jackson came in."

"Because I needed help with my buttons on my wrists," he explained as he held up one arm.

"But when Jackson came in, he happened to see that I was crying."

"And you know how Kayla cries, Dad. It wasn't like I could miss that. So I asked her what was wrong." He frowned. "And then we had to talk about it."

Looking down at Jackson, Kayla murmured, "He was so sweet, I started crying harder."

"But that's when you started yelling about the time, Dad. And then Kayla got all flustered. So then we had to make a plan." Smiling at her, Jackson's voice warmed. "We had a good one, didn't we, Kayla?"

"We did, but now it's out in the open." She looked at Sean and smiled.

Just like he hadn't been gaping at them both.

His heart was beating so fast, Sean could hardly trust himself to speak. "Want to show me what's in that bag, guys?"

"Oh! Sure." Jackson held it up for him to take.

Then...well, the air got thick with expectation. His hand shook as he curved his fingers around the thin, rectangular item inside. He swallowed as he lifted it to see what that pregnancy test said.

Pregnant.

Kayla was pregnant. They were going to have a baby. "I...I didn't know we were..." Suddenly aware of Jackson standing there, he coughed. "I mean, this is a surprise."

And didn't he just sound like an idiot?

"It was to me, too."

Finally lifting his gaze from the test, he met Kayla's brown eyes and saw they were filling with tears again. And shining right through were about a dozen emotions—hope and excitement and… worry?

She was worried that he wasn't happy.

"Kayla, oh my gosh. Come here, honey." He wrapped his arms around her, then curved out his right arm and brought Jackson into the fold.

"You're happy, right?" Kayla asked in a small voice.

"I'm the happiest I've ever been. Our little family of three is going to become a family of four."

"He's happy, Kayla. I told ya."

"Are you happy to have a little brother or sister, buddy?"

"Uh-huh. Plus, Kayla will get to be a mommy now, too."

"No, Jackson," Kayla said. "I've already been a mommy to you. I love you that much."

Jackson rolled his eyes, though his cheeks flushed with happiness. "You know what I mean, Kayla. Now you'll get to carry a baby around all the time."

She laughed. "That, too."

When they broke apart, Sean held up the bag again. "Jackson, go put on your jacket, okay? Give me a moment with Kayla."

Looking from one to the other, Jackson said,

"Okay, fine. But don't forget that we're gonna be late."

"Close the door, son."

When the door closed and they were all alone, Sean said, "You've made me very happy, sweetheart. I'm thrilled."

"Me, too."

Feeling like he'd been missing out, he rubbed her arm. "So, what's been going on? Are you feeling okay?"

"A little queasy, but just fine." She exhaled. "Boy, talk about an unexpected blessing!"

Thinking about a morning a little over a year ago, when he looked up and saw her walking toward him across the room at Loaves of Love, Sean pulled her into his arms again. "I'm starting to think that the best things happen as surprises. This baby. Meeting you again."

"I agree one hundred percent."

Just as he was showing her how happy he was with kisses, Jackson's voice rang through the air.

"We're going to be late, guys! Come on!"

Breaking apart, Sean reached for Kayla's hand and led her toward the door. "We're coming. Settle down!"

"What about Edna? Are you not worried about what she's going to say if we show up late?" Kayla asked.

"Nope. I have no doubt that she's going to understand completely."

And with that, he helped Kayla with her coat, slipped on his blazer and they walked out of the house. At last.

Sean knew the wedding was going to be wonderful and the reception was going to be a great party, but he was already looking forward to coming home again.

They had a future to plan.

* * * * *

Be sure to look for the next book in Shelley Shepard Gray's A Matchmaker Knows Best series, available soon wherever Harlequin Heartwarming books are sold!